INTERNATIONAL TRADE IN HEALTH SERVICES AND THE GATS

Current Issues and Debates

D1718954

INTERNATIONAL TRADE IN HEALTH SERVICES AND THE GATS

Current Issues and Debates

Edited by Chantal Blouin,
Nick Drager, and Richard Smith

THE WORLD BANK
Washington, D.C.

ISBN-10: 0-8213-6211-9   e-ISBN: 0 8213-6212-7
ISBN-13: 978-0-8213-6211-2   DOI: 10.1596/978-0-8213-6211-2

Library of Congress Catologing-in-Publication Data has been applied for.

CONTENTS

PREFACE AND ACKNOWLEDGMENTS

Trade liberalization can affect health in multiple ways. Sometimes the impact is direct and the effect is obvious, as when a disease crosses a border together with a traded good. Other times the effects of trade liberalization are more indirect. For example, reducing trade tariffs may lead to lower prices for medical equipment and health-related products; changing international rules concerning patent protection affects access to essential medicines and technology transfer; and liberalization of trade in health services can alter national health systems. There is a link between increased trade and economic growth, which itself can lead to reduced poverty and higher standards of living, including better health. It is important to link the trading system with sound social policies to move toward a more equitable distribution of the potential economic benefits of trade openness.

One of the key challenges faced by ministries of health arising from trade rules is accurately assessing and responding to the risks and opportunities for population health and human development of the increasing openness in health services under GATS.

This book attempts to address this challenge head-on, providing analytical tools to policymakers, in both the health and trade ministries, who are involved in the liberalization agenda more widely, and the current GATS (General Agreement on Trade in Services) negotiations more specifically. The book includes an overview of current evidence on the health sector implications of the liberalization of health services trade in selected countries; focusing especially on developing countries. We hope that it will be a tool for trade capacity building and for facilitating national dialogues on what are the best policy options on health services and trade agreements. The topic is a controversial one, so we ensured that the different chapters reflect a range of views on the GATS and health services. The objective is to provide information that will contribute positively to the debate on GATS. Moreover, although we focus largely on the GATS negotiations, the book should not be seen as limited to the multilateral sphere. Regional and bilateral trade negotiations are omnipresent now and the health issues raised here are relevant to these negotiations as well.

The book is, of course, the product of a collaborative effort by many organisations and individuals. Building on its recent work on globalization and health, the WHO partnered with researchers and analysts in order to develop the materials included. The first phase of this work led to the presentation and discussion of draft chapters and case studies at a workshop in Ottawa, Canada, in July 9–11, 2003. Bringing together more than 70 participants, this forum allowed for vigorous discussion among trade and health experts and representatives of government ministries and agencies, non-governmental organizations, professional associations, aid agencies and academic institutions from more than 20 countries (The North-South Institute provided technical support, while the Canadian Public Health Association undertook logistical support for the workshop. The University of Ottawa's Institute for Population Health hosted the event.) The second phase of this work led to revisions to the chapters; the results of which are presented here. A third phase will see the methodologies suggested here being implemented in a variety of national contexts to begin the process of gathering together consistent evidence on the extent of, and impact of, trade on health, which will then be reported at a later date.

In bringing this phase to fruition, we would like to thank all the collaborators. First, the contribution of the authors of each chapter in the book, and also to the authors of the various country case studies summarized herein: Susan Cleary, Francisco León, Alfred Inis Ndiaye, Cha-aim Pachanee, Cintia Quiliconi, Soledad Salvador, Guang Shi, Untung Suseno, Michael Thiede, Stephen Thomas, and Suwit Wibulprasert. We also benefited from the participation and comments of Benedikte Dal, Ross Duncan, John Foster, Jens Gobrecht, Ajay Gupta, Margaret Hilson, Laurie Hunter, Ron Labonte, Susan Joekes, Paul Mably, Aaditya Mattoo, Blanka Pelz, Matthew Sanger, Ted Schreker, Scott Simon, David Strawczynski, and David Warner. We are also grateful to the remaining participants to the Ottawa workshop, who also contributed greatly to the improvement of the quality of the chapters. Our thanks also go to UNCTAD, OECD, WTO, and the South Centre for their contribution. For its support in the preparation of the final version of this book, we would like to thank Stephen McGroarty of the World Bank's Office of the Publisher as well as the reviewers who contributed their time and energy to improve the quality of the manuscript. Finally, we would like to thank the sponsoring agencies for this project: the Canadian International Development Agency (CIDA), Health Canada, the International Development Research Centre (IDRC), the World Bank (WB), and the World Health Organisation (WHO). The views and positions expressed in the book are the views of the authors, and should not be seen as representing official policy of the organizations or governments which supported its publication.

CONTRIBUTORS

Rudolf Adlung, World Trade Organization

Obijiofor Aginam, Carleton University

Chantal Blouin, The North-South Institute

Antonia Carzaniga, World Trade Organization

Rupa Chanda, Indian Institute of Management, Bangalore

Carlos Correa, University of Buenos Aires

Nick Drager, World Health Organization

David P. Fidler, Indiana University School of Law

Jens Gobrecht, World Health Organization

Jane Lethbridge, Consultant

Martine Julsaint, South Centre

Mina Mashayekhi, United Nations Conference on Trade and Development

Julia Nielson, World Bank

Didar Singh, Consultant

Richard Smith, University of East Anglia

Elisabeth Tuerk, United Nations Conference on Trade and Development

David Warner, University of Texas at Austin

ACRONYMS AND ABBREVIATIONS

CPC	United Nations Provisional Central Product Classification
DWP	Doha Work Programme
EBOPS	Extended Balance of Payments Services Classification
EC	European community
ENT	economic needs test
ESM	emergency safeguard mechanism
EU	European Union
FATS	foreign affiliates trade in services
FDI	foreign direct investment
GATS	General Agreement on Trade in Services
GATT	General Agreement on Tariffs and Trade
GPA	Government Procurement Agreement
HIT	health information technology
ICN	International Council of Nurses
ICT	information and communication technology
IFI	international financial institutions
IFPMA	International Federation of Pharmaceutical Manufacturers Associations
IHR	International Health Regulations
ILO	International Labor Organization
IMF	International Monetary Fund
IOM	International Organization for Migration
ITC	International Trade Centre
LDCs	least developed countries
MDGs	Millenium Development Goals

MFN	most favored nation
MRA	mutual recognition agreement
MSITS	Manual on Statistics of International Trade in Services
NAFTA	North-American Free Trade Agreement
NAMA	non-agricultural market access
OECD	Organisation for Economic Co-operation and Development
OSs	*Obras Sociales*
SARS	Severe Acute Respiratory Syndrome
SIA	sustainability impact assessment
SMEs	small and medium-sized enterprises
TBT	Technical Barriers to Trade (Agreement on)
TRIPS	Agreement on Trade-Related Aspects of Intellectual Property Rights
UNCTAD	United Nations Conference on Trade and Development
UNHCHR	Office of thse United Nations High Commissioner for Human Rights
UNICEF	United Nations Children's Fund
WHO	World Health Organization
WPDR	working party on domestic regulation (in the GATS)
WTO	World Trade Organization

TRADE IN HEALTH SERVICES AND THE GATS: INTRODUCTION AND SUMMARY

Richard Smith, Chantal Blouin, Nick Drager

Why This Book?

Globalization is one of the key challenges facing health policymakers in the twenty-first century. While effects on health from, for example, cross-border flows of infectious disease and the advertising of unhealthy lifestyles are important aspects of globalization, a significant challenge concerns the globalization of the health sector itself: direct trade in health-related goods, services, and people (patients and professionals). Trade in health services will be affected by changes in general trade liberalization, international legislation, and international institutions; in return, it will itself impact on national economies (see WHO and WTO, 2002).

However, to date the health sector has been relatively unaffected by trade, as it remains a predominantly service-oriented sector. Throughout history, most trade liberalization has concerned the movement of "goods," and, to a lesser degree, people, since these can be "stored" and therefore transported. However, while services (such as banking, education, and telecommunications, as well as health) account for only about 20 percent of global trade (on a balance of payments basis), this sector is the fastest growing. Much of this increase in service-related trade has resulted from changes in technology, which make e-commerce and telemedicine technical possibilities; from easier travel and border restrictions, which make temporary movement of patients and professionals feasible; and from the rise of transnational corporations, which makes the ownership and management of health care facilities more fluid.

A recent, and critical, development in international legislation concerning trade and health services has been the World Trade Organization (WTO) negotiations aimed at the further liberalization of trade in services: the General Agreement on Trade in Services (GATS).[1] The GATS system was initiated in 1994 during the "Uruguay Round" of WTO negotiations, where initial commitments in health services were made by a handful of countries. More recently, negotiations began following the WTO meeting in February 2000, with initial requests for specific commitments made by the end of June 2002, initial offers due by the end of March 2003, and finalized agreement by the end of January 2005 (an up-to-date outline of GATS negotiations and health services can be found in Chapter 2 of this book). This pace of development of the new GATS commitments, and especially their binding nature, has created a fresh imperative to establish how health services will be affected.

More specifically, it has raised concerns that the spread of globalization threatens to outpace the ability of governments and nations to adjust to the new commitments, let alone guide them (Adlung, 2002; Price and Pollock, 1999). In this respect, the potential risk associated with trade in *health* services is further increased with the added complication of conflicts, or misunderstandings, between the trade and health sectors; this causes further confusion in estimating the potential benefits and risks of trade liberalization in health services. National ministries of trade (and perhaps finance and foreign affairs) often make GATS commitments in isolation from health ministries, yet their decisions have an impact on health, of which they have limited knowledge. Conversely, ministries of health typically have very limited knowledge of trade issues. A critical factor in globalization and trade in health services is therefore to address this asymmetry of information by enabling ministries of health to make informed and comprehensive presentations to ministries of trade concerning decisions to be taken under the GATS.

The core purpose of this book is to inform policymakers from both trade and health about the nature and implications of international trade in the health sector, and thus to assist them in the formulation of trade policy and in international negotiations in the health sector. The book is the culmination of several key elements of work concerning trade in health services that the WHO has commissioned. This work has been focused around providing health policymakers with tools to assist them in evaluating the liberalization of national health systems utilizing currently available data, in formulating the development of systems to improve the collection of data relevant to these decisions, and in participating in the negotiation process.

There is an animated international debate about the impact of GATS on public services in general and health in particular. The book is also intended as a contribution toward a more informed debate, by providing different perspectives on the GATS. Indeed, some of the authors place more emphasis on the opportunities linked to trade in health services, while others focus more on the risks associated with making GATS commitments in this area.

Given the limited amount of empirical evidence specifically on trade commitments and health services, the editors recommend that policymakers choose a cautious approach and take careful stock of their capacity at the national level to mitigate the risks and take advantage of the benefits of trade in health services, before they make binding commitments.

An Overview of the Book

Chapter 2 considers developing country strategies for GATS negotiations. For this purpose, it first describes the broader challenges arising from the interface between the GATS as a commercial agreement vis-à-vis the right to health and the particular public/essential nature of health services. The chapter then gives a brief overview of the state of play of current GATS negotiations. Next the chapter discusses more specific challenges: first, challenges arising from the impact the current GATS negotiations may have on domestic regulations; second, challenges that arise from an overall lack of data and understanding about the health and developmental implications of liberalizing services trade; and third, challenges arising from a lack of political and/or negotiating clout that developing countries face in the WTO context.

Chapter 3 provides an outline of the current situation with respect to GATS commitments and negotiations in health services. This overview covers the current level of commitments in trade in health services under the GATS, by member states, sector, and GATS mode, and discusses reasons why the pattern is as it currently stands (generally low, and mainly involving developed nations). The chapter then moves on to explore the available limitations that countries may, and have, agreed to under the GATS, as well as the possible implications of trade under GATS, both in terms of possible risks and benefits.

Chapter 4 provides a detailed step-by-step outline of the legal obligations under the GATS, with a view to assisting policymakers to assess their options in the context of the negotiations. This chapter also highlights some of the questions policymakers might wish to consider in assessing whether or not to make commitments under the GATS, in terms of what might be the costs and benefits vis-à-vis health policy outcomes. The chapter also addresses what sort of flanking, or corresponding regulatory or policy measures, might need to accompany any commitment.

Chapter 5 examines the important legal aspects of making commitments under GATS. Coming to grips with the legal aspects of trade agreements and GATS is vital for health policymakers, as they contain legal rules that may affect health policy. This chapter attempts to provide an understanding of the core international legal implications of GATS for health policy, specifically whether GATS helps or hinders WTO members' capacity to protect health and provide health services. Lessons in this respect are gathered from historical international legislation, most prominently through the General Agreement on Tariffs and Trade (GATT) and the Agreement on Trade-Related Aspects of Intellectual Property Rights (TRIPS). Through providing a brief analytical overview of the international legal implications of GATS, the chapter thus provides health policymakers with a tool to navigate the international legal waters through which health policy must now traverse with respect to trade in services.

Chapter 6 moves on to consider the task before policymakers of assessing whether liberalization in health services will or will not improve access to health services, and to what extent it will contribute to economic welfare. The existing theoretical and empirical literature on trade in services generally points to the positive economic impact of decreasing and eliminating barriers to foreign services suppliers. The question for policymakers, then, is to what extent the conclusions and policy recommendations derived from the general findings on the benefits of liberalization in services are applicable to health services and insurance. This chapter presents a methodology to assess the impact of such policy reforms. In recent years, the European Commission has developed a methodology to conduct sustainability impact assessment of trade negotiations. This chapter briefly presents this methodology and how it can be used and applied in health services. It also summarizes the findings of the country studies commissioned in the context of this project.

The book moves toward its conclusion in Chapter 7 by considering what the literature has to say about trade within the four GATS modes. This chapter provides an overview of a set of four background papers commissioned by the WHO relating to each of the four GATS modes. The book then concludes with a chapter that discusses the next steps for policymakers, highlighting the importance of national assessment of trade in health services. (Such an exercise would benefit from the analytical framework proposed in the Annex.) The framework is designed to cover issues relating to all four modes of the GATS, and to cover aspects of the general economic and health environment, modal characteristics of trade in health services, and institutional, legislative, infrastructural, and other factors of importance in assessing health services trade and preparedness for GATS negotiations. It is designed to assist countries in gathering information to help policymakers understand the nature and implications of international trade in the health sector, and thus assist them in formulating trade policy as well as participating in international negotiations concerning the health sector. In doing so, the framework also identifies information and data gaps, and thus helps prioritize, streamline, and coordinate data collection in this area, as well as helping to avoid duplication of information and effort in assessing the opportunities and risks involved in engaging in wider trade liberalization in health services. The remainder of this introductory chapter summarizes the key findings and recommendations of the book.

"Top Ten" Key Questions Concerning Trade in Health Services and the GATS

Why are Current Levels of Trade in Health Services Low?

It is clear from the various chapters within this book that the *overall* level of GATS commitments in health is extremely low, which itself is seen as a reflection of an overall low (although increasing) level of trade within health services. Indeed, apart from education, no service sector has fewer GATS commitments than health. Further, of those who have made commitments, the number of sectors committed is positively related to levels of economic development. That is, developed countries appear to find it either easier or more economically beneficial to submit relatively extensive schedules than do developing countries.[2] Overall, of the four relevant subsectors, medical and dental services are the most heavily committed (62 members), followed by hospital services (52 members), and services provided by midwives, nurses, etc. (34 members). This general pattern suggests that it is politically easier or more economically attractive for administrations to liberalize capital-intensive and skills-intensive sectors than labor-intensive activities.

Given that commitments and negotiation activity are so low in health compared with other service sectors, the key question is therefore why they are so low, and whether this indicates that countries should actually be unconcerned about trade in health services or GATS commitments in this area. In this respect, two reasons might be suggested for such low levels of current activity.

The first is the presence of government monopolies offering services free or below cost. This would especially affect commitments under Mode 3 (commercial presence), but also other modes as well. However, although this may be a part of the reason, total monopoly situations are rare, and most countries have both a public and a private health sector. Second, there do not appear to be any "pace setters" in the health sector, compared, for example, to the role played by the United States, the European Community, and other OECD countries in areas such as telecommunications and financial services.

Nonetheless, this does not imply that trade in health services will not assume greater significance in future rounds of GATS negotiations. For example, it may be argued that the whole process of GATS is so new that other sectors, which were already more liberalized, were easier to commit to first, and once these are underway, attention will turn to other areas. It may also be argued that new technologies are making health more amenable to trade. Similarly, saturation in other markets may lead to health being seen as a growth area, especially as more countries increase the role of the private sector in health services. Overall, however, the lesson seems to be that there is no reason to suggest that trade in health services will remain at a low level, and that once developed countries have "saturated" their own markets they will be likely to move on to see how to exploit other markets. At the same time, it might be suggested that while developed countries have their trade focus on other sectors, developing countries might take advantage of this vacuum in trade to pursue their own agendas, either in health or in other sectors linked with health.

How will GATS Legally Affect a Country's Health Policy?

Two core issues determine the answer to this question. First, does the specific health-related service in question fall within the remit of GATS? GATS applies to health-related services provided for profit, but controversy exists about GATS' application to government-provided services. GATS excludes services provided pursuant to the exercise of governmental authority as long as such services are not provided on a "commercial basis" or "in competition" with other services. How WTO members define these terms will determine whether government-provided health-related services fall within, or are excluded from, GATS. Although many legal experts expect the exclusion to be interpreted and applied narrowly, the ambiguity provides an opportunity for the health policy community to influence the interpretation of this exclusion in a way that is sensitive to health policy concerns. For example, WTO members can clarify what "commercial basis" and "in competition" mean in a way that excludes the provision of most government-provided health-related services. Important here is also influencing the WTO to insist that the "burden of proof" concerning whether a government-supplied service benefits from the exclusion should fall on the WTO member claiming that the exclusion does not cover a government-supplied service (i.e., a WTO member complaining about a possible GATS violation).

Second, when a health-related service falls within GATS, what GATS "rules" are most significant in affecting health policy? These are fourfold.

1. The general obligations and disciplines of GATS affect health policy. Essentially, these are obligations that apply to trade in all service sectors covered by GATS, and comprise the most-favored-nation (MFN) obligation, and various

obligations that relate to domestic regulatory powers. The MFN obligation probably does not significantly affect health policy. However, the general obligations affecting domestic regulatory powers may be significant, as they may interfere with the ability of a member to regulate services domestically, such as in regard to licensing and qualification requirements, or technical standards. At present, however, WTO members have negotiated no disciplines on domestic regulatory powers in the area of health-related services. Overall, in terms of the general obligations and disciplines of GATS, their present impact on health policy is not particularly troubling. The general obligations that are universally binding are not large in number or worrying for health policy. The low level of specific commitments made to date in health-related sectors mitigates the effect of the general obligations linked to specific commitments. More concerns may arise in the future, however, if the level and nature of specific commitments in health-related sectors increase and as WTO members negotiate additional multilateral disciplines on trade in services.

2. Rules governing the making of specific commitments and progressive liberalization will also affect health policy. Many suggest that rules on specific commitments allow WTO members to retain flexibility and discretion in calibrating where and how much to liberalize trade in services. What this perspective obscures, however, is that the policy freedom and flexibility WTO members have to make specific commitments disappears once specific commitments are made, perhaps locking WTO members into liberalization commitments that may turn out to be bad policy moves. Further, the flexibility of the specific commitment provisions cannot be isolated from the duty to participate in successive negotiating rounds to progressively liberalize trade in services. The political dynamic created by the duty to negotiate progressive liberalization may, over time, be detrimental to a government's ability to provide and regulate public-interest services such as health. The GATS rules on making specific commitments require that members exercise great care and foresight in listing the types of access restrictions or national-treatment restrictions they want to maintain or adopt in the future. The broad scope of GATS therefore creates an enormous challenge for members, with pressure to undertake the complex and difficult process of scheduling specific commitments with little margin for error.

3. In the event a health-related measure affecting trade in services violates GATS, the treaty contains exceptions to its obligations, including an exception specifically on health. The health exception justifies violations of GATS rules when the measures in question are "necessary to protect human, animal, or plant life or health." WTO members attempting to use this exception must demonstrate that their measures are the least trade-restrictive measures reasonably available to them to achieve the level of health protection sought.

4. The GATS' "institutional framework," and particularly the dispute settlement mechanism, are also important parts of GATS for health policy. Other contexts demonstrate that the WTO dispute settlement mechanism will not adopt a deferential attitude toward members, arguing that their behavior protects human health. At the same time, these rulings suggest that the WTO dispute settlement process is capable of producing rulings that recognize the importance of protecting human health within a system designed to liberalize international trade.

The relationship between GATS and health policy may be most significantly shaped by the ongoing and subsequent efforts to progressively liberalize trade in health-related services, and the negotiation of further multilateral disciplines on domestic regulatory powers. The challenge for health policy communities is to manage this international legal process in an informed and sophisticated manner in order to ensure that the evolving law of GATS recognizes and respects WTO members' rights to promote and protect health. For this, it is vital that countries have a clear idea of the effect that liberalization will have on their respective health systems.

What Effect Might Liberalization have on National Health Systems?

The effect of liberalization on a country's health system will crucially depend upon the extent to which the private sector does, or is able to, participate in the provision of health services. A potential concern with GATS is that it may cause countries to overlook the issue of commercial health service provision and finance in the move to discuss the level to which foreign participation in the market may occur. However, the core issue remains whether a country wishes to have, or expand, private sector involvement in the provision and/or finance of health services. This will be an issue related to, for example, national budget priorities, the desire to increase available resources, questions about the efficiency of resource use, ensuring that public policy objectives (such as universal provision of high-quality care) are met, and so forth. This issue cannot be answered here, but that it *is* a key issue needs to be stated.

If such commercialization of health care is desired, the question becomes whether to allow participation by foreign suppliers. It is only at this stage that the GATS comes into the equation; the GATS only deals with the treatment of foreigners, not nationals, and the GATS has nothing to say on the debate over whether to allow private provision per se. This may involve some of the following considerations: the desire to increase the efficiency of national private providers by exposing them to competition; the use of foreign suppliers to meet key shortages in the short- to medium-term; the desire to have access to new technologies or skills that may not be available from national suppliers; and the desire to increase the facilities and services available to health care consumers beyond what the domestic suppliers can provide. Equally, consideration must be given to how to ensure the quality of foreign providers and the impact of foreign suppliers on local suppliers and on the system for health care as a whole.

What are the Likely Benefits from Greater Trade in Health Services?

Foreign investment in health facilities represents a transfer of resources whose ramifications reach beyond the health sector, including indirect effects on growth, income, and employment, and in other sectors, such as construction, transport, and communication. Health tourism can become an area where developing countries are competitive exporters. Some countries with health personnel surpluses can also make important economic gains from remittances from the temporary movement of health professionals. From the standpoint of public health it might prove too narrow a view to consider only the direct effects on a population's health status of increased foreign presence in, for example, a country's hospital sector. Broader routes of causation, leading from the liberalization of trade and investment to development and from development to better population health, may be equally significant in this connection.

In addition to the economy-wide benefits, trade in health services can have positive impacts on the national health system in a variety of ways. Foreign investors can bring in additional resources, new technologies, and new management techniques that can improve the provision of services and financing of the system. These can improve working conditions and therefore reduce the likelihood that health professionals leave the country. Foreign insurers may contribute to reduce the heavy reliance on out-of-pocket payments for health services found in many developing countries. The potential of trade in health services can be harnessed to benefit the whole health system, not merely a small group of patients. However, this will require a strengthening of the stewardship and regulatory functions of national governments.

What can be Done to Limit the Possible Risks of Trade?

A key concern with respect to liberalizing trade in health services is the effect on equity of access and quality of care. There are limits to the extent to which governments can influence the level and structure of trade in health services. However, it is important to bear in mind that:

1. GATS does not impose any constraints on the terms and conditions under which a potential host country treats foreign patients, so, for example, foreigners may

be charged extra for treatment and these proceeds used to enhance the quantity and quality of basic domestic supplies;

2. There are no legal impediments in GATS that would affect the ability of governments to discourage qualified staff from seeking employment in the private sector, whether at home or abroad, such as through deposit requirements or guarantees that would make it financially unattractive for young professionals to capitalize immediately on taxpayers' investment in their education by seeking higher incomes; and

3. It is difficult to see any crowding-out effects, to the disadvantage of resident patients, that could not be addressed through adequate regulation that would not normally fall foul of GATS provisions. For example, a country might require all private hospitals to reserve a minimum percentage of beds for free treatment for the needy, to offer some basic medical services in remote rural areas, or to train beyond the number required for the purposes of these institutions.

Beyond these sorts of considerations, there are a number of key limitations that may be made by members in their GATS commitments. *Horizontal* limitations apply across all committed sectors, and typically reflect economy-wide policy concerns and objectives. These include, for example, restrictions on the physical presence of foreign suppliers, foreign equity ceilings, or restrictions on the legal form of establishment (e.g., joint ventures only). In contrast, *vertical* limitations refer to specific limitations under each GATS mode. For Modes 1 and 2, these mainly concern the nonportability of insurance entitlements. Mode 3 and 4 limitations tend to be covered under horizontal limitations. For example, in Mode 3, some countries have reserved the right to restrict the commercial incorporation of foreign health care providers, and in Mode 4, quota-type restrictions, mainly setting a ceiling on numbers of foreign employees or denying access to all persons not considered to be specialist doctors, have been frequent. Furthermore, economic needs tests (ENTs) have also been frequently referred to in limitations under Modes 3 and 4, mostly for hospital services but also for medical and dental services.

When, and How Best, Might Negotiations be Undertaken?

From what we have seen in this book, there is no point in hasty liberalization. The consequences should be carefully considered, and in particular the timing and pace of liberalization must be well thought out. In a public monopoly environment, the production, financing, regulation, and control of a service tend to go hand in hand, whereas the move toward competitive systems necessarily implies a separation of tasks and functions. Liberalization may therefore presuppose regulation to meet the multiplicity of legitimate objectives involved. This is a challenging task, not least for developing countries lacking regulatory experience. However, there is nothing to prevent administrations from joining forces to exploit possible synergies and/or mandating competent international organizations to propose model solutions. Regulatory approaches developed for telecommunications in recent years, under the auspices of the International Telecommunication Union, could inspire work in WHO and comparable bodies in other areas as well. The technological and economic forces working toward global market integration are unlikely to leave the health sector unaffected, and timely action by governments would seem to be desirable.

What is the Relationship between Trade in Health Services and Other Sectors?

Trade policy becomes a health policy issue not only for how it affects health systems, but also for how it influences the many social, environmental, and economic determinants of health. Health services, although an *important* determinant of health, are not the *primary* determinant of health, especially in developing countries. Rather, the greatest predictors of population health are education, income (and thus employment), gender, nutrition, and access to clean water and sanitation. Thus, any assessment of the impact of trade liberalization should include the impact of trade policy commitments in other areas, such as education, water, and sanitation services; equitable access to which is strongly associated with population health.

Clearly, each population health determinant is influenced by domestic public policies, but crucially these domestic public policies are influenced by numerous bilateral, regional, and global trade agreements, of which GATS is just one. It is therefore important for developing countries to consider important nonmedical (social, environmental, economic) health determinants, how they are presently considered in policy discussions of nonhealth sectors (e.g., environment, education, transportation, energy, finance, social services, housing) and what analytical and human resource capacity is available in the health ministry, or in collaboration with university researchers and nongovernmental organizations, to engage in assessments of nonhealth policies on health determinants.

Should Trade Liberalization be under GATS or Other Trade Agreements?

Thus far, discussion has focused mostly on GATS. However, the core question concerning trade liberalization in health services is whether these reforms should be undertaken under the GATS or under other trade agreements? There are many issues relating to this question, the two most important of which appear to be:

1. Can GATS commitments in one area be used effectively as a bargaining chip to negotiate better market access or to achieve other goals with trading partners in another area? For example, a commitment in health services may be offered in exchange for a reduction in agricultural subsidies from other members of the WTO.
2. Will foreign investors see binding trade reforms under GATS as an insurance policy that their entry to a market, and their nondiscriminatory treatment, is guaranteed? If so, will this encourage investor confidence and lead to greater foreign investment in the sector where the commitments were made?

Whether a country should consider liberalizing trade in health services in the context of a regional trade agreement, but not under the GATS, will depend upon the country's assessment of, among other things, whether its trade interests are regional or global (e.g., while some countries may feel more comfortable opening up to foreign investment from their neighbors, their export interests—such as in temporary movement of personnel—may be more global in character). Other factors to consider include the extent to which the key shortages expected to be met by trade can be met from the parties to the regional agreement, as opposed to on a global basis; the relative costs and benefits of negotiating effort, relative negotiating power, and the scope for leveraging the outcome of one process in the context of another.

Of course, even if countries do not make commitments under the GATS on health services, trade itself will continue as it has for some time, independent of the GATS. Thus, whether a country decides to make GATS commitments on trade in health services or not, it will still need to deal with many of the issues and challenges that arise from that trade. So, should a country commit under GATS or not? This hinges almost entirely on one crucial issue.

What is the Single Most Important Issue in Determining Whether to Commit under GATS?

Virtually all chapters in this book raise the issue of policy reversal as perhaps the most important element of doubt over whether liberalization should take place within GATS or without.

Making commitments under GATS is very different from undertaking liberalization unilaterally within a country's own policy framework. By committing a sector to GATS, the country must abide by specific GATS rules on market access and national treatment in relation to that sector, as well as the general GATS rules governing all services. Unlike a country's own unilateral decisions, which can be reversed if they are found to be damaging, the GATS commitment is binding and effectively irreversible. This requires there to be a far higher threshold of certainty before countries decide to make any commitments—particularly in crucial service sectors such as health—under GATS. In assessing the likely impact of GATS on health, the central questions facing policymakers are therefore actually very simple, and very stark:

1. Will increased trade in these services lead to better health outcomes?
2. Will increased liberalization of trade (more competition from foreign private health care companies) lead to better health outcomes?
3. Will making a GATS commitment in these sectors offer any additional advantage that will lead to better health outcomes?

Of course, the implication here is clear:

> "if the answer to any of these is negative, or in doubt, then a country should not make GATS commitments."

Overall, it is concluded that members who would like to open their health sector to foreign providers should consider "experimenting" with liberalization outside of GATS before making GATS commitments. Members can liberalize trade in health-related services unilaterally, if they wish, without accepting binding commitments in their national GATS schedules of specific commitments. Such unilateral liberalization would allow WTO members to experiment with such policies in a way that permits them to reverse course on market access or national treatment if the experiment produces unsatisfactory results. Although this seems straightforward, answering these questions will require a considerable level of information and analysis.

How Might a Country Best Obtain the Information Necessary to Inform Policy?

Data on the impact of trade liberalization on health, health services, or the economy are scarce. That data are scarce really reflects three interrelated issues: that there has been no imperative to assess the data before (for instance, routine data tend not to be broken down in to health sector categories that would be required); there is no existing "tool" that may be used to determine what, and how, such data may be collected; and that countries often lack human and physical capital to collect the required data. An attempt has been made in this book to address these issues through a proposed framework for country analysis, located in the Annex.

The framework is designed to assist countries in gathering information that would help policymakers understand the nature and implications of international trade in the health sector, and thus assist them in formulating trade policy as well as in participating in international negotiations concerning the health sector. In doing so, the framework will also assist in the identification of information and data gaps, and thus help prioritize, streamline, and coordinate data collection in this area; it should also help to avoid duplication of information and effort in assessing the opportunities and risks involved in engaging in wider trade liberalization in health services. Furthermore, by proposing a common format and a standard questionnaire, the framework will hopefully facilitate the establishment of a common database and data collection techniques and greater sharing of experiences and data across countries, thus enabling cross-country learning and comparative assessment of the effects of autonomous or GATS-related liberalization.

The framework is designed to gather information from a variety of sources, and in a variety of formats (quantitative and qualitative). It is therefore not possible, or necessarily desirable, to produce a "mathematical" algorithm for determining a country's approach to trade liberalization in health services (within or without the context of GATS). Rather, the framework pulls together, in a systematic manner, the most relevant items of information that policymakers will need to assist them in this respect and to work through the complex economic, sectoral, social, and international issues that surround trade liberalization and health services. In this way, the framework achieves three goals. First, it creates awareness and sensitization of issues with respect to trade liberalization and health services. Second, the framework helps users to identify and formulate policy, at the national, bilateral, regional, and multilateral levels. It is expected that the framework exercise will help countries to identify areas and issues on which to focus and prioritize in terms of policy measures and initiatives at various levels, with a view to facilitating trade in health services while ensuring the associated gains and mitigating the associated adverse effects. Third, the framework should help to identify gaps in data and information, and in existing data collection systems and procedures. It is expected that identification of such limitations will provide the basis for establishing appropriate procedural, organizational, and institutional structures and systems to improve the state of data and information relevant to understanding and assessing trade in health services.

Notes

1. Further information on GATS is available at http://www.wto.org/english/tratop_e/ serv_e/ serv_e.htm.

2. This generally applies, although there are some interesting anomalies, such as Canada not undertaking commitments in any of the four relevant subsectors (medical and dental services; services provided by midwives, nurses, physiotherapists, and paramedical personnel; hospital services; and other human health services such as ambulance services and residential health facility services), and the United States and Japan scheduling only one, while Burundi, The Gambia, Lesotho, Malawi, Sierra Leone, and Zambia have all included at least three subsectors.

References

Adlung, R. 2002. Health services in a globalizing world. *EuroHealth* 8: 18–21.

Price D., and A.M. Pollock. 1999. How the World Trade Organization is shaping domestic policies in health care. *The Lancet*; 354: 1889–92.

WHO and WTO. 2002. *WTO agreements and public health: a joint study of the WHO and WTO Secretariat.* Geneva.

Yach, D., and D. Bettcher. 1998a. The globalization of public health I: threats and opportunities. *American Journal of Public Health* 88: 735–38.

Yach, D., and D. Bettcher. 1998b. The globalization of public health II: the convergence of self-interest and altruism. *American Journal of Public Health* 88: 738–41.

2

STRATEGIC CONSIDERATIONS FOR DEVELOPING COUNTRIES: THE CASE OF GATS AND HEALTH SERVICES

Mina Mashayekhi, Martine Julsaint, Elisabeth Tuerk

Introduction

This chapter aims to address some of the many challenges developing countries face in current negotiations on services trade, including health services, and more particularly in determining the appropriate interface between the public policy objectives of providing accessible and universal health services and the potential difficulties of strengthening the provision of health services, including to the poor and marginalized, through a market-oriented approach. After a brief discussion of the context in which the liberalization of health services takes place, the chapter gives a short overview of the state of play of current GATS negotiations. Next, the chapter discusses specific challenges for developing countries: first, challenges arising from the impact the current GATS negotiations may have on domestic regulations, particularly regulations for public services, but also more broadly,

This chapter was written by Mina Mashayekhi, head of Trade Negotiations and Commercial Diplomacy Branch (TNCD), DITC, UNCTAD; Martine Julsaint Kidane and Elisabeth Tuerk, both also with UNCTAD, TNCD Branch. The views expressed are those of the authors and do not necessarily reflect the views of UNCTAD or its member states. The authors are grateful to Verona Collantes for helpful comments.

domestic regulations that are pursuing health objectives; second, challenges that arise from an overall lack of data and understanding about the health and developmental implications of liberalizing services trade; and third, challenges arising from developing countries' lack of political and/or negotiating clout in the WTO context. Finally, the chapter also suggests a series of specific negotiating tools to help address this lack of influence. While it is neither possible nor intended to provide comprehensive, ready-made solutions for these challenges, this chapter aims to suggest possible ways to tackle some of these challenges—at least in part. For this purpose, the chapter groups the four challenges discussed into two groups, challenges arising from the content of GATS disciplines and obligations, and challenges arising from the particular dynamics of the WTO GATS negotiations.

The impact of globalization and technological progress is profoundly transforming the services sector, including the health services sector. Dynamic growth in trade and investment is an important feature of the services sector in the past two decades. Services trade is estimated at US$1.57 trillion, with an increase of 6 percent over the period 2001–2002 (WTO, 2003b). The share of trade in services of developing countries has increased from 18 percent in 1995–1998 to approximately 20 percent in 2003. As a consequence, a whole new set of challenges and opportunities has emerged and needs to be faced by policymakers, regulators, negotiators, and private operators. The health services sector therefore would need to be examined within this broader context of profound economic transformations and the Millennium Development Goals (MDGs), as many of the MDGs are poverty- and health-focused. The MDGs call for: eradication of extreme poverty, with the target of halving poverty between 1990 and 2015 (Goal 1); marked improvements in the health of the poor by reducing child mortality by two-thirds (Goal 4); improvement of maternal health by reducing the maternal mortality ratio by three-quarters (Goal 5); combating HIV/AIDS, malaria, and other diseases, with the target of halting the progress of the disease by 2015 and reversing the spread of the disease (Goal 6); and creation of a global partnership for development, including through cooperation with pharmaceutical companies providing access to affordable, essential drugs in developing countries (Goal 8). Evidence suggests that many countries are far behind in meeting these goals. More broadly, overall economic development and poverty reduction are affected by ill health. In addition to the health-related objectives, the UN Millennium Declaration also calls for an open, equitable, rule-based, predictable, and nondiscriminatory multilateral trading and financial system. These broader development goals and wider context require concerted and targeted national and global strategies and actions to build the capacity of national health systems to provide health services according to the needs of people and irrespective of ability to pay, thereby increasing the access of the poor to essential health services.

Ensuring that health services meet the needs and expectations of the people, including the poor and marginalized, depends on governments setting the rules for the entire health system, i.e., responsible stewardship. National health authorities are faced with a number of competing priorities and have to assess how changes in the economic environment can be harnessed in order to improve national health systems and benefit the population. Thus, there is a need to carefully consider the regulatory framework and liberalization of the health sector.[1] This requires that each country map out its path to universal access to essential health services and to liberalization based on epidemiological and economic analysis and based upon priorities of communities. The need to reconcile this complex set of objectives with those of economic efficiency and international competitiveness raises a dilemma, particularly for developing countries. Currently, this dilemma manifests itself in the new round of GATS negotiations.

Context and State of Play: GATS and Services Trade Negotiations

Since 2000, the negotiations on services have proceeded in accordance with Article XIX (Negotiation of Specific Commitments) of the GATS, and were subsequently incorporated into the Doha Work Programme (DWP) (WTO, November 2001d). Development has been made a key consideration in trade negotiations. In fact, the Doha Declaration seeks to place the needs and interests of developing countries at the heart of the DWP. More specifically, in paragraph 15 it provides for negotiations on trade in services to be conducted with a view to promoting the economic growth of all trading partners and the development of developing and least developed countries (LDCs). It reaffirms the Guidelines and Procedures for the Negotiations on Trade in Services (WTO, March 2001c) as the basis for continuing the negotiations with a view to achieving the objectives of the GATS, as stipulated in its Preamble,[2] in Article IV (Increasing Participation of Developing Countries) and in Article XIX (Progressive Liberalization).

The DWP calls for initial requests for specific commitments to be submitted by June 30, 2002, and for initial offers to be submitted by March 31, 2003. Bilateral consultations on requests for market access began in July 2002. By mid-July 2005, the total number of initial offers presented was 68, representing 92 Members (counting the 25 Members of the European Union (EU) as one) Including LDCs, this leaves more than 55 offers outstanding.[3] LDCs, where special modalities apply, are expected to make commitments that are limited in terms of sectors, modes, and scope. Most developing countries are still in the process of identifying their specific sectoral and modal interests, the barriers to their services exports, the potential impact of responding to the requests for liberalization by developed countries on their services sectors, and ways and means of overcoming supply constraints through implementation of GATS Articles IV and XIX.2. While a number of those countries in Central Europe acceded to the EU on May 1, 2005 had not made offers before, others have. The process of request and offer is taking place in the broader context of an important increase in the services trade (which was estimated at US\$1.57 trillion) and major domestic unilateral liberalization of services sectors, partly driven by structural adjustment programs of International Financial Institutions (IFIs).Major trading partners and IFIs encourage developing countries to lock in these reforms in the GATS negotiations.

The Fifth WTO Ministerial Conference in Cancun, Mexico, held in September 2003, was supposed to serve as stocktaking of progress in the negotiations. However, because of deadlock in other negotiating areas, particularly agriculture and the Singapore Issues, the conference concluded without a declaration indicating the way forward. While the services paragraph of the draft ministerial text was not among the most controversial ones, some developing countries have stressed that the draft ministerial texts for Cancun did not contain any reference to the Guidelines and Procedures for the Negotiations on Trade in Services, nor to GATS Articles IV and XIX.2; thus, in their view, some issues have not been adequately addressed. This particularly relates to supply of services through movement of natural persons, the issues of assessment of trade in services, and the review and evaluation of progress in the negotiations (as provided for in paragraph 15 of the Guidelines). Subsequently, the so-called July Package[4] provided that revised offers would be submitted by May 2005 and, in its Annex C also contained specific references to Mode 4, as well as least-developed countries. Basically, the July Package reiterated previous objectives and commitments set out in the GATS Guidelines and the DWP, while emphasizing the need for a high quality of offers in sectors and modes of export interest to developing countries and no a priori exclusion of any service sectors or mode. In that context, WTO members have discussed specific indicators for progress in respect of meaningful commitments on Mode 4 to help spur forward the process of negotiations.[5]

There are several reasons why services are particularly important in the DWP. These include: (a) their role in the growth and development of the whole economy and their direct link with poverty reduction; (b) their linkages with other market access negotiations; and (c) their role in achieving an overall balance of negotiations. However, since Cancun, the negotiations on services have been proceeding even though the other areas under negotiation, particularly agriculture and non-agricultural market access (NAMA), have not all picked up. Whereas the services negotiations modalities were adopted in March 2001 in the form of Guidelines and Procedures for Negotiations on Trade in Services, after the July Package establishing a "framework for modalities" the objective for agriculture and NAMA is to adopt a the Modalities provided for in Doha at the Hong Kong Ministerial in December 2005. Overall, this indicates that the initial deadline for the conclusion of the Doha Round of Negotiations (by January 1, 2005) was not attained, leaving members with a longer negotiating perspective and therefore more time to prepare requests and offers based on impact assessment evaluation and anchored in national policy priorities and objectives.

Health Services Sector and the GATS Negotiations

The economic importance of the health services sector is on the rise. This results, among other reasons, from increased demand for health care, the phenomenon of consumerism (including in the health services sector), a shortage of health personnel in some developed countries, aging populations requiring tailor-made products and services, the information/technology revolution, the increased mobility of consumers and service providers, and the combination of increasing medical costs and decreasing public health care budgets, which requires the containment of costs in health care. Moreover, in developed countries, as the population ages, they will continue to face an increasing scarcity of health workers, and the demand for and benefits of allowing labor mobility will increase for them. These trends are major driving forces for the expansion of trade in health services. While global health expenditures are estimated at US$3 trillion, trade in health services, although growing, remains relatively small: globally, cross-border trade is estimated to comprise less than one percent of global health expenditures, or US$30 billion (WHO, January 2002).

Revealed Comparative Advantage of Developing Countries in Trade in Health Services

Many developing countries have a revealed comparative advantage in health services. They owe this comparative advantage to their lower production costs, including in the area of health education; their skilled health professionals; their ability to provide unique services such as traditional medicine; their potential to combine health care and tourism; and their natural resources with perceived curative benefits. Thus, competitiveness in this sector depends on the cost structure, the quality of health facilities and infrastructure, and the availability of skilled health professionals, as well as natural endowments, cultural affinities, and geographical proximity (Adams and Kinnon, 1998). Some developing countries have developed effective export strategies. India, Cuba, China, Thailand, Jordan, South Africa, and the Philippines are important suppliers of health services. India and China are establishing hospital and specialty clinics in foreign markets. Thailand and Jordan have developed the sector with the objective of establishing regional health centers. The Philippines, Jamaica, Cuba, and India receive remittances through movement of their health professionals. An average of 5,700 nurses moved abroad for work annually between 1995 and 2001, primarily to the United Kingdom and to Saudi Arabia. Already in 2000–01, 5,967 non-E.U. nurses were admitted to the U.K. Nursing and Midwifery Council. The main suppliers were the Philippines (3,396) and South Africa (1,086) (UKCC, 2002). Important outflows also took place to the United States (during the 1980s). In fact, between 1997 and 2000, out of 26,500 foreign nurse applications for U.S. registered nurse licenses, 36 percent were from the Philippines (Dole, 2001). More recent data indicate that in the United States, 3.9 percent of registered nurses were trained abroad, with the major sources being the Philippines (43 percent), Canada (16.1 percent), the United Kingdom (7.8 percent), and India (9.6 percent) (OECD, 2002). Also, outsourcing of health services is becoming more important for some developing countries, e.g., Brazil and India, and telemedicine, catering for the needs of remote and rural regions, can reduce health care costs.

Box 2.1: GATS and the Human Right to Health

Civil society groups and trade unions have expressed the concern that the GATS agreement poses threats to the accessibility and quality of health care services worldwide (see: Third World Network, The Corner House, Save the Children, and Public Services International). As a response, these groups are calling on the WTO to incorporate principles encompassing the human right to health. For some of these groups, this is essentially a call to exclude health from the GATS negotiations. Coalitions of physicians, public health activists, and trade unions from southern countries are also joining in the calls for action. Human rights aspects form an increasingly important component in this debate. In the spring of 2002, the Commission on Human Rights adopted a Report of the High Commissioner looking into the liberalization of trade in services and human rights. Subsequently, in the summer of 2003, Paul Hunt, the Special Rapporteur on the Right to Health, conducted a mission to the WTO, among others, discussing the impacts of the GATS agreement on the human right to health.

In the spring of 2004, at its 60th session, the Commission on Human Rights discussed the Special Rapporteur's mission report. Among other things, the report noted, that "[t]he effect of the liberalization of these 'modes' of service supply on health and health-related services will depend on the specific nature of a country's national health system, the regulatory environment, the Government's policies and the level of development and infrastructure of the country. While accepting that increased trade in health services could increase available resources and improve the state of health care in some cases, it could also lead to regressions in enjoyment of the right to health..."

Box 2.1: GATS and the Human Right to Health (Continued)

The report continues by describing the effects of increasing private participation in health services provision: "A two-tier system could lead to specialized surgery responding to profitable areas (for example, selective surgery); 'cream skimming,' where services are provided to those who can pay more but need less; the 'brain drain,' with health-care professionals moving toward the higher paying private sector focused on patients who can pay, and possibly diverting resources from rural and primary health care towards specialized centers. Thus, while increased trade in services might lead to an improvement in health services for some, it could also generate increased discrimination in the provision of health services—particularly discrimination on the basis of social status—and a withdrawal of resources from the poor towards the wealthy."

Next, the report outlines the contribution of a human rights approach to services trade liberalization to face these challenges. Specifically, it states that "This is the situation that a human rights approach to trade in services can help to avoid. While some trade and development theorists accept that there will be some 'losers' in the process of trade liberalization and development, but this can be justified through overall gains to welfare, a human rights approach focuses on protecting the rights of all, particularly the potential 'losers,' and seeks to design policies accordingly. The right to health requires that health facilities, goods and services shall be accessible and of good quality. If increased trade in services were to lead to a reduction in rural primary health care, or reduced access for the poor because of user-fees, prima facie this would be inconsistent with the right to health. Equally, if increased trade in services were to lead to substandard health facilities, goods and services, this too would prima facie be inconsistent with the right to health."

After a brief description of the GATS agreement[a] and its basic features, the Special Rapporteur also addresses the "lock-in effect." Specifically, he "...questions the appropriateness of the requirement of compensatory adjustments if a decision to modify or withdraw a commitment is linked to the existence of a negative impact on the enjoyment of the right to health." Finally, the "Special Rapporteur" emphasizes the importance of a WTO member undertaking a right to health impact assessment before making a commitment to open up the health service sector to international competition. In this way, the WTO member can decide on the correct form, pace and sequence of trade liberalization according to national needs and consistent with the right to health."

Source: UNHCHR, 2002; UNHCHR, 2004.

a. See also Consumers International 2001, Dommen 2003, Hilary 2001, and Türk and Krajewski 2003.

Scope, Coverage, and Definitional Issues

The scope and coverage of the GATS is broad as defined in Article I. Article I.1 GATS covers "measures by members *affecting* trade in services." Measures affecting trade in services does not convey any notion of limiting the scope of the GATS to certain types of measures or to a certain regulatory domain, but rather indicates a broad scope of application. In fact, it could include regulations relating to goods, which are associated with the supply of services. Article XXVIII defines measures broadly to include "any measure by a member, whether in the form of a law, regulation, rule procedure, decision, administrative action or any other form." In addition, Article I: 3 of GATS includes under the "measures by members" measures taken by central, regional, or local governments, as well as all measures taken by "nongovernmental bodies in the exercise of powers delegated by ...governments or authorities." In regard to GATS coverage of subnational regulatory measures, the GATS only requires members to take such reasonable measures as may be available to it to ensure compliance by subcentral bodies. Article I further provides that the category of "services" includes any service in any sector except services supplied in the exercise of governmental authority.

By including Mode 3, akin to foreign direct investment (FDI), the GATS also extends the traditional way of considering trade as cross-border trade only. Similarly, the GATS as a trade agreement goes further than mainly disciplining measures imposed at the border, e.g., tariffs, and also addresses "beyond the border issues." The GATS broadly defines trade in services to cover four modes of supply of services, namely Mode 1: cross-border through mainly electronic transaction, e.g., telemedicine, telediagnosis, teleanalysis, outsourcing, and e-commerce; Mode 2: movement of consumers, e.g., tourism to consume health services; Mode 3: commercial presence through the establishment of branch, subsidiary, joint venture, etc., e.g., hospitals; and Mode 4: supply of services through movement of natural persons such as nurses and doctors. Supply of a health service often requires a multimodal approach to market access commitments as well as a multisectoral approach, given its linkage with business and professional services, insurance (health or social security), construction, tourism, etc. Even without such a broad approach, the health services sector covers medical and dental services, veterinary services, and services provided by nurses, midwives, physiotherapists, and paramedical personnel, which are covered under professional services and hospital services, and other human health services and social services, which are covered under the health-related and social services sector of the Services Sectoral Classification List.[6]

MFN Obligation and Exemptions

One of the main obligations for WTO members under the GATS (a general obligation) is the obligation to accord most-favored-nation (MFN) treatment. Essentially, MFN means that a WTO member must provide the "like" services and service suppliers of any WTO member with treatment no less favorable than it accords to those "like" services and suppliers of any other country. When deciding on their liberalization commitments at the end of the Uruguay Round, members could—individually—opt for maintaining a number of measures that were inconsistent with MFN treatment. The condition is that these measures were included in a list (schedule of MFN exemptions) and that they met the requirements set out in the GATS Annex on MFN exemptions. In fact, some 70 countries took MFN exemptions for some 380 measures (Mashayekhi, 2000). The agreement also mandates an MFN review, to be undertaken by the Committee on Trade in Services (CTS). The first reviews consisted of information exchange exercises designed to provide information on the status of MFN exemptions and whether the conditions that created the need for the exemptions still prevail. The reviews were being conducted along sectoral lines. Thus far, a few countries mentioned that they had eliminated their MFN exemptions in particular sectors.

There is, however, divergence of views on the mandate of any MFN reviews. Some delegations consider that the main objective of such reviews is to arrive to the removal of all MFN exemptions, which are no longer justified and that MFN exemption should be removed after 2005. Other Members insist on the fact that this exercise is merely a review, that MFN exemption can be maintained beyond 2005, and that their removal should be dealt with in these, and future, trade-liberalizing negotiations. Without reaching any explicit agreement on these diverging views, members, in the June 2005 services cluster agreed that they had completed the 2nd MFN review, and that there would be a 3rd review of MFN exemptions, scheduled to begin in 2010. If the issue of the mandate is not dealt with it is very likely that at the 3rd review Members will simply be restating their earlier views. Some members will hope that this 3rd review will lead to a substantial elimination of the remaining exemptions. They stress that the Agreement's language in Annex on Article II, in para 6 states that "in principle, such exemptions should not exceed a period of 10 years…" suggesting that any exemptions maintained after 2005 should be the exception rather than the rule. Others refer to the same para stating that the exemptions "… shall be subject to negotiation in subsequent trade-liberalizing rounds", suggesting that accordingly, the review should focus on information exchange, and MFN exemptions can be retained according to individual Members' preferences.

An OECD study indicates that out of 88 members that have taken commitments in health and social services, only one has made an MFN exemption (OECD, 2001). However, this does not take into account those MFN exemptions that are listed under professional services but are health-related (e.g., services provided by nurses, midwives, and physiotherapists; medical services; and dental services). Table 2.1 lists all such MFN exemptions as they appear in members' MFN-exemption lists,

TABLE 2.1   MFN Exemptions Relevant to the Health and Related Service Sectors

	Cyprus (GATS/ EL/25)	Jordan (GATS/ EL/128)	Bulgaria (GATS/ EL/122)	Tunisia (GATS/ EL/87)	Dominican Republic (GATS/ EL/28)
Sector or subsector	Human health services	Medical labs	Medical and dental services	Bilateral social security agreements	Dental, physiotherapy, medical, paramedical, and nursing services
Description of measure indicating its inconsistency with Article II	Provision to Cypriot citizens of medical treatment, not available in Cyprus, in selected countries with which bilateral agreements have been signed or will be signed in the future.	Licenses may be issued to non-Jordanians for the practice of medical testing and laboratory administration only if Jordanian nationals are granted reciprocal treatment. Exception to the reciprocity requirement may be granted to foreign directors of private hospital labs.	Public medical insurance, subsidization and compensation plans and programs, which cover the cost and expenses relating to medical and dental services provided to foreign citizens in the territory of the Republic of Bulgaria, are granted on the basis of reciprocity in the framework of bilateral agreements.	Extension of the social security and health benefits to citizens of other countries.	Dentists, physiotherapists, doctors, paramedical personnel, and nurses from the countries mentioned in column 3 may exercise their profession on the basis of reciprocity.
Countries to which the measure applies	All countries with whom medical cooperation might be desirable. (Agreements already exist with medical centers in Greece, the U.K., and Israel.)	All	Countries with which such bilateral agreements are or will be concluded.	All countries	All countries
Intended duration	Indefinite	Indefinite	Indefinite	Not specified	Indefinite

TABLE 2.1   MFN Exemptions Relevant to the Health and Related Service Sectors (*Continued*)

	Cyprus (GATS/ EL/25)	Jordan (GATS/ EL/128)	Bulgaria (GATS/ EL/122)	Tunisia (GATS/ EL/87)	Dominican Republic (GATS/ EL/28)
Conditions creating the need for the exemption	The measure is necessary due to the existence or possible future signing of new bilateral agreements between Cyprus and third countries with whom Cyprus has geographical proximity or other special links.	Need to ensure equal access to foreign markets for Jordanian medical laboratories.	Obligations under international agreements.	To preserve the social security rights of nationals of the two contracting parties concerned.	Reciprocity legislation in force.

citing the sector concerned, the description of the measure, the countries it applies to, the duration of the measure, and the reason for undertaking the measure. The members who chose to keep these measures have done so for a variety of reasons, including the preexistence of bilateral agreements for cooperation in the health sector and the desire to ensure reciprocity of market access for certain health professionals. Members will probably maintain the MFN-inconsistent measures, including those that pursue health goals in the current review. Moreover, it must also be noted that some MFN-exemption measures, which do not apply to health services, cite health as the reason for the application of the measure.[7]

Transparency—Ensuring Good Governance and Effective Market Access

Transparency is another key obligation of the GATS. The transparency obligation requires members to publish or otherwise make available information relating to all measures that apply to services trade and that affect the operation of the GATS agreement. Members must also notify new or changed laws, regulations, or administrative guidelines that affect trade in services covered by their specific commitments. Transparency is deemed crucial for this area of trade because it enables foreign services suppliers to access information concerning the regulations of foreign markets.[8] Current discussions in the WTO focus more particularly on the achievement of fuller transparency of laws and regulations forming part of the discussions surrounding the development of future disciplines on domestic regulation (under Article VI.4). Developing countries need to ensure that this will not increase the administrative burden on them.

With respect to the health sector, transparency is relevant in several ways. With respect to a country's own domestic market, transparency is an important element of good governance and important for health ministries and other relevant ministries/authorities. In fact, transparency can assist to ensure that the adequate health regulations are in place and that they are communicated to the trade or other officials who are responsible for notifying WTO members of such measures. The challenge here may be to improve coordination between health ministries (issuing such regulations) and other ministries, including trade ministries. But transparency is also important with respect to foreign markets. Specifically, it is important as it allows foreign providers wishing to access markets to have the relevant information on the regulations and standards that they will have to comply with. From the perspective of developing countries, such information may be particularly useful with regard to cross-border supply, including through outsourcing (e.g., medical transcription of records) or movement of natural persons under Mode 4 (e.g., movement of nurses and doctors), two of the areas where developing countries seem to have a comparative advantage. Transparency is also particularly crucial in the context of health-related financial regulations (such as health and social insurances).

A more general point in the discussion on transparency relates to the need for transparency not only on the side of the regulatory authority but also on the part of the service suppliers. Indeed, public health objectives require suppliers to provide transparent records and accounts. In fact, the cost of inadequate provision (or of nonprovision) of services can be detrimental, especially for developing countries, which already face many resource constraints, thus calling for increased transparency on the side of the services suppliers.

Market Access and National Treatment—Positive List Approach to Commitments

The Structure of the GATS clearly separates the general obligations and disciplines that are accepted by members upon their signature of the agreement (e.g., the unconditional MFN obligation and transparency) from specific commitments that are the subject of specific negotiations, the results of which are included in members' schedules of commitments (i.e., market access, national treatment, and additional commitments). This is the so-called positive list approach to scheduling commitments. The schedules of specific commitments enable governments to adapt their level of commitments in terms of sectoral and modal coverage, market access, and national treatment (with appropriate limitations and qualifications) through gradual liberalization to their level of development. The positive list approach permits a progressive implementation of the potentially far-reaching market access and national treatment obligations, also allowing to selectively determine the exact scope of a Member's commitments (e.g. the inclusion or not of services supplied in governmental authority).

The mandate for negotiations on specific commitments is found in Article XIX of the GATS, which instructs members to start a new round of services negotiations by the year 2000. These negotiations cover both granting access to members' markets and granting foreign services and service supplier's national treatment, both of which can be accorded on a sector-by-sector and mode-specific basis with attachment of appropriate limitations and conditions.

Market Access The market access commitments taken by a member (according to Article XVI) broadly imply according all other WTO members equal access to supplying services on an MFN basis for all sectors and modes of supply for which the member has agreed to such commitment. More specifically, a full market access commitment obliges the member in question to refrain from putting in place the specific measures included in the taxative list in Article XVI (Krajewski, 2003).These measures are: limitations on the number of suppliers; limitations on the total value of services transactions or assets; limitations on the total number of service operations or on the total quantity of service output; limitations on the total number of natural persons; measures that restrict or require specific types of legal entity or joint venture; and limitations on the participation of foreign capital.

National Treatment The national treatment commitments that members can decide to take (according to Article XVII) broadly oblige the member in question to grant foreign services and service suppliers treatment no less favorable than the one accorded to "like" domestic services and services suppliers. However, this obligation is more complex than initially perceived. In fact, the text of the agreements, as well as WTO dispute settlement, has shown that the GATS national treatment obligation has a de jure but also a de facto aspect. Once a member has agreed to accord national treatment, this obligation implies that the treatment must be equally de jure (on the face of the measure being implemented) and de facto (in regard to its effects). This means that a measure, even if it de jure does not discriminate between foreign and domestic services and service suppliers, may still be found to be a de facto violation of national treatment.

Box 2.2: Malaysian Commitments on Health Services

Malaysian commitments on health services are a good example of taking deeper commitments in specific activities of this sector, complementing them with carefully designed limitations. Malaysian commitments are limited to private health services only, with conditionalities allowing the government to ensure local participation. In addition, Malaysia has entered into commitments in relation to business services.

The commitments provide for market access and national treatment under Modes 1, 2, and 3 for private hospital services. On Mode 3, access is conditioned by an economic needs test (ENT) and is allowed only through locally incorporated joint-venture corporations with Malaysian individuals or Malaysian-controlled corporations or both, limiting foreign shareholding in the joint venture corporation to 30 percent. Moreover, the joint venture should operate a hospital with a minimum 100 beds. With respect to national treatment, the establishment of feeder outpatient clinics is not permitted.

Under professional services, Malaysia has also taken commitments in medical specialty services. These cover a number of very specialized subsectors such as forensic medicine, nuclear medicine, geriatrics, and microvascular surgery. With respect to Modes 1 and 2, both market access and national treatment have no limitations. With respect to Mode 3, the provision of services is limited to supply only by a natural person. Mode 4, in turn, is limited to intracorporate transferees with specific national treatment limitations relating to practice only in private hospitals of at least 100 beds, at a specified location and with changes requiring approval. Moreover, setting up of individual or joint group practices is not permitted.

Finally, Malaysia also made commitments under Article XVIII (the GATS provision on "additional commitments") stating that the qualifying examination to determine competence will be conducted in the English language. A number of other business services commitments that relate to health, e.g., management consulting services relating to advisory and guidance in the field of pharmacy, are also included.

Source: Malaysia, 1994. Schedule of Specific Commitments, GATS/SC/52, 15 April 1994.

In other words, in order to treat the foreign and domestic suppliers equally, it may be necessary to apply formally different measures to each group. Moreover, it is important to note that the national treatment obligation only implies that members cannot accord foreign services and service suppliers treatment *less* favorable once they have taken a commitment. The rule does not imply that they cannot give them treatment *more* favorable than to the domestic industry.

Finally, it is important to highlight that the national treatment obligation applies to subsidy-type measures as it does to other measures. This entails that if a member wishes to subsidize certain services, as may often be the case for services such as health, but does not wish to extend the subsidy to foreign service suppliers operating in its territory, the member must inscribe a limitation to any national treatment obligation.[9] Indeed, members not only have the option of taking full market access and national treatment commitments or no commitments. They can also take partial commitments by inscribing limitations in their schedules, as provided for in Articles XVI and XVII.[10] The possibility to make conditional (or limited) commitments may be particularly important in sectors such as health, where for social or other reasons, members may deem it unwise to grant full access and national treatment in their markets. It must, however, be clearly stated that conditions in schedules are not necessarily a long-term solution as they are susceptible to being the object of negotiations for removal in subsequent negotiating rounds directed toward progressive liberalization.

GATS 2000 Negotiations: Proposals and the Request/Offer Phase

During the earlier, proposal phase of GATS 2000 negotiations, the health sector was not included, except for the areas covered in the Mode 4 proposals by India and Pakistan and a group of developing countries. From developed countries, there have so far not been any vocal export interests for binding health services. In the first phase of the current negotiations, when members submitted their initial negotiating proposals, several developing countries expressed their interests in the liberalization of health services. This is the case for countries such as Colombia, Cuba, and India, who indicated that this was a sector of interest to them. It can be expected that these countries (and possibly others) have followed up these initial expressions of interest with concrete initial requests targeting specific markets and will have further discussed this in bilateral consultations with their trading partners.[11] Developing countries design their negotiating positions in light of their national trade, developmental, and other objectives—but also as a function of the requests that they receive from their trading partners and of the bargaining process of the negotiations.[12] This raises the question whether some members will choose to carve out their health sectors from the negotiations while requesting other members to take liberalization commitments in this area. A quick glance at the initial offers submitted to date **shows** that offers for liberalization of specific health-related service sectors remain limited. The United States, the European Community, and Canada, for example, have stated that, for them, health services are not a focus area of negotiations. To date, it seems that many other developed countries have adopted similar positions. At the same time according to the CTS Chair's July 2005 report to the Trade Negotiations Committee (TNC)[13], there were 10 offers in health services, all of which were made by developing country

Members.[14] According to the report, three developing country Members indicated their interest in further liberalization of the health sector, one of which stressed the importance of supplying these services through modes 1 and 2, including through insurance portability.

Requests Subsequent to the proposal phase, a few developing countries have included this sector in their requests, particularly in relation to the movement of natural persons but also in respect to the other modes. These requests from developing countries are put to both developed and other developing countries. Developing countries have targeted a variety of measures. Among others, their negotiating requests specifically ask major trading partners to:

- remove limitations under which individual medical doctors are allowed to enter only for purposes of studies or training and not to render professional services;
- remove quantitative restrictions and numerical quotas as contained in horizontal commitments so as to enable health professionals (including medical and dental services, midwives, nurses, physiotherapists, paramedical personnel, or speech therapists) to enter and deliver health services on a demand-driven basis;
- remove requirements of residency, nationality requirements, and quantitative restrictions so as to enable health professionals (specifically medical doctors, dentists, dieticians and nutritionists, dental assistants, midwives, nurses, physiotherapists, and paramedical personnel) to enter and deliver health services on a demand-driven basis;
- unlink independent professionals from juridical persons contained in horizontal commitments and remove the residency requirement;
- take full commitments in health services with respect to Mode 4, unlink independent professionals from juridical persons contained in horizontal commitments, remove ownership of hospitals to nationally licensed physicians, to remove prohibitions on investors owning hospitals in Mode 3;
- remove ENTs;
- recognize qualifications of the medical and dental services professionals and nurses; and
- put in place a visa system that ensures the fulfillment of the horizontal and sectoral commitments undertaken.

Offers Among the offers submitted, some contain elements related to health services. More specifically, several members (e.g. Bahrain, Hong Kong, Korea, India and Trinidad and Tobago) offered new health-related commitments (i.e. introduced sectors, sub-sectors or modes that had previously not been scheduled). Hong Kong, for example, in it is initial offer, made new commitments on five health-related sub-sectors, namely, hospital services; other human health services; medical and dental services; services provided by midwives, nurses, physiotherapists, and paramedical personnel; and (part of) veterinary services. As to the nature of the commitments, however, except for Mode 2, where it made full commitment (for veterinary services, including Mode 1), all of the other modes were kept unbound. Subsequently, Hong Kong's revised offer did not introduce any further changes in this context.

India's initial offer on medical and dental services, and services provided by midwives, nurses, physiotherapists, and paramedical personnel, in part, mirrors the improvement it has made on its Uruguay Round commitment on hospital services (e.g. Mode 2 "none" and Mode 3: increasing the foreign equity threshold, as well as attaching certain technology transfer requirements). In addition, India's new Mode 3 commitment in these subsectors contains the condition that "[p]ublicly funded services may be available only to Indian citizen or may be supplied at differential prices to persons other than Indian citizens."

Also Korea made new commitments in its initial offer, more specifically on veterinary services. In its revised offer, it introduced a few technical changes regarding insurance (including health and accident insurance) and improvements to its offer in veterinary services. Similarly, Pakistan, in its initial offer, included new commitments for veterinary services and services provided by midwives, nurses, physiotherapist, and para-medical personnel, clearly stating however (in the sectoral column) that "[t]he offer does not include services provided by public institutions whether owned and operated by federal, provincial, district, Tehsil or municipal Authorities"). Mauritius offered a new Mode 1 commitment for market access in direct (life and non-life) insurance, albeit with the condition that only companies established and incorporated in Mauritius are allowed to sell insurance.

Trinidad and Tobago also offered new commitments. For example, under professional services, Trinidad and Tobago complemented its pre-existing commitments in dental and veterinary services, with new commitments for medical services (including both, general and specialized medical services) and services provided by nurses. Interestingly, Mode 3 is being kept largely unbound, Mode 2 (and in part Mode 1) would largely be fully open ("none"). Bahrain, in its initial offer suggested new commitments in social services (full commitments on all 4 Modes for both, national treatment and market access), which subsequently, in its revised offer, it decided to withdraw. In its revised offer, it then suggested new commitments in medical and dental services, veterinary services and services provided by midwives, nurses and physiotherapists. Generally, these new commitments suggests "unbound" for Mode 1 and 3, "none" for Modes 2, and "unbound, except as indicated in the horizontal section" for Mode 4. Only veterinary services also contain a "none" for Mode 3 in the market access column. Furthermore, Bahrain's revised offer introduced new commitments for hospital services, for other human health services, and for social services. While the offer in social services is towards full openness (e.g. none in all four modes of supply), the other two sub-sectors are more nuanced. For Mode 3 in market access in hospital services, for example, Bahrain suggested the condition that "a private hospital may be established by Bahraini doctors with no less than 5 years of continues (sic) experience or by organizations, companies and societies established in Bahrain."

Several other members, e.g. Mexico, India, New Zealand, and the European Community, made improvements to existing health related commitments. Among others, improvements to the offers were of the following nature: New Zealand's changed its Mode 1 commitments in veterinary services, which was previously "unbound due to technical infeasibility," to "none" (with no further health-related changes in the revised offer). In the case of the European Community, some members provided (or amended) their definitions/criteria for ENTs. For example, for medical, dental, and midwives services, Germany's ENT has the following criteria: local demand and population. Several European members also adopted common criteria for services provided by pharmacists, specifically, population and geographic density of existing pharmacies. Subsequently, in its revised offer, the EC expanded the geographical scope of certain Mode 3 commitments in medical, dental and midwives services (to Lithuania and Sweden).

India's initial offer introduced improvements to its Mode 3 market access commitment on hospital services, where it increased the foreign equity ceiling from 51 percent to 74 percent and attached new conditions relating to transfer of the latest technology and approval requirements. Pakistan, in turn, in its initial offer, improved its Mode 3 market access commitments in hospital services by eliminating certain limitations. In addition, Pakistan introduced some technical changes in medical and dental services sub-sectors. Improvements were also offered by Egypt, which, in financial services (including life, health and personnel accident insurance) eliminated certain Mode 3 market access limitations (i.e. two related to ENTs, and one relating to foreign capital equity thresholds (which had, however, already phased out). The Dominican Republic introduced minor changes to its commitments for dental and medical services, social services, as well as hospital services and other human health services.

Other countries did not offer any health related changes. Albania, while already having commitments on medical and dental services, veterinary services, services provide by midwives nurses, physiotherapist and paramedical personnel, as well as for hospital services and other human health services, did not introduce any health-related changes in its initial offers. The situation is similar with Kenya, whose initial offer does not introduce any changes to its pre-existing commitments in non-life insurance. The same is true for, Norway, which did not (neither in its initial nor in its revised offer) include any changes to its previous commitments in medical and dental services, veterinary services and deliveries and related services, nursing services, physiotherapeutic and para-medical services. Finally, also the Philippines' offer does not introduce any changes in health related services.

On the whole, the initial offers on health-related services are limited. Considering that current commitments are not very deep (including in Mode 4) and there is a steadily increasing demand for health-related services (especially for services to be delivered through the movement of natural persons) globally, there is room for member countries to request for more opening. While to date there are a few offers on health services, they are mostly made by developing country WTO Members. Frequently, they are also made by WTO members who had previously undertaken health-related commitments). However, it remains to be seen to what extent future offers by industrialized countries will truly match the expectations set out in developing countries' requests.

Movement of Natural Persons: Mode 4—The Need for Commercially Meaningful Commitments

So far, specific commitments made under GATS have been asymmetrical in terms of limited coverage of Mode 4. This trend is continued by the initial offers developed countries have submitted. Thus far, these offers do not contain any major improvements in this respect. For developing countries, however, commercially meaningful liberalization in Mode 4 amounts to a litmus test for the real development content of the Doha Work Programme and its claim to be a Doha Development Agenda (UNCTAD, 2003). In fact, with the right policy and regulatory framework at the national and international levels, Mode 4 liberalization could be a win-win welfare situation for developed and developing countries. Economic analysis shows that if entry quotas were increased by an amount equal to 3 percent of developed countries' labor forces, there would be an increase in world welfare of $US156 billion per year (Winters, 2003).

Still, potential gains from Mode 4 liberalization are most important for developing countries. The most evident way in which trade in Mode 4 benefits developing countries is through the provision of a steady and continuous inflow of remittances. Currently, such remittances amount to nearly US$100 billion a year and exceed the level of official development assistance (World Bank/IMF, 2004). However, the total amount of resources remitted may be two or three times

Box 2.3: GATS and Movement of Nurses

In recent years, the international movement of nurses has been on the rise. Two main reasons for this trend are, first, the search for better employment opportunities and quality of life by developing country workers, and, second, the large nursing shortages in many developed countries. Bilateral labor agreements have also facilitated the movement of nurses. This pattern of migration (South to North), however, may give rise to problems of exploitation and abuse in the form of lower worker protection rights, wages, and benefits, among others. As a response to these concerns, nurses associations worldwide have begun organizing and lobbying their governments on this issue. Thus far, the more active groups are mostly from developed countries, especially those facing a high influx of foreign workers. In fact, some groups from the North, such as Grassroots Women based in Canada, are advocating on behalf of foreign nurses and support southern groups like the Filipino Nurses Support Group to push for policies to better the treatment of foreign nurses. Among other things, these groups are calling for:

- the recognition of qualifications,
- workers' rights and labor standards,
- equal pay, and
- opposition to unregulated privatization schemes that lead to exploitative arrangements.

In developed countries, nurses associations such as the New Zealand Nurses Organization, Registered Nurses Association of Ontario, or the American Nurses Association are calling upon their governments to protect their domestic public health systems and workforce. The U.K. nursing association has developed a code of ethical recruitment. The main areas of concern and policy suggestions shared by these groups with regard to GATS and trade liberalization in general are:

- threats to Governments' ability to regulate,
- downward harmonization of professional qualification recognitions,
- threat to quality and universal access to health care,
- deteriorating working conditions and wages,
- lack of transparency and participation by relevant stakeholders in negotiations, and, as a response,
- the goal of ensuring that public health services are excluded from international trade negotiations.

The International Council of Nurses (ICN),[a] whose global membership represents both developed and developing country members, aligns itself with both southern and northern interests. Its call for action essentially promotes equity, sound regulation, advancement of the nursing profession, and participation in decision making. ICN believes that ensuring an adequate supply of

Box 2.3: GATS and Movement of Nurses (Continued)

qualified nursing personnel is key to the provision of quality health care. The right of the individual nurse to migrate and the resulting beneficial effects are likewise recognized. However, the ICN places great importance on ethical recruitment, policies on definition, scope, and protection of title, and discourages the practice of nurse recruitment from countries without sound human resource planning and governance frameworks (these include high standards for personal/ professional growth and performance, public sanction, participation of the profession in public policy, accountability to the public, and proper recognition and remuneration, as well as ensuring an adequate supply of nurses at home and providing incentives for return).

Source: International Council of Nurses, submissions to the WTO Workshop on Domestic Regulation, and Yan 2002.
a. Presentation by Judith Oulton, International Council of Nurses on Applicability of the Accountancy Disciplines to Nursing, WTO Workshop on Domestic Regulation, 29–30 March, 2004.

greater, since a large number of transactions are effected through informal channels. Dynamic gains for the home country are significant, because remittances increase investment and domestic savings; promote development of other sectors of the economy and trade; ensure transfer of technology, entrepreneurship and knowledge; and build human capacities.

The problem of nursing shortages is seen in both developed and developing countries and serves as a point of departure between the perspectives of developing and developed country nurses. Developing countries that face nursing shortages— such as the Caribbean, the Philippines, and India—are contending with "brain drain" from the loss of workers, particularly of skilled and experienced health providers, abroad. In the Philippines in particular, concerns have been raised regarding the very high turnover rates (between 40 and 80 percent) of nurses in leading hospitals, the overseas recruitment of the "best and the brightest" and the well-experienced and sufficiently trained, and the flight of nursing faculty members themselves. In 2002, 13,536 nurses, representing about one-fourth of the total nurses employed by all Philippine hospitals, left the country.[15] As teams of nurses working in critical wards such as surgery and intensive care units move abroad, some hospitals have resorted to a temporary closure or discontinuance of some of their services or have gambled by utilizing the services of novices and less-experienced personnel. Those who were left behind are forced to work overtime, as they have to attend to patients needing emergency care.

Several academics and groups linked to health-related professions and practices have initiated moves to address the issue of the nursing shortage in the

Philippines. Some of their suggestions for regulating nurses' movement include: requiring *compulsory service to local hospitals* for some specified number of years before they are allowed to work abroad; *paying an equivalent amount* for their training and the partial cost of their education in case they do not complete the mandatory domestic employment requirement; devising some form of *rotation schemes* to ensure the availability of an ample supply of qualified nurses domestically (which is also an assurance that their chance to work abroad is only for a limited amount of time); *improving the package of incentives* for nurses and other health professionals to entice them to stay and work for local hospitals; *encouraging return migration* by acknowledging their training abroad and giving them some visiting scholar or other honorary positions and encouraging them to serve as trainers; requiring those who leave to *post some bond* to ensure their return to the country; and creating a body (or a mechanism) to serve as a repository of data and information on nurses and to deal with human health–related concerns and policies. Consideration is also being given to legislative measures to alleviate this situation.

In the Caribbean, there has been an effort to combat this problem, for example through the development of a managed migration program by the Regional Nursing Body of the Caribbean.[16] The Commonwealth Countries adopted an International Code of Practice on Ethical Recruitment in 2002.

On the other hand, developed country nurses associations feel that recruiting foreign nurses not only further exacerbates problems back home but also only provides a short-term solution for the receiving country. The American Nurses Association, for example, points to the deteriorating working conditions of the nursing profession in the United States as one of the major causes of its shortage of nurses. Improving such conditions and promoting nursing education, they say, is the long-term solution. Ensuring the temporal nature of movement is of course an important way of alleviating brain drain. Some countries such as the Netherlands have devised mechanisms to ensure that movement to their markets remains temporary, and have decided to invest in monitoring the return and in training programs for skills that would be useful to service suppliers upon return to their home countries. Costs linked to brain drain need to be balanced against gains through brain circulation, including through remittances transferred to the home country which support inter alia development of infrastructure such as educational and health facilities and capital for entrepreneurial initiatives. In fact, some health professionals have returned with higher skills and training, and invested in local skill development and strengthening of the health infrastructure.

Obviously, while allowing for regulatory measures to combat possible negative effects, there is still a need for options on how GATS can be used to promote liberalization in Mode 4. One of the ways to approach this could be through a model schedule. Such a model schedule could combine specific commitments for natural persons with certain skills on short-term intracompany visits and short-term visits to fulfill contracts." Short-term" could be defined in each case as a stay of less than a year. Reflecting these classes of movement as a Service Provider Visa in the national migration laws would help streamline temporary entry.[17] A set of additional commitments could be made under Article XVIII of the GATS, which would aim to enhance the transparency of visa procedures and limit the trade-impeding impact of measures such as qualifications requirements and administrative procedures. In such a model schedule, emphasis could be on broad horizontal commitments, eliminating ENTs, and ensuring a basic minimum level of access across all sectors, supplemented by sector-specific commitments such as those concerning specific categories of health professionals where deeper liberalization is possible. Nevertheless, under this approach, lack of recognition of qualifications would remain one of the major barriers to Mode 4-related supply. More recently, additional approaches were discussed, including moving discussions on Mode 4 by adopting a set of common categories of persons, or by addressing certain issues (e.g. transparency, or qualification requirements) in current negotiations on domestic regulation. In addition, the least-developed countries have recently submitted a group request on Mode 4.

Mutual Recognition Agreements

Commitments on market access and national treatment are not always sufficient for a foreign service supplier to be able to supply a market. Indeed, if the country of import of the service does not recognize the qualifications of the provider, the value of any market access granted is questionable/diminished. The recognition of qualifications is a crucial element for the provision of health services. This is one area where the protection of public health and information asymmetries makes it essential that the government set out the level of qualification required for the provision of services. Such professions as nurses and doctors are particularly affected by the need for the recognition of qualification.

In Article VII, the GATS allows members to enter into mutual recognition agreements (MRAs) enabling them to recognize the education or experience obtained, requirements met, or licenses or certifications granted in one or several other countries. The article further requires that negotiations to such agreements be open to all members who can demonstrate that their qualifications are equivalent. However, to date, the number of MRAs and their impact on services trade has been rather limited.

An OECD study shows that many MRAs notified under the GATS take place within the context of broader regional cooperation or integration initiatives.

However, there are also some instances where countries have used other processes outside of MRAs to assess the qualifications of foreign service providers (OECD, 2003).

In the current GATS negotiations, discussions on MRAs are principally related to market access issues as well as to transparency requirements. Indeed, nonrecognition basically impedes on market access commitments. The establishment of a monitoring and coordination mechanism for ensuring effective access to MRAs could be an important contribution to addressing these problems. In addition, there is need to examine the accession clauses of existing MRA agreements to ensure that—indeed—it is possible for new members to join under the same conditions as the members of the MRA. Also, one could suggest that those members who have formed such agreements take a more proactive approach to ensure effective access of developing countries to mutual recognition agreements through inviting others to join such agreements and actively pursuing mutual acceptance of equivalence. Currently, members are also discussing how to better implement Article VII. Among the implementation issues raised is the question of whether MRAs by professional associations can be considered as agreements and arrangements between members under Article VII.

GATS Rules (Safeguards, Subsidies, and Government Procurement)

At the conclusion of the Uruguay Round some of the rules relating to trade in services had not been negotiated conclusively. Members therefore decided to conclude the GATS but include several mandates for further negotiations. The negotiations on a group of issues referred to as GATS Rules, and which pertain to an emergency safeguard mechanism (Article X of GATS), government procurement (Article XIII), and subsidies (Article XV), are currently taking place. These negotiations are mandated to be completed before the conclusion of the market access negotiations. As they are still ongoing these negotiations provide health policymakers and other interested stakeholders with an opportunity to focus on the regulatory issues and the linkages between these negotiations and domestic health policies.

Emergency Safeguard Mechanism/Measures An emergency safeguard mechanism (ESM) for services would allow members to adapt to changing circumstances in the context of liberalization (e.g. by addressing adjustment costs, brining on board those who lose out from liberalization, and creating a breathing space to build capacities), by temporarily suspending their obligations under the GATS. Several members have stated that having such measures would help persuade domestic constituencies and trading partners to accept greater liberalization, in view of the particular vulnerability of services suppliers in developing countries, who lack experience with liberalized markets and who are usually SMEs. Several fundamental issues relating to this safeguard are still under discussion, including the desirability and feasibility of such a measure. Owing to its temporary nature, allowing time for addressing the necessary adjustment by local suppliers of services and employment and other structural concerns, an ESM could provide an opportunity for affected industries to restructure. The importance of an ESM is therefore based on the understanding that liberalization involves adjustment costs and that imperfection in factor mobility and asymmetry of information may negatively affect resource allocation. Since a multilateral assessment of the implications of liberalization in trade in services has not been completed, governments remain cautious in the presence of uncertainties about its potential impacts. Emergency safeguard measures could take various forms, including the suspension of specific commitments or the adoption of positive measures in favor of domestic suppliers. The initial deadline for the negotiations on emergency safeguard mechanisms was missed and has since been further extended. The current deadline is for any eventual results of the negotiations to enter into effect no later than the date of entry into force of the results of the current round of services negotiations (WTO, March 2004).

Subsidies Negotiations on subsidies are based on the need to address the trade-distorting impact of subsidies granted by members. Developed and developing countries are not concerned in the same way by this issue. Indeed, developing countries consider that they are negatively affected by the subsidies that developed countries provide to their service suppliers, which lead to unfair competition. This is especially the case since many developing countries cannot match such subsidies because of scarce resources. They therefore tend to be in favor of limiting subsidies relating to services. However, they also feel that in some circumstances they may need to subsidize their service industries in order to build competitive services sectors and meet social objectives. Measures could be classified under three main categories: *export-enhancing subsidies*, through which a country would attain a larger market share in comparison to that in the absence of the measure; *import-displacement subsidies*, through which a country would import less than in the absence of the measure; and finally, *investment-diverting subsidies*, which distort the flows, volume, and direction of foreign direct investment (FDI) in relation to what would have been expected in the absence of the measure.[18]

Health sector subsidies are targeted to ensure that health services are provided universally, including to the poor and marginalized. Cross-subsidization may be an important tool to that effect. However, it is questionable whether these subsidies with social objectives fall under the mandate of Article XV, which explicitly targets trade-distortive effects of subsidies. Article XV recognizes the role of subsidies in relation to the development programs of developing countries and takes into account the needs of members, particularly developing countries, for flexibility in this area. Further work is required to define the subsidies covered by any new disciplines, to identify services-related support measures that could be considered as subsidies, and, in particular, to analyze their effect on trade in services.

Government Procurement Article XIII exempts from the MFN, market access and national treatment provisions of GATS all services purchased by governmental agencies for governmental purposes and without a view to commercial resale, or with a view to use in the supply of services for commercial resale. The same article provides that there shall be multilateral negotiations on government procurement of services within two years of entry into force of the WTO (i.e., beginning in 1997). So far, these negotiations have not yet produced any concrete results.

Most developing countries do not wish to participate in the existing Plurilateral Agreement on Government Procurement (GPA), which includes some services because of the lack of effective special and differential treatment provisions and costs of implementation. Among others reasons, this is because of the general perception that by opening their government procurement to international tendering, they will allow foreign firms to capture a significant part of their domestic business, while their firms will be precluded from gaining access to foreign government procurement markets owing to financial and technological weaknesses or owing the various other barriers.[19] Government procurement is also used as a means to promote development of domestic industry or technology and to support the competitiveness of small- and medium-sized enterprises. Developing countries have been reluctant to embrace the initiative to establish disciplines on transparency in government procurement because they are concerned that this may prejudge their use of government procurement as a tool for pursuing social and development objectives, particularly if there are any elements that go beyond strict transparency requirements and impact market access, and also because of the high cost of implementation of such an agreement.

Previously, there had been confusion as to how the mandate in GATS relates to the GPA and the mandate under the Doha Ministerial Declaration for possible negotiations on transparency in government procurement. With the 2004 July Framework (suspending discussions on government procurement), its impact for the respective services negotiations remains unclear to date. There has not been much progress on the GATS negotiations on government procurement so far. In its most recent contribution, the main *demandeur,* the EC, have narrowed their focus, now calling for mainly procedural disciplines. They argue that such rules would be particularly important to ensure the effective opening of government procurement markets.

GATS Rules—Issues for Consideration from a Health Perspective The different negotiations in the rules agenda could well have an impact on members' health sectors. For example, a safeguards mechanism may also be useful with regard to sensitive sectors such as the health sector. While current criteria in the goods area relate to injury or threat thereof to the domestic industry, one could also envisage going beyond industry considerations, so as to include health considerations as sufficient grounds for launching a safeguard action. But even when staying within the narrow remits of industry considerations, to some extent, excessive provision of services may be detrimental, particularly in the high revenue-generating services. Countries may wish to avoid the phenomenon of useless duplication of high revenue-generating services (catering to the wealthiest in society) while basic services (for the poor or in rural areas) are still lacking. Health authorities should therefore be able to warn trade officials when a sudden increase in imports is distorting the domestic market and when action needs to be taken. At the same time, a safeguards mechanism could also create the potential for protectionist abuse, further undermining developing countries' export opportunities through Mode 4 (or even Mode 1). Eventually, the potential for protectionist abuse would depend upon the question of the criteria used in defining an emergency situation, and the procedures and threshold required for triggering the mechanism. In addition, there is need for including strong special and differential treatment provisions for developing countries.

Future disciplines on subsidies would relate to the problem of insufficient provision of health services at affordable costs. Indeed, members currently have the flexibility to use subsidies, including social-oriented subsidies (in case of a national treatment commitment, as long as they are not discriminatory). The question remains whether these types of subsidies could be considered trade-distortive and whether any future disciplines would require a special carve-out for subsidies related to essential services, which would include health services.

Finally, the negotiations regarding government procurement may be important for those health services that are purchased by the government or by public hospitals. For example, in some countries the government provides free medical and dental services for children in school. As the definite relationship between the provision of essential services and government procurement remains to be determined (Cossy, 2005), it is crucial to closely follow these negotiations to ensure that such public service provision of services remains possible.

Regulatory Challenges—the Need for Flexibility

The supply of services—and their (international) trade—need to be carefully regulated. This is a widely recognized fact. The rationale for regulating services ranges from economic to noneconomic objectives, covering the need to address market failures (e.g., information asymmetry, fear of excessive entries) as well as social objectives (e.g., the accessibility and availability of services) and ethical issues related to the supply of services. All of these aspects—economic, social, and ethical—are pertinent to health services.

Thus, today, the health sector tends to be heavily regulated. The principle reason behind this is that governments aim to achieve national health objectives in spite of the many market failures of the sector. Indeed, governments have to find a solution to the often-distorted market situations, which—left to their own devices—would not necessarily provide a sufficient supply of health services at affordable costs for the entire population. Regulatory frameworks are frequently a response to overcome these challenges.[20] Consequently, negotiations that affect this regulatory framework may therefore have vast implications for a country's health system. Such consequences may go beyond what are impacts on the regulation of health services *per se*. A group of nongovernmental organizations (NGOs) has highlighted the constraints that GATS disciplines could have on services such as marketing which, in turn, could be used to promote certain health outcomes (regulations for the marketing of baby foods illustrate this point) (Equinet et al., 2003). This is even more problematic in the case of developing countries, as they often do not yet have strong regulatory systems in place.

Currently, many services sectors, including the health care sector, are undergoing regulatory reform. This usually entails two features: deregulation, which involves removal of outdated and costly regulations, sometimes reflecting the traditional role of government in the services sectors; and reregulation, i.e., the adoption of more appropriate, market-oriented regulations. Both deregulation and reregulation are linked to liberalization.

While in some services sectors (i.e., telecommunications) there is, at least to some extent, an "agreed model" of liberalization across countries, this is less the case with respect to health services. Rather, health regulations in various countries go down individual national paths (Krajewski, 2003). While there might still be lessons learned from sectors such as telecommunications, international rules for services trade need to recognize this diversity and specificity of the health sector. The last years have seen much controversy about the extent to which the GATS recognizes this diversity. Frequently, it is claimed that the GATS induces and locks in liberalization, while recognizing the right to regulate.[21] At the same time, it does not give guidance—perhaps for good reasons—about what constitutes an appropriate regulatory framework.[22] Most importantly, however, there are concerns that GATS commitments would preclude the sort of trial-and-error approach that is crucial for domestic regulatory processes. Being able to experiment with regulatory approaches, adapting and changing them in case of failure or in case of changed circumstances, is particularly important in developing countries, where regulatory frameworks are still at early stages of development. Thus, a trial-and-error-process, allowing for learning by doing, is crucial.

The two areas where the GATS may encroach most upon this trial error process—and upon domestic regulatory prerogatives in general—are the GATS approach toward public services and the GATS negotiations on domestic regulation.

GATS and Public Services—Strategic Challenges from Ambiguity

The Public/Private Interface from a GATS Perspective Approaching GATS negotiations from a developmental and health perspective raises the question of whether health services and their supply should be covered by an international trade agreement at all. This question is particularly relevant for the so-called "public services" aspects of the health sector. While this (broader) question is beyond the scope of this paper, the following discussion seeks to describe the interface between GATS and so-called "public" or "essential" services. It should be noted that a number of different approaches have been followed in open markets to provide for universal service provision, e.g., through pooling of funds for universal services and its allocation based on competitive tenders or through imposition of a universal service levy of one percent on gross operating revenues of companies to finance a fund dedicated to providing universal access in remote areas or consumer subsidies. These approaches have to be adapted to the local conditions of each country and not all have been successful in achieving universal access.

Approaching the question from the perspective of public as opposed to private ownership of health service providers requires looking at the definitional aspects of the GATS. At a first glance, the GATS appears to be neutral as to whether service providers are *privately* or *publicly owned*. When defining whether a service is "owned" by a member, the GATS explicitly says that a service supplier could be public or private, indicating no preference.[23] In addition, the GATS contains language that is commonly understood to allow "public monopolies."[24] There are, however, concerns about the extent to which GATS induces and locks in privatization, and about the practical implications that increasing private sector involvement may entail for public providers. While fundamental in nature, these concerns are beyond the scope of this paper.[25]

A second way to approach the interface between GATS and public services is to ask whether the GATS, in its obligations, recognizes the specific nature of public or essential services. The GATS' national treatment and most favored nation obligations are central in that context. In essence, once a sector is committed to full national treatment, WTO members may not accord different treatment to domestic and foreign "like" services and "like "service suppliers,[26] turning the determination of what are "like" services or service providers into the central issue. However, this question of "likeness" also serves as an example for the interface between the GATS and public services: are public health services (and service providers)— because of their essential nature for a large number of citizens (including the poor and marginalized)—"unlike" private health services (and services providers) that tend to serve the wealthier segments of society? To date, this question remains shrouded with uncertainty.

Both the legal text of the GATS as well as WTO jurisprudence have failed to provide guidance about which elements and factors should be relevant for the definition of "likeness of service suppliers." What seems clear is that WTO panels and the appellate body have focused on the characteristics of the *service* in question rather than on the characteristics of the *supplier*. In the *Bananas* case, the panel simply stated that "...to the extent that entities provide these like services, they are like services suppliers."[27] Thus, it is not certain what factors future panels (or the appellate body in future appeals) will take into consideration when deciding what are like services, and consequently like service suppliers. It remains to be seen whether factors such as the "public or developmental interest" in health services or their contribution to the progressive realization of the right to health will be relevant. Similarly, it remains open whether panels or the appellate body will recognize the fact that public heath service providers, because of their universal services mandate, may need to operate under commercial circumstances that differ from those of their private counter parts, eventually requiring subsidies and other assistance from the government. Essentially, these questions are open, to be decided in future WTO cases. For a sector like health, these questions are highly important, particularly as some WTO members are moving toward entering into commitments in the sectors.[28] Currently, negotiations about national treatment commitments are proceeding in uncertainty about the eventual impact and breadth of such commitments.

A third way to approach our question about the relationship between the GATS and "public services" is to look at the scope of the GATS. According to Article I, the GATS covers all services, except for services "supplied in the exercise of governmental authority." A service supplied in the exercise of governmental authority is further defined as a service that is "neither supplied on a commercial basis nor in competition with one or more service suppliers."[29] Thus, the notions of "commercial" and "in competition" determine the scope of the GATS.[30] A closer look at these concepts suggests that the GATS does not exclude particular services just because of a possible "public or developmental interest" in their supply.[31] Thus, while health services are characterized by both a public and developmental interest in their supply, whether such a service is eventually covered by or excluded from the GATS rather depends on whether this service is supplied on a noncompetitive and noncommercial basis. These characteristics describe mainly the economic conditions of the supply of a service. Generally, a service supplied "on a commercial basis" can be defined as a service supplied on a profit-seeking basis. Services are supplied "in competition" if two or more service suppliers target the same market with the same or substitutable services. This is typically the case if they have common end-uses.

However, to a large extent, the notions of "noncompetitive" and "noncommercial" also depend on the legal and political framework in which the service is provided. For example, drinking water could be distributed by a government department or by a state-owned company on a monopoly basis and at a very low, subsidized price. As this would essentially prevent the distributor from making a profit, it could be argued that drinking water distribution is a service that would fall outside of the scope of GATS. If, however, a government chooses to introduce elements of commercialization and competitiveness into the provision of water through privatization policies, it may thereby submit this sector to GATS disciplines.

Thus, a WTO member wishing to exclude a particular service from the scope of GATS must ensure that this service is supplied on a nonprofit and noncompetitive basis. However, this is difficult, given that—apart from a few clear-cut cases— there is a great deal of ambiguity as to what is the meant by "noncompetitive" and "noncommercial."

Ambiguity—Potentially Far-Reaching Consequences Thus, several of the provisions that are key for identifying the interface between GATS and public services are essentially unclear. This ambiguity may have vast consequences. For example, a WTO member may enter into far-reaching GATS commitments assuming that the "public services" aspect of these sectors (e.g., universal provision of health services) is not covered by the GATS in the first place. Subsequently, the member may realize that other members have different perceptions in regard to the real scope of the agreement.[32] Similarly, a member may enter into specific commitments, for example in national treatment, assuming that this only implies to refrain from discriminating between foreign and domestic private services providers, while continuing the subsidization of domestic public or essential services providers. Subsequently, the member may realize that others have different perceptions about the breadth of the GATS national treatment commitment and about the notion of "likeness." A final example is a situation in which a member considers another member's GATS commitments more far-reaching in terms of covering public (health) services and their supply, counting on export opportunities (i.e., in Mode 4) that had never been contemplated by the liberalizing member. Thus, there are valid reasons for eliminating—or at least reducing—the current ambiguity, both from a defensive and from an offensive perspective.

One could assume that multilateral, negotiated solutions and interpretative understandings to reducing such ambiguities appear rather unlikely (and maybe even undesirable).[33] Consequently, WTO members may wish to consider individual approaches to clarification. While such clarification would not relate to the agreement as such, it would at least clarify the scope of members' individual GATS commitments. Some members have moved in this direction by "carving out" services sectors and subsectors that they want to reserve for public or quasi-public management.

Strategic Responses: Using Schedules for Individual Solutions   There are various ways in which members can carve out all or parts of the public sector provision of certain services. These ways differ according to the *types* of conditions members have attached to their specific commitments and whether these conditions are *sector–specific* or *horizontal*. Another difference is whether the conditions carve out the public services aspect from the *overall specific obligation* or whether the condition only retains the ability to use *certain regulatory tools* for the public services part of the sector.[34] The European Community schedule (European Communities, 1995) is an example of a horizontal limitation, carving out certain regulatory tools. Specifically, the EC schedule allows regulators to use certain tools for "services considered as public utilities at a national or local level." An explanatory footnote to the EC schedule adds that "[p]ublic utilities exist in sectors such as related scientific and technical consulting services, R&D services on social sciences and humanities, technical testing and analysis services, environmental services, *health services*, transport services, and services auxiliary to all modes of transport" (emphasis added).

Thus, health is listed as a sector where public utilities exist. However, this still leaves open the question of what the public utilities aspects are in the health sector. Here the wording of the conditionality comes into play. What is interesting is that the EC schedule refers to "services *considered* as public utilities" (emphasis added). This language appears to indicate that the EC schedule reserves the right to define, on an *ad hoc* basis, what services are *considered* public utilities. Thus the European Community included what can be called a "self-defining" interpretation, a scheduling tool that is expected to grant considerable flexibility to the European

Community to define and alter what services are considered public utilities according to its social priorities. The fact that the list in the footnote is "indicative" means that services not currently listed could be "considered" as public utilities in the future. As indicated above, health services are, however, already listed in the footnote.

Looking at the EC schedule for health services reveals that there are commitments for hospital services and social services (convalescent and rest houses, and old people's homes). For the two sectors committed, Modes 1 and 4 remain unbound (Mode 4 subject to horizontal commitments).Mode 2 is fully open and Mode 3 is committed, with a series of country-specific conditionalities mostly requiring authorizations or economic needs tests.[35] In its initial offer, the European Community does not suggest any changes specifically relating to its public services carve-out. There are some cases where members— individually or jointly— made suggestions regarding the definition or criteria of their economic needs tests. In the case of services provided by pharmacists, for example, EC members adopted the common criteria of population density and geographic density of existing pharmacies.

Another approach toward public sector carve-outs is taken in the Nordic/Swiss schedules, which exclude the "public works function whether owned and operated by municipalities, State or federal governments or contracted out by these governments."[36] The relevance of this approach may be most obvious for public services such as water or energy, or may be a municipality subcontracting the operation of its health facilities.[37] While this approach also seems to grant flexibility, much depends on how the terms "public service function" or "public works functions" are interpreted. However, neither the Swiss nor the Nordic commitments contain a specific list of what is contained in the "public works function," much less a specific reference as to whether health is included.

Looking at the Swiss schedule reveals that, apart from full Mode 1 and 2 commitments, commitments for medical and dental services (market access) and additional conditional commitments for national treatment, Switzerland doesn't have any health commitments.[38] Similarly, to the European Community, neither Switzerland nor Norway, in their initial offer, suggested any changes to their commitments in so far as they relate to public services or health services.

A third approach is to carve out public services by explicitly limiting the commitments to private services. Mexico and Malaysia take this approach in the health sector.[39] Here, the first column of the services schedule (the column explaining the sector in question) clarifies for each sector listed that it relates to "private" services only. Again, neither the Mexican nor Malaysian, in their initial offer had suggests any changes to this approach to covering private services only.

Fourth, there is the U.S. and Estonian approach to public services.[40] This approach clarifies in the first column of the services schedule (the column explaining the sector in question) that the commitment only covers services "contracted by private industry."[41] This suggests that the decisive aspect—whether a service is covered by a commitment or not—is whether or not the *consumer* of the service is *private industry*, as opposed to the *public sector* or *private individuals* for personal consumption. While this approach is relevant for public services such as energy, water, or telecommunication, the concept of private industry consumption does not appear to apply broadly for health services.

Looking at the U.S. health commitments reveals only commitments for hospital and other health care facilities (in Modes 2 and 3), these being subject to detailed limitations. For example, the scope of the commitment is limited to cover "direct ownership and management and operation by contract of such facilities on a 'for fee' basis." The Mode 3 commitment subjects the establishment of hospitals and other health care facilities to needs-based quantitative limits, or—as in the case of New York—places prohibitions on "corporate ownership of an operating corporation for, and limited partnerships as operators of, hospitals or nursing homes." Another interesting limitation, perhaps less relevant for public services but clearly relevant for developing countries' export opportunities, is found in the Mode 2 national treatment commitment. This states that "federal or state government reimbursement of medical expenses is limited to licensed certified facilities in the United States or in a specific U.S. state." Again, neither the United States nor Estonia, in their initial offers, suggests any changes relevant to the approach described above.

This analysis of selected developed country members' schedules suggests they have realized the ambiguities of the way the GATS deals with public services. The schedules discussed have either tried to remedy the ambiguities of the Art. I "public services exclusion" by carefully limiting the sectoral breadth of the commitments or by excluding the public services/works dimension altogether. Also, they seem to try remedying the deficiencies that might arise from the definition of what are "like" services or service suppliers. The European horizontal limitation on subsidies may well have been inscribed against this background.

There are, however, limits to these responses. Most importantly, any limitations or clarifications included via a member's schedule only apply to the specific obligations that WTO members enter into through their schedule. Thus, even if carved out from market access and national treatment obligations, the "public works function" (in the case of the Nordic/Swiss approach) still is covered by the GATS' general MFN obligation. A second problem is that conditionalities may be hard to put in place. GATS provisions such as Articles IV (increasing participation of developing countries) and XIX (recognizing the particular need of developing countries for flexibility to carefully design their commitments) can help to strengthen the argument for conditionalities. Also, pointing to the human right to health, and governments' obligation to progressively realize it, may increase developing countries' bargaining leverage. This may be helpful in cases where countries have decided to take a defensive approach and consequently aim to attach a set of conditionalities to their commitments, or refrain from undertaking commitments in the first place. At the same time, conditionalities with a health component, such as public reimbursements of health expenditures being limited to expenses occurred within the country, can effectively be used to limit developing countries' exports via Mode 2. Another limitation of the scheduling approach is that, in many cases, conditionalities are time-bound. Under the mandate of progressive liberalization, WTO members are negotiating further liberalization of health services trade—which frequently entails the elimination of conditionalities.

Current Negotiations on Domestic Regulation—Strategic Challenges from a Double-Edged Sword[42]

GATS Article VI.4 and Its Negotiating Mandate: Coverage of Domestic Regulation In addition to the question of public services, concerns about the GATS have been loudest with respect to the current negotiations on domestic regulation. Article VI.4 provides both some basic disciplines on domestic regulation and a mandate for negotiations to develop further disciplines. The overall goal is to provide predictability and certainty for operators and to ensure the effectiveness of specific commitments.

Along these lines, Article VI.1 requires WTO members to ensure that, in sectors where they have undertaken specific commitments, "...all measures of general application affecting trade in services are administered in a reasonable, objective and impartial manner."

Next, Article VI.2 provides for an obligation to maintain and institute judicial, arbitral, or administrative tribunals or procedures for prompt, objective, and impartial review of administrative decisions affecting trade in services and—where justified—appropriate remedies.[43] Article VI. 3 provides that where authorization is required for the supply of a service on which a specific commitment has been made, the competent authorities should "within a reasonable period of time" after the submission of a complete application inform the applicant of the decision concerning the application and at, the request of the applicant, provide information concerning the status of the application "without undue delay." Article VI.4, in turn, provides for a work program for negotiations of future disciplines: "With a view to ensuring that measures relating to

Box 2.4: Accountancy Disciplines

The Disciplines on the Accountancy Sector may permit lessons to be learned for approaching health services in the current negotiations on domestic regulation. Adopted in 1998, the Accountancy Disciplines are applicable only for members who have made commitments on accountancy services, and the disciplines will only enter into force together with the results of the current round of services negotiations.

The disciplines provide that "members shall ensure that measures not subject to scheduling under Articles XVI or XVII of the GATS (relating to licensing requirements and procedures, technical standards, and qualification requirements and procedures) are not prepared, adopted, or applied with a view to or with the effect of creating unnecessary barriers to trade in accountancy services." The disciplines also require members to ensure that such measures are not more trade-restrictive than necessary to fulfill a legitimate objective (i.e., establish a necessity test). The protection of consumers, the quality of the service, professional competence, and the integrity of the profession are specifically referred to as legitimate objectives.

From a systemic point, it is important to note that the work on disciplines for the accountancy sector clarified—to a certain extent—the relationship between Articles VI (domestic regulation), XVI (market access), and XVII (national treatment), insofar as there should not be any overlap between Article XVI and XVII on the one hand and Article VI on the other hand. Thus, the accountancy disciplines cover only nondiscriminatory and nonquantitative measures. However, there still remains considerable ambiguity as to a clear distinction between coverage of the different provisions.

Today, the question is whether some of the guidelines and disciplines could be generalized and be made applicable to professional services, including those in the health sector. (Note, however, that current disciplines do not aim at harmonizing domestic regulations relating to professional services.) This may be even more so, as certain activities of the health sector, such as nurses, dentists, and midwives are "professional services" in terms of GATS sectoral services classification. The WTO Secretariat sent a questionnaire to professional bodies, including those in the health sector, asking among other things, whether accountancy disciplines could apply to their profession. Some professions found the disciplines too general and limited, while other professions preferred to focus on market access and national treatment. Thus, this survey has not yet made it fully clear whether the main elements and concepts of these disciplines are applicable, consequently raising the need for further examination of how the main principles of future disciplines could apply to individual sectors.

The International Council of Nurses (ICN) for example, advocates for national regulatory systems and global standards that are responsive to the evolution of nursing and patient care. Specifically, any regulation should: (1) have standards based on clear definitions of professional scope and accountability and ensure and safeguard competence; (2) promote universal standards

Box 2.4: Accountancy Disciplines (Continued)

of performance and foster professional identity and mobility, taking into account local needs and circumstances; (3) acknowledge the role of interested parties in standard-setting and administration; (4) provide and be limited to those controls and restrictions necessary to achieve their objectives; (5) be coherent, sufficiently broad, and flexible to achieve the objective and still permit freedom of innovation, growth, and change; (6) provide honest and just treatment for those parties; and (7) recognize the equality and interdependence of professions. On the issue of establishing disciplines under the ambit of the WTO for the nursing profession, the ICN believes that a significant number of countries support the idea but at same time maintain the following concerns: lowering of standards; implications of the necessity test as it relates to regulatory autonomy; fear of the impact of dispute resolution outcomes on the ability to provide safe health care. Concerns were also expressed especially for poor countries, which lack resources to develop regulatory mechanisms and, consequently, would encounter problems in adhering to any disciplines that might be institutionalized.

Source: Disciplines on Domestic Regulation in the Accountancy Sector—Adopted by the Council for Trade in Services on 14 December 1998, S/L/64; ICN presentation to the WTO Workshop on Domestic Regulation, March 2004 Geneva.

qualification requirements and procedures, technical standards and licensing requirements do not constitute unnecessary barriers to trade in services, the Council for Trade in Services shall… develop any necessary disciplines. Such disciplines shall aim to ensure that such requirements are *inter alia*: (a) based on objective and transparent criteria, such as competence and the ability to supply the services; (b) not more burdensome than necessary to ensure the quality of the service; (c) in case of licensing procedures, not in themselves a restriction on the supply of the service."

Article VI.4—Constraining Policy Flexibility for Health or Facilitating the Movement of Natural Persons? The extent to which these negotiations matter for health services becomes obvious when looking at the broad scope of the negotiating mandate. In accordance with Article VI.4, disciplines on domestic regulation cover measures relating to qualification requirements and procedures, technical standards, and licensing requirements. The use of the term "relating to" makes the reach of such disciplines also broad.[44] For example, the European Community has suggested that "[c]ertain self-regulatory measures should be subject to disciplines."[45] Similarly, a recent contribution by a group of countries (Chile, Hong Kong, Korea, Switzerland, Taiwan and Thailand) specifically addressed the application of regulatory disciplines to different levels of governmental (including regional and local) and non-governmental bodies[46], and, more specifically relating to technical standards, Switzerland recently suggested to cover both, mandatory and voluntary standards.[47]

One could think of a range of domestic health measures that would be covered by the mandate of these negotiations. Governments typically seek to ensure a certain quality of medical and hospital services, either by requiring licenses and prior authorization of the supply of these services, or by applying quality standards to the supply of services. Licensing requirements and standards are regulatory instruments within the scope of GATS Article VI.4.

However, the mere fact that certain regulations are covered by Article VI.4 and the negotiations conducted thereunder does not imply that such regulations be prohibited. Rather, whether or not a government (national or subnational) will be able to implement such a domestic regulation will depend upon the content and nature of the measure in question and upon the obligations set out in the international rules that apply to such national health regulations. Currently, the latter are still in the making, in the GATS working party on domestic regulation (WPDR). Three topics are central to the current negotiations in this body. All of them give rise to concerns when applied to health services and their regulation and developing as well as developed countries may wish to carefully consider them. During the last years, similar concerns have also been repeatedly voiced by civil society groups.

The first set of concerns relates to the fact that some suggest that, in the future, a so-called "necessity" or "proportionality" test should be applied to domestic regulations.[48] If developed to the full, such a necessity or proportionality test may result in balancing trade with other national policy imperatives (Neumann and Tuerk, 2003). Depending on its ultimate wording, the future obligation could also include a so-called "least trade-restrictive" criterion. It is questionable, however, whether the design and development of national health policies should be subject to such a least trade-restrictive test. Such an obligation to choose the least trade-restrictive among various alternative available options appears to be particularly problematic for developing countries.[49] Given their scarce resources, developing countries need to carefully determine where to invest these resources: maximizing health and developmental benefits, or minimizing negative effects on international trade. A less trade-restrictive option may frequently entail more administrative or other burdens, thus giving rise to questions of priority.

Before moving forward with the negotiation of such disciplines, trade negotiators may wish to consult with their health policy counterparts about the range of policy options that may be affected by such disciplines. Some countries, for example, require hospitals to offer some of their services on a nonprofit or pro-bono basis.

Clearly, there may be alternative regulatory mechanisms, the trade-restrictive impact of which are less pronounced.[50] A second, related question is whether such necessity tests interfere with WTO members' choices about which legitimate policy objectives they wish to pursue. Normally, necessity tests are phrased in a way that contains an open or an exclusive list of legitimate objectives.[51] Usually, human health is among those policy objectives explicitly recognized as legitimate. At the same time, there are other policy objectives, e.g., cultural, ethical, or human rights objectives, that are not explicitly mentioned. Thus there may be questions about whether they are legitimate, and who should judge their legitimacy. For the GATS, the necessity test in the accountancy disciplines is an interesting example of a necessity test with an open-ended list of legitimate objectives. Paragraph II of the disciplines states that "[l]egitimate objectives are, *inter alia*, the protection of consumers (which includes all users of accounting services and the public generally), the quality of the service, professional competence, and the integrity of the profession." It is interesting that several of these legitimate objectives are not typically mentioned in other necessity tests. The necessity test in the accountancy disciplines may therefore serve as an example of a necessity test with legitimate objectives that are specifically designed to suit the circumstances of a particular services sector. This may be harder to achieve in the case of a necessity test applying to all services sectors in a cross-cutting way.

The extent to which legitimate objectives are solely within the prerogatives of WTO members has also been addressed in WTO case law. In the so-called *Sardines* case, the appellate body interpreted a provision related to the necessity test in Article 2.2 TBT (a necessity test containing an open-ended list of legitimate policy objectives). In this case, the appellate body declared its authority—at least in the context of TBT Article 2.4—to question the legitimacy of certain policy objectives.[52] Specifically, it agreed with the panel that the second sentence of Article 2.4 implies that WTO tribunals, i.e., panels and the appellate body, must examine and determine the legitimacy of measures' objectives. It is important to note, however, that this was done in the context of legitimate policy objectives that were not explicitly included in the list of "legitimate" objectives.

In the context of GATS Article VI.4, the exact nature of the necessity test is yet to be determined.[53] In fact, more recent submissions to the WPDR take a more careful and nuanced approach towards the issue of necessity. To avoid taking a decision on which legitimate objectives are to be included in any exhaustive or indicative list (implicitly excluding others), some members suggest using the notion of "national policy objectives." It remains to be seen what regulatory challenges will ultimately be arising from these negotiations, in particular the different formulations of the necessity test, and how they will affect developed and developing countries, especially their domestic regulations pursuing health objectives.

For developing countries, however, future disciplines on domestic regulation may not only bring about regulatory challenges at home, they could also play a role in facilitating developing countries' supply of health services to the North. As mentioned earlier, developing countries may have an interest in supplying health services via Mode 1, outsourcing; via Mode 2, health consumers abroad; or via Mode 4, the movement of health personnel, etc. Qualification and licensing requirements may constitute a major impediment to realizing such trade opportunities. Consequently, the necessity test, by ensuring that measures relating to qualification requirements are not more trade-restrictive or not more burdensome than *necessary*, might indeed appear to be the way to go. Thus, disciplines on domestic regulation could—in theory—prove beneficial for developing countries, at least in this limited area. Similarly, mutual recognition of qualifications, a topic closely linked to the VI.4 agenda, may be a step toward facilitating Mode 4 exports for developing countries.

The third main concern voiced in the context of VI.4 disciplines on domestic regulation surrounds the negotiation of the so-called "a priori comment process." Under the guise of increasing transparency, part of the overall effort to strengthen good governance, some WTO members have proposed to negotiate international rules obliging WTO members to notify proposed laws and regulations and to solicit comments from interested parties (WTO, May 2000)[54]. Similar provisions in the Agreement on Technical Barriers to Trade (TBT) not only oblige WTO members to notify, request comments, and discuss these comments upon request, but also to "take these written comments and the results of these discussions into account."[55] This may have far-reaching consequences for the regulatory prerogatives of WTO members, including in health sectors (Fuchs et al., 2002).

While such resistance had also originated from the North, including from WTO members who are *demandeurs* for other areas of the VI.4 negotiations, the proposal's effects on developing countries would most likely outweigh those on industrialized countries by far. While transparency may offer a series of benefits (notably, promoting good governance, enhancing predictability of the trading environment, making specific commitments more effective, or ensuring economic efficiency),[56] they also promise to create a series of challenges, particularly for developing countries. Challenges are even bigger with respect to the so-called a priori transparency mechanisms. Most important in that context is the fact that developing countries themselves will hardly have the administrative resources and political clout to actively use such a mechanism to their own benefit. Rather, they will be subject to most of the comments and will have to invest scarce administrative resources in that process. Also, the regulatory processes of developing countries are less developed and consequently most open and vulnerable to outside influence. Finally, for some developing countries, such a process is simply unconstitutional.

Thus, reviewing the two negotiating items, transparency (including a priori transparency) and necessity (including the issue of legitimate objectives), that are currently under discussion in the VI.4 negotiations, the two appear to offer both benefits and challenges for developing countries. The same applies to an assessment of current options from a heath perspective. Consequently, any move forward should be undertaken after a careful consideration of the pros and cons of the relevant option. This would also include a strategic analysis of those elements of the VI.4 package, which appear—at least at a first glance—promising from a development and health perspective.

Strategic Responses—Carefully Assessing Promised Benefits In order to determine an adequate negotiating position for developing countries, one would have to assess whether potential benefits from greater market access and national treatment outweigh the potentially negative effects of international rules (necessity test and a priori transparency) that have the potential to constrain domestic regulatory processes. When considering potential benefits, a series of aspects merit attention: First, there is the potential that strong disciplines on VI.4 may assist to ensure access to Northern health services markets. This could prove helpful for exporting health services through Mode 1 (cross-border, including through off-shoring and outsourcing), Mode 2 (consumer of health services abroad), and Mode 4 (movement of health personnel).However, before relying on the potential benefits that strong future VI.4 disciplines may bring about, it is important to recall the original idea of VI.4. Ultimately, disciplines on VI.4 should "underpin" market access commitments undertaken by WTO members.[57]

Thus, most likely, future VI.4 disciplines will not take effect across the board, but only where—and to the extent that—members have undertaken commitments. Thus, in the absence of commitments (on Modes 1, 2, or 4), future VI.4 disciplines will not provide any value. Counting on VI.4 to substitute market access that is supposed to be negotiated under the request offer negotiations does not appear to be the way to go. Next, regarding MRAs, the chances that multilateral negotiations in the WTO will truly result in strong disciplines for MRAs—applicable for both North and South—are more than slim. MRAs have proven a sticky issue. Even negotiating processes that combine countries less diverse than those forming the broad membership of WTO have failed to comprehensively address MRAs and related issues. Particularly in sensitive sectors such as health, progress has proven difficult to achieve. Thus, it is highly unlikely that multilateral negotiations in that direction will make much progress. Consequently, including MRAs in a negotiating package may only on its face render the package more development-friendly.

While these are initial pointers, it remains to be seen how current negotiations will actually move. It appears that, overall, caution is warranted in regard to the strategy of using future VI.4 disciplines for qualification requirements as a way to ensure access to Northern health services markets.

Challenges in the Process of Negotiating—the Need for Data and Clout

Lack of Data and Understanding about the Effects of Health Services Liberalization (in the Multilateral Context)

Lack of Data—Need for Informed Negotiations As shown above, a strategic analysis of the pros and cons of certain negotiating packages is a main challenge in international trade negotiations. While strategically assessing the outcome of package- deals and trade-offs is key, services trade negotiators face additional, more fundamental, challenges. This is particularly true for developing country negotiators. Even after more than a decade of multilateral services trade liberalization, the effects of services liberalization remain far from well understood (Raghavan, 2002). Negotiators and services trade policymakers not only suffer from an overall lack of data, but also from a lack of understanding in regard to the economic, social, and other effects of services trade liberalization. While economic theories predict large gains of services trade liberalization (mainly in terms of increasing the efficiency of services markets), the real impacts—particularly from a distributional point of view—remain far from understood. This is true for most services sectors, including health. Understanding health services liberalization is particularly problematic, as health policies and their objectives go beyond allocative efficiency. Adequately addressing social and distributional questions arising in health policymaking requires a mix of skills that is not necessarily present among trade policy makers and trade economists. In developing countries this situation is compounded by an overall lack of information about their health sector as such.

This is particularly problematic in light of the current push for further liberalization that developing countries face in the bilateral request offer negotiations. Locking-in liberalization policies without a comprehensive understanding of their effects does not sound promising. This is even more so, given that to date, the GATS agreement does not contain an effective safeguards mechanism, and that experience—albeit in the trade in goods context—points to the limited value of the agreement's general exception for health.[58]

Strategic Responses: A Thorough and Comprehensive Assessment—A Tool to Address Informational Deficits Conducting a thorough and comprehensive assessment of services trade liberalization could offer a means to address such informational deficits. This potential has been acknowledged by GATS Article XIX, which establishes assessment as a precondition for further negotiations. It is unfortunate, however, that to date, assessment has not yet produced tangible and usable results.[59] With respect to health, the many discussions under the assessment agenda item have not addressed health-related objectives. Nevertheless, the benefits of a proper assessment—both at the national as well as at the international level—are obvious. So far, developing countries have been actively participating in the assessment exercise.

To date, a number of common observations have emerged from initial developing country submissions on assessment (*Mashayekhi and Julsaint, 2000*). These include developing countries' views that:

1. an overall balance of rights and obligations for all WTO members has not been attained (referring to a lack of meaningful concessions by developed countries);
2. the increase in share of world services exports has been small for developing countries;
3. the objectives of Article IV have not been achieved, due to trade barriers and supply constraints that developing countries face;
4. benefits from privatization and liberalization are not automatic, and that appropriate preconditions, including technological capacity building and complementary policies, are crucial to realize benefits;
5. policy flexibility and proper sequencing of liberalization are other key elements to realizing the benefits of liberalization;
6. priority attention needs to be given to ensuring access to universal and essential services; and
7. nascent services sectors and small- and medium-sized enterprises of developing countries require capacity building and other assistance from developed countries.

It is crucial that WTO members adequately reflect on these observations, and that they are effectively addressed in the results of the market access negotiations. This may lead to a reconsideration of market openness, and increasing focus on reregulation, depending on the assessment of evolving market realities.

Ongoing efforts on assessment are necessary to further improve the understanding of these challenges. Efforts to obtain insight into the impact of trade liberalization in developing countries should be taking place at the national, regional, and multilateral levels.

Conducting a thorough and comprehensive assessment at the national level would allow WTO members to gain a better understanding of their health services sectors, their deficiencies, and their opportunities. This, in turn, would allow them to better design their negotiating positions. Developing countries may require assistance—financial and technical—to achieve this. Conducting a thorough and comprehensive assessment at the international level would allow WTO members to share their national experiences with services trade liberalization, including in the health sector. Again, sharing experiences will improve overall understanding, with direct results for negotiating positions.

However, the value does not lie in the assessment exercise per se, but rather depends on its content and focus. To date, services trade assessment has been an exercise, predominantly efficiency-oriented and focusing on business perspectives. Thus far, the WTO, the Organisation for Economic Co-operation and Development (OECD), the World Bank, and the International Trade Centre (ITC) have been mainly focusing on efficiency and business perspectives in their assessment-related activities.[60] In turn, the United Nations Conference on Trade and Development (UNCTAD) has focused on an assessment of the nexus between trade and development, while the World Health Organization (WHO) and United Nations High Commissioner for Human Rights (UNHCR) have contributed to assessments, from a health and human rights perspective.[61] For example, the approach recommended by the UNHCR assessment is a cautious one, suggesting that the making of trade policy and trade rules should be based on sound evidence that—in addition to leading to increased investment and economic growth—the particular strategy will promote the enjoyment of human rights. With respect to health, UNHCR noted that increased private investment can lead to: 1. the establishment of a two-tiered services supply with a corporate segment focused on the healthy and wealthy and an underfinanced public sector focusing on the poor and sick; 2. brain drain, with better trained medical practitioners and educators being drawn toward the private sector by higher pay scales and better infrastructures; 3. an overemphasis on commercial objectives at the expense of social objectives, which might be more focused on the provision of quality health, water, and education services for those who cannot afford them at commercial rates; and 4. an increasingly large and powerful private sector that can threaten the role of the government as the primary duty bearer for human rights by subverting the regulatory system through political pressure or the co-opting of regulators.

Thus, to be truly beneficial from a health-policy perspective, the breadth of assessment as feeding into the WTO negotiations should be broadened to also include health dimensions, both from a developmental and a human rights perspective. The relevant intergovernmental organizations may offer valuable contributions, both in the assessment discussions in the WTO, as well as in the conduct of national services trade assessments.

In light of their scarce resources and their limited information about their services economies, developing countries would be obvious beneficiaries of such an assessment. For example, an assessment would help them improve their understanding about the complexities of health services trade, including the developmental implications of such trade. Also, this would place them in a better position for designing their country-specific negotiations positions. Finally, a true political will to conduct a useful assessment exercise would consider it a vital input in the bilateral negotiations—as requested by GATS Article XIX. Thus, this would allow developing countries to gain time and to avoid being pressured into accepting liberalization commitments without having understood their implications. Ultimately, this would ensure that services trade liberalization is properly sequenced, a requirement broadly acknowledged by trade and other economic policymakers. In addition to feeding into the bilateral request offer process, an assessment could also be valuable for other items on the GATS agenda.

Lack of Political and Negotiating Clout

Bilateral Requests and Offers—Lack of Balance A second main challenge developing countries face in the current market access negotiations originates in the essentially bilateral nature of the current request offer phase. A bilateral negotiating relationship may accentuate situations where countries face pressure to accept certain liberalization commitments. This is particularly likely to occur in relationships between developing and industrialized countries, where power imbalances are most likely. Such power imbalances may also lead to situations where negotiating pressure is accompanied by political pressure, or—may be more frequently—by claims (and promises) about the beneficial effect of liberalization in sectors of export interest to developed countries, (and about the detriments of increasing exports in one particular mode of services trade, for example in Mode 4, where developed countries have a comparatively defensive stance). Again, assessment may be a possible tool to address such complex situations.

Strategic Responses: A Transparent Assessment, Negotiating Context, and Negotiating Tools—To Address Deficits in Negotiating Clout Developing countries face important challenges, many of which are due to a lack of bargaining power and leverage, when negotiating trade issues. Other difficulties relate to limited capacity, both in terms of financial and human capital, and asymmetry of information and experience. These challenges are evident in the GATS negotiations and are exacerbated by the bilateral nature of the request and offer modalities.

Assessment Most importantly, a through and comprehensive assessment would assist developing countries to prepare their negotiating positions. Questions to be addressed in such assessments would include the following: what are the macroeconomic, political, social, and trade environments, and how do they relate specifically to health; what are the health status of the population and the strengths and weaknesses of the current health system; and what are the costs and benefits of different options to be pursued in trade negotiations on health services?[62] To prepare for an informed nationally-driven decision-making process with positive health outcomes from trade negotiations there is a need to put in place a multistakeholder dialogue and coordination mechanism, to include relevant government authorities from health ministries but also trade, services sectoral officials, representatives of health professions regulators, and the civil society to ensure selection of priorities and strategic options and to create the conditions and plan for a successful implementation process prior to the taking of commitments in the GATS framework. Data and information gathering and assessment of trade in health services are other elements of informed decision making which, would also require coordination with a number of organizations involved in this area, including WHO, the International Labor Organization (ILO), UNHCR, UNCTAD, professional associations, and NGOs.

Thus, thorough and comprehensive assessment would also engage a broader constituency and other stakeholders in the debate. Building on the expertise of various intergovernmental organizations and also involving organizations such as the WHO or relevant bodies dealing with the right to health and the right to development would allow the assessment to go beyond strict economic considerations. This could also involve organizations at the national level, including health policymakers, think tanks and nongovernmental organizations.

An assessment would thus render the negotiating process more open and transparent, reducing the potential for pressure and power politics. Together with a multilateral report back and monitoring of bilateral negotiations, the informed presence of relevant other intergovernmental (and nongovernmental) organizations in some of the WTO deliberations, as well as their monitoring of bilateral and multilateral negotiating processes, could render bilateral negotiations less prone to abuse and power politics. Carrying out the assessment exercise, including the sharing of experiences (both in the conduct of assessments as well as with their results) at the multilateral level, would help to create and strengthen alliances between developing countries, which may face similar challenges with respect to their national health policies and health services sectors.

Finally, a thorough and comprehensive assessment, together with an open debate about its results, would provide a proper context for the current negotiations. In addition to facilitating the development of national negotiating positions, an assessment would allow a better understanding of the validity of claims about the potential benefits and challenges of liberalizing health services in various modes of delivery. Also, this would place such claims in the context of a broader debate on the pros and cons of liberalization, and more broadly, of privatization. An assessment could also feed into the review of progress, as established by paragraph 15 of the Negotiating Guidelines.[63] Under this agenda item, WTO members review the progress of negotiations and the extent to which Article IV (on increasing participation of developing countries in trade in services) has been implemented through the negotiations. Information about trade in health services, particularly Mode 4, would constructively contribute to this multilateral review exercise.

Thus, without providing a ready-made solution to the difficulties of power imbalances as they occur particularly in the bilateral request/offer negotiations, assessment may provide one of many valuable contributions toward remedying this, and other, problems.

Context and Negotiating Tools The broad political and economic contexts in which GATS negotiations take place can also be a determining factor in how negotiations will proceed. As the backdrop to negotiations, this context can considerably alter public and political expectations and will often set parameters for both the debate and its outcome. The context of negotiations can be determined by independent events, for example the HIV/Aids pandemic, the implementation of the MDGs, and increasing prominence of the human right to health. Similarly, the negotiating context can be determined through specific actions. This may include the publication of assessments of problems associated with privatization of health services (for example, by UNHCR and WHO), political statements, or more general propaganda on substantial welfare gains from liberalization. This may result in the creation of a proliberalization or antiliberalization context.

In addition to the broader context, there is a range of more specific negotiating tools available to developing countries to advance their positions. Many of these tools have been used by both developing and industrialized countries. They have resorted to such tools either in the GATS negotiations or with regard to other trade-related issues.

These tools are interrelated, and include:

Coalition building and the forming of alliances: grouping with other negotiating parties has proven useful for combining resources or negotiating power. Examples include MERCOSUR, like-minded groups, LDC groups, and alliances among some developing countries for Mode 4 (which also includes movement of natural persons in the health sector). Alliances can be formed among developing countries, but they can also include industrialized countries e.g., "Friends of Mode 4."

- *Partnerships:* partnerships can also go beyond strict negotiating parties and include International Government Organizations (IGOs) or civil society groups. To date, negotiators have used the findings from the research community, both IGOs and NGOs, to press for a particular point of view. Proliberalization research findings have been used both prior to and during the Uruguay Round to include services in multilateral trade negotiations and to push for liberalization of sectors such as financial and telecommunication services. More recently, research findings that a reduction in services trade barriers, which spurred cross-border trade in services and reduced inefficiencies from services monopolies by 10 percent and price markups from imperfect competition by a similar percentage, could increase the income of developing countries by US$900 billion (9.4 percent) by 2015 from 1997 levels (World Bank, 2002) have been put forth. These reinforce the position that openness in services positively influences growth performance, while downplaying the downside of flawed reforms. UNCTAD, WHO, the Pan American Health Organization (PAHO), and UNHCR have provided constructive input to the broader discussion on GATS and its impact on health and human rights and development, particularly in regard to tailoring commitments under the GATS to national policy ends and ensuring that improving affordability and access should be core objectives of liberalization of trade in health services. The NGOs' role in the Trade-Related Aspects of Intellectual Property Rights Agreement (TRIPS) and Public Health Declaration and Decision was key in raising the moral and human dimension of trade policy decisions. In addition to remedying lack of negotiating clout, IGOs and NGOs could assist in the implementation of negotiated commitments or in the conduct of national assessments. With their specific expertise in respect to health policies and regulatory requirements, IGOs and NGOs could assist developing countries with devising flanking policies to strengthen supply capacity in developing countries.
- *Development Benchmarks:* establishing standards, yardsticks, or other levels that can operate as a reference point or target for negotiations. Examples include the modalities for special treatment of LDCs, or the WHO's policy objectives for furthering the health status of the population: (1) equitable access to care, which is equal utilization of health services for the same need combined with vertical equity, which is users contributing according to their economic capacity; (2) quality of care, which relates to the standard of the health care system; and (3) efficient use and allocation of resources. The latter

could be used to determine whether or not a country would enter commitments, what kinds of commitments, and with what types of limitations and conditions. Another useful set of development benchmarks has been proposed by a group of 18 developing countries, which have submitted a communication on review of progress as established in paragraph 15 of the Guidelines in March 2004. This communication proposes that the Council begin a "systematic and careful review" of the commitments being offered to developing countries in order to determine the extent to which commercially meaningful market access and national treatment commitments are granted, and proposes to begin this review with the movement of natural persons. According to the co-sponsors of the document, developed countries have not responded to the requests made and interests expressed by developing countries as the offers do not show any real improvement to the existing commitments in Mode 4. The communication sets forth elements to be used as criteria or development benchmarks to assess the extent of market access as follows: expansion of commitments in categories de-linked from Mode 3; elimination of restrictions attached to Mode 4 commitments; establishment of transparent and objective criteria as an additional commitment under Article XVIII, the introduction of a Service Provider Visa to remove cumbersome and nontransparent administrative procedures and regulations relating to work permits and visas; and common understanding on the categories of natural persons to enhance the predictability of commitments.

- *Monitoring and review mechanisms:* regularly observing and discussing negotiating developments may help participants bring to light and discuss both their successes and areas that could use improvement. In the WTO context, members have established processes for reviewing the implementation of agreements. With respect to GATS, paragraph 15 of the Negotiating Guidelines and Procedures for the Negotiations on Trade in Services provides that an evaluation of the results attained be conducted before the completion of the negotiations. More specifically, this review shall assess the progress of negotiations in terms of the objectives of Article IV (increasing participation of developing countries in trade in services, particularly in sectors and modes of interest to them). Obviously, this includes health services, specifically exports through Mode 4 as the results of the preliminary assessment by the Group of 18 developing countries, mentioned above, indicate.
- *Parallel avenues, justifications, and arguments:* pursuing an issue through an alternative avenue, or pursuing it with other, supporting arguments could assist in strengthening the case and increasing chances of success for the *demandeur.* For example, the United States has pushed for a priori transparency and regulatory issues, both in the discussions on Article VI.4 and in the bilateral request offer

negotiations. On the developing country side, one could consider using both Article IV and Article XIX. to maintain flexibility in liberalization and setting conditionalities, i.e. as part of a defensive argumentation. The same two provisions could also be used from an offensive perspective, i.e. providing arguments toward increasing developing countries exports. Health may be a relevant consideration in both approaches. Another example relates to the lack of clarity regarding the definition of public services and likeness. These can be tackled both through multilateral approaches or through country-specific commitments, which would carve out public services according to national definitions and public health objectives.

- *Timing:* setting timelines could assist in providing impetus to negotiations. For example, in the Negotiating Guidelines, members have set timelines for the submission of initial requests and initial offers, including those related to health services. Similarly, they have repeatedly set timelines for the negotiation of emergency safeguards mechanisms—albeit with limited success.

- *Sequencing and linking:* requiring one stage of negotiations to precede another, or conditioning progress on one issue with progress on another, are two closely related options. A health-related example is to require health impact assessments prior to making market access commitments in health-related services sectors and modes.

- *Blocking:* refusing to negotiate on an issue or refusing to agree to a certain outcome may appear unproductive—and consequently is used in a less obvious and noticeable manner. For example, developed countries are using social concerns to refuse offering commercially meaningful Mode 4 commitments.

- *Flexibility in outcome:* allowing for alternatives in outcomes may make the overall result more acceptable. Alternatives could relate to the content of obligations, their legal nature, or the timing when negotiating partners would be bound by the outcome. Examples are reference papers (allowing for slight variations in the content of obligations); precommitments (allowing commitment now to future liberalization); a plurilateral rather than multilateral approach (allowing for variations in the scope/addressees of obligations); and the reference to possible policy and regulatory reform as an additional commitment (content of obligation). Examples of flexibility in terms of the legal nature of the outcome are the guidelines for the granting of credit for autonomous liberalization (stopping short of creating a legal "right" to credit) and the Japanese proposal on domestic regulation suggesting different approaches to the legal nature of its specific provisions on the Article VI.4. proposal (e.g., containing best endeavor language, for example in para 18).

The above list is not exhaustive, nor does it provide for clear delineations among the different categories. Individual developing countries must design their own negotiating strategies and determine how these tools can most effectively be used to pursue trade and health objectives in the services negotiations. Some instances where a well-designed negotiating strategy might be particularly important include: the ongoing bilateral request/offer negotiations, in particular the Mode 4 negotiations (including requests and offers in health-related activities); the multilateral rule-making negotiations, in particular the negotiations on the establishment of an emergency safeguard mechanism (the potential applicability of a safeguard mechanism to Mode 4, including health services exports, is increasingly mentioned); the parallel pursuit of bilateral and multilateral negotiations; and more broadly, the current efforts to put the DWP back on track and to ensure balanced outcomes in different areas of negotiations.

Conclusions and Policy Recommendations There is an urgent need to reconcile the objective of trade liberalization with noneconomic factors such as consumer protection, equity, human rights, quality and standards, cultural, ethical, and national security considerations. This need is particularly urgent with respect to GATS negotiations aiming to liberalize trade in health services. To ensure that negotiations towards the further liberalization of services trade will deliver development dividends is a major challenge for developing countries, as the regulatory framework of services is complex and is primarily aimed at dealing with nontrade concerns and noneconomic objectives. Specific policy measures are required to address the negative and adverse effects of globalization, privatization, and liberalization on health and to strengthen positive outcomes and ensure the achievement of MDGs on poverty and health. Premature and rapid liberalization in the health service sector could generate considerable costs in efficiency and social impact that would worsen growth performance and health outcomes and ultimately erode political support for further opening up of the sector. Therefore, a well-calibrated and sequenced approach to liberalization is highly preferable in this essential services sector.

A series of guiding principles could be particularly important in that context:60 In line with the MDGs, the following aspects may warrant attention.: 1. international rules and institutions should promote global public goods, including universal access to health services; 2. growth needs to be inclusive, equitable, and sustainable, and this requires policy coherence among trade, development and noneconomic policies; 3. strong national health policies, institutions, regulatory framework, and programs are essential; 4. access and affordability of health services should be integrated fully in negotiations on trade in services; 5. a comprehensive multistake-holder approach, including cooperation and monitoring mechanisms, along with the participation of all the relevant agencies involved in health policy formulation and health services, is key to the adoption of a sustainable and informed approach to health services negotiations. 6. GATS does not oblige any country to liberalize its health services. Liberalization needs to be based on a thorough impact assessment of potential costs and benefits for the health systems and policies. Liberalization would need to be gradual, appropriately sequenced and calibrated, selective, and preceded by appropriate macroeconomic policies, human resource and regulatory infrastructure, domestic investment, and home-grown external policies; 7. special attention is needed to increase the transfer of financial and technical resources and capacity-building measures to ensure the development of developing countries, particularly the LDCs, and particularly in respect to building competitive services sectors, including the health sector, and building the capacity of health workers; 8. ensuring commercially meaningful commitments in Mode 4 through, e.g. streamlined visa, licensing and work permit requirements; separating temporary stay from permanent migration in visa regimes by creating a Service Provider Visa; removing ENTs; improving transparency; and facilitating recognition of qualifications; 9. putting in place mechanisms to alleviate brain drain and increasing the benefits of brain circulation.

It is hoped that this paper will serve to stimulate thought among developing country negotiators and policymakers in both Trade and Health Ministries as to the best strategic approach toward trade in health services in the ongoing services negotiations. A proactive role in setting the agenda, combined with a thorough understanding of the negotiating issues (both in Geneva and in the capitals) and increasing economic and social analysis of the effects that services trade liberalization has on individual countries' economies, their health sector, and ultimately the health of their populations, may effectively promote negotiating outcomes that will result in a multilateral trading system supportive of development in the South.

Notes

1. WHO, 2001.

2. (*wishing* to establish a multilateral framework…for trade in services…as a means of promoting the economic growth of all trading partners and the development of developing countries; *recognizing* the right of members to regulate, and…the particular need of developing countries to exercise this right; *desiring* to facilitate the increasing participation of developing countries in trade in services, and the expansion of their service exports…).

3. Report by the Chairman to the Trade Negotiations Committee, Special Session of the Council for Trade in Services, TN/S/20, 11 July 2005.

4. Doha Work Programme, Decision Adopted by the General Council on 1 August 2004, WT/L/579, 2 August 2004.

5. Communication from Bolivia, Brazil, Chile, China, Colombia, Cuba, the Dominican Republic, Ecuador, Egypt, Guatemala, India, Indonesia, Mexico, Nicaragua, Pakistan, Peru, the Philippines, and Thailand. Review of Progress as established in paragraph 15 of the Guidelines and Procedures for the Negotiations on Trade in Services.

6. Classification List: MTN.GNS/W/120.

7. For example, the Austrian MFN Exemption list provides as a justification for an MFN exemption concerning road transport that this is done "to take into account regional specificity of the provision of road transport services and to protect the integrity of road infrastructure, health, and environment."

8 For a thorough discussion of the GATS' transparency provisions and their potential benefits, see Mashayekhi, 2004a and 2004b.

9. The national treatment obligation does not, however, require a member to take measures outside its territorial jurisdiction. The member would therefore not have to extend the subsidies to a service supplier located in the territory of another member. See WTO Document "Scheduling Of Initial Commitments In Trade In Services: Explanatory Note." This note is a revised version of a draft entitled "Scheduling of Commitments in Trade in Services: Explanatory Note," 22 December 1992.

10. Article XVI specifically lists the measures that members must inscribe in their schedules if they wish to maintain such limitations. Article XVII provides no such list of measures but simply states that the commitments may be "subject to any conditions and qualifications."

11. The requests exchanged between members are confidential documents, so no wide-ranging analysis of what countries have requested of each other in terms of health services can be done.

12. The negotiating context and tools used by members in the negotiations can have a significant impact on the results of the negotiations. See, for example, Mashayekhi and Tuerk, 2003.

13. Report by the Chairman to the Trade Negotiations Committee, Special Session of the Council for Trade in Services, TN/S/20, 11 July 2005.

14. Note that this figure relates to offers in the health services sector, excluding health related services such as nurses, paramedical services, midwives, or dental services.

15. Philippine Overseas Employment Authority statistics.

16. International Council of Nurses, 2002.

17. Communication from Argentina, Bolivia, Chile, China, Colombia, the Dominican Republic, Egypt, Guatemala, India, Mexico, Pakistan, Peru, the Philippines, and Thailand, TN/S/W/14, 3 July 2003.

18. UNCTAD, TD/B/COM.1/62

19. The counterpoint to this argument is that the services so obtained would be provided at more competitive prices than local firms could achieve (otherwise the local firms would win the contracts), thus stimulating development and growth elsewhere in the economy. Where the balance between these two concerns lies is a matter for judgment by each country.

20. Health and Social Services, Background Note by the Secretariat, S/C/W/50, 18 September 1999.

21. The two goals, liberalization of services trade and the right to regulate, are recognized in the Preamble of the GATS. The goal to liberalize services trade is, for example, enshrined in the second recital, which reads "[w]ishing to establish a multilateral framework of principles and rules for trade in services with a view to the expansion of such trade under conditions of transparency and progressive liberalization…" The right to regulate, in turn, is recognized in recital four. Specifically, it reads "[r]ecognizing the right of members to regulate, and to introduce new regulations, on the supply of services within their territories in order to meet national policy objectives…"

22. The GATS, like many other international trade agreements, mostly formulates its obligations in the negative, i.e., establishes what countries are prohibited to do (i.e., depending on their specific commitments, WTO members shall not discriminate, shall not put in place quantitative restrictions, or shall not put in place certain requirements that are more burdensome than necessary). The GATS does not, however—and maybe for good reason—set forth what WTO members should do, i.e., what is "good regulation" to implement. An exception to this is the Reference Paper on Telecommunications which, to some extent, establishes regulatory principles on issues such as interconnection, public availability of licensing criteria, independence of the regulator, and allocation of scarce resources.

23. GATS Art. XXVIII (n) states that "a juridical person is: (i) 'owned' by persons of a member if more than 50 percent of the equity interest in it is beneficially owned by persons of that member." "Juridical Person" is defined in Art. XXVII (l) as "privately-owned or governmentally-owned."

24. GATS, Art. VIII. For a discussion of these aspects, see Cossy, 2005.

25. For some initial ideas on the relationship between GATS and privatization, see Ostrovksy, Speed, and Türk, 2005.

26. In other words, a government must accord the same "equal" conditions of competition to foreign services and service suppliers of other members as it accords to its own "like" services and services suppliers. Specifically, a member is obliged to provide "not less favourable treatment" to foreign service providers. It is however, allowed to provide "less favourable treatment" to its domestic service suppliers. Similarly, in the case of MFN, the GATS reads that "…each member shall accord immediately and unconditionally to services and services suppliers of any other member, treatment no less favourable than it accords to like services and services suppliers of any other country." For a discussion of the GATS national treatment and most favored nation obligations, see Zdouc, 2004. See also, Krajewski, 2003a.

27. *EC-Bananas III, para 7.332. European Communities-Regime for the Importation, Sale and Distribution of Bananas*, WT/DS27/R/ECU, adopted 25 September 1997, as modified by the appellate body. See also, W Zdouc, 2004.

28. Para 5 of the Negotiating Guidelines states that "There shall be no a priori exclusion of any services sector or mode of supply." WTO, 2001c.

29. GATS, Art, I para 3 lit. c.

30. Note that the Annex on Financial Services contains its own attempt to clarify the language used in Art I. 3 GATS and its application to the services covered by the financial services annex. See Art 1. (b) and (c) of the Annex on Financial Services.

31. For a thorough discussion of the legal aspects surrounding GATS Art I, see generally Krajewski, 2001. See also Krajewski, 2003b.

32. It is interesting to note that the European Communities are now, in the GATS framework, trying to renegotiate the schedules of some of their members who had negotiated their GATS commitments independently, before acceding to the European Union. Arguably, the fact that some of these members have not put any public services carve-out is an issue under discussion in this context.

33. For a discussion of possible multilateral solutions, see Krajewski, 2001.

34. For a more detailed discussion of these approaches, see: Ostrovksy, Speed, and Türk, forthcoming.

35. The same applies to services such as medical, dental, and midwife services, and services provided by nurses, physiotherapists, and paramedical personnel.

36. Sweden, 1994; Norway, 1994; Switzerland, 1994. Strictly speaking, Liechtenstein also belongs to this category, Liechtenstein, 1994.

37. In that case, however, questions about government procurement might arise. For a discussion about government procurement and public services (the example of water), see Cossy, 2005.

38. Switzerland retains its right to require Swiss nationality to practice independently.

39. Malaysia, 1994; Mexico, 1994.

40. The Republic of Estonia, *Schedule of Specific Commitments*, GATS/SC/127 (October 5, 1999); The United States of America, *Schedule of Specific Commitments*, GATS/SC/90 (April 15, 1995).

41. For both countries, this clarification only applies to two of the four environmental services subsectors mentioned, namely sewage services and refuse disposal services.

42 . More a more comprehensive analysis of current discussions on domestic regulation, see Mascareignes, Tuerk, forthcoming.

43. This obligation, however, is a qualified one, as it is also stipulated that this requirement is applicable where this would not be inconsistent with constitutional structure or the nature of the legal system.

44. The broad categories of measures in Article VI.4 have been defined by the WTO secretariat as follows: *qualification requirements:* substantive requirements relating to education, examination requirements, practical training, experience, or language requirement that a professional service supplier is required to fulfill in order to obtain certification or a license; *qualification procedures*: administrative or procedural rules relating to the administration of qualification requirements, such as organizing of qualifying exams; where to register for education programs; conditions to be respected to register; documents to be filed; fees; mandatory physical presence conditions; alternative ways to follow educational programs or to gain a qualification/equivalence; *licensing requirements*: comprising substantive requirements other than qualification requirements, compliance with which is required in

order to obtain a formal permission to supply a service; licensing procedures: administrative procedures for submission and processing of an application for a license, including time frame for processing of a license, documents and information required for the application; and technical standards: requirements that may apply both to the characteristics or definition of the service and to the manner in which it is performed, e.g., a standard may stipulate the content of an audit that is similar to a definition of a service, another standard may lay down rules of ethics or standards of conduct to be observed by auditors, etc. See background paper by the WTO Secretariat, 1996.

45. WTO, 2001a.

46. Application of Regulatory Disciplines to Different Levels of Governments and Non-Governmental Bodies, Communication from Chile; Hong Kong, China; Korea; Switzerland; The Separate Customs Territory of Taiwan, Penghu, Kinmen and Matsu; and Thailand, Room Document, WPDR, 27 April 2005.

47. Proposal for Disciplines on Technical Standards in Services, Communication from Switzerland, S/WPDR/W32, 1 February 2005.

48. WTO, 2001a. See also WTO, 2003a; this paper refers to the revised draft (3 May 2003). See also: WTO, 2000b, as well as WTO, 2002 for an overview of the work WTO members have carried out to date on that issue in the WPDR. For the most recent contribution by the WTO Secretariat, see WTO Secretariat, 2003.

49. The question of whether a measure restricting trade should be considered necessary only if there is no less-restrictive and reasonably available alternative measure to achieve the same policy objectives is what is termed the "third aspect." See Honeck, 2004. Other aspects are the scope of measures subject to the "necessity test," and the policy objectives that may related to a necessity test. See also WTO Secretariat, 2003.

50. For a discussion of this and other examples, see Krajewski, 2003a.

51. This is the case, both in the GATT and GATS general exceptions, but also in the TBT necessity test. See GATT Art XX, GATS Art XIV, TBT Art 2.2.

52. Article 2.4 TBT states that WTO members need not use international standards as a basis for their technical regulations "when such international standards or relevant parts would be an ineffective or inappropriate means of the fulfillment of the legitimate objective pursued," and does not contain any list of legitimate objectives. Art 2.2 TBT includes an open-ended list of legitimate objectives and states that "such legitimate objectives are, *inter alia:* national security requirements, the prevention of deceptive practices, protection of human health or safety or animal or plant life or health, or the environment." When interpreting Article 2.4 TBT, the appellate body explicitly stated that "'legitimate objectives' referred to in Article 2.4. must be interpreted in the context of Article 2.2," the TBT provision setting out the necessity tests and the indicative list of legitimate objectives according to which the necessity of a measure needs to be judged.

53. WTO Secretariat, 2003.

54. More recently, see also Horizontal Transparency Disciplines in Domestic Regulation: Proposal by the United Sttes, 2 May 2005 (room document). See also certain elements in Proposal for Disciplines on Technical Standards in Services, Communication from Switzerland, S/WPDR/W32, 1 February 2005

55. TBT, Art. 2.9.4. See WTO Secretariat, 1996;WTO, 2001b.

56. Mashayekhi, 2004a.

57. Here the notion of market access is used in the broader term, encompassing both market access and national treatment commitments.

58. Note however, that the most recent panel and appellate body reports in the US Gambling case-albeit not directly related to health issues—adopted a more far reaching and flexible interpretation of the GATS provision on general exceptions. See also Fidler, David, and Correa, Carlos, GATS and Health-Related Services, the WTO Decision in US-Gambling: Implications for Health Policy Makers, Trade and Health Notes, June 2005.

59. This is the case, despite the fact that assessment has been recognized as a standing agenda item on the Council for Trade in Services.

60. For an overview of the assessment-related work undertaken by various intergovernmental organizations, see Mashayekhi and Julsaint, 2002.

61. See, for example, WHO, 2002.

62. Drager, McClintock, and Moffitt, 2000.

63. WTO, 2001c. 60. See also: Drager and Beaglehole, 2001 and WHO, 2004.

References

Adams, O., and C. Kinnon. 1998. A public health perspective. In *International Trade in Health Services: A Development Perspective.* UNCTAD/ITCD/TSB/5, WHO/TFHE/98.1. Geneva: UNCTAD-WHO.

Buchanan, J., T. Parkin, and J. Sochalski. 2003. *International nurse mobility: trends and policy implications.* Geneva: WHO .

Consumers International. 2001. The General Agreement on Trade on Services (GATS): An impact assessment by Consumers International.

Cossy, M. 2005. Water services and the GATS—selected legal aspects. In Weiss, E.B., L. B. DeChazournes, and N. Bernasconi-Osterwalder, eds., *Fresh water and international economic law.* Oxford University Press.

Dole. 2001. Philippine Department of Labor and Employment, press release, 29 May 2001, Manila

Dommen, C. 2003. No sell-out on trade. In the Human Rights Commission, *Bridges between trade and sustainable development,* Year 7, No. 3, April.

Drager, N., and R. Beaglehole. 2001. Globalization: changing the public health landscape. *Bulletin of the World Health Organization* 79 (9): 803.

Drager, N., E. McClintock, and M. Moffitt. 2000. *Negotiating health development: a guide for practitioners.* Geneva: Conflict Management Group and WHO.

Equinet, International People's Health Movement, and Save the Children UK. 2003. The GATS threat to public health. A joint submission to the World Health Assembly, World Development Movement, May.

Estonia, Republic of. 1999. Schedule of Specific Commitments, GATS/SC/127(October 5).

European Communities. 1995. Schedule of Specific Commitments, GATS/SC/31 (Apr. 15).

Fuchs P., E. Tuerk, and M. Krajewski. 2002. Environmental implications of the general agreement on trade in services (GATS) and of future GATS negotiations. Scoping study for the German Forum for Environment and Development, funded by the Federal Environment Ministry of Germany; Series UBA-TEXTE. Berlin: Federal Environmental Agency (Umweltbundesamt UBA), April.

Hilary, John. 2001. The wrong model. Save the Children.

Honeck, D. 2004. GATS and necessity. Presentation in the Workshop on Domestic Regulation 29–30 March, Geneva.

Kenneth, M., J. Neumann, and E. Tuerk. 2003. Second guessing national policy choices: necessity, proportionality and balance in the WTO services negotiations. A CIEL Issue Brief for the WTO's 5th Ministerial, September.

Krajewski, M. 2001. Public services and the scope of the GATS. Research paper (CIEL Washington, D.C.) at http://www.ciel.org/Publications/PublicServices Scope.pdf (visited Jan. 16, 2004).

Krajewski, M. 2003a. *National regulation and trade liberalization in services.* London: Kluwer Law International.

Krajewski, M. 2003b. Public services and trade liberalization: mapping the legal framework. *J. Int'l Econ.* L. 341.

Liechtenstein. 1994. Schedule of Specific Commitments, GATS/SC/83 (April 15).

Malaysia. 1994. Schedule of Specific Commitments, GATS/SC/52 (April 15).

Mashayekhi, M. 2000. GATS 2000 negotiations, options for developing countries. Working Paper 9, South Centre, Geneva.

Mashayekhi, M. 2004a. GATS, transparency, and domestic regulations to the WTO. Paper presented at the WTO Workshop on Domestic Regulation, Geneva, March 29–30

Mashayekhi, M. 2004b. Disciplines on domestic regulations: options for developing countries. Forthcoming,

Mashayekhi, M., and M. Julsaint. 2002. Assessment of trade in services in the context of the GATS 2000 negotiations. Working Paper 13, South Centre, Geneva.

Mashayekhi, M., and E. Tuerk. 2003. The WTO services negotiations: some strategic considerations, T.R. A.D.E. Working Paper 14, South Centre, Geneva,

Mexico. 1994. Schedule of Specific Commitments, GATS/SC/56, (April 15).

Neumann, J., and E. Tuerk. 2003. Necessity revisited—Proportionality in WTO law after Korea-beef, EC-asbestos, and EC-sardines. *Journal of World Trade* 37 (1).

Norway. 1994. Schedule of Specific Commitments, GATS/SC/66 (April 15).

OECD (Organisation for Economic Co-operation and Development). 2001. Trade in services: a roadmap to GATS MFN exemptions. Paris: OECD, TD/TC/ WP(2001)25/FINAL, p 15.

———. 2002. International migration of physicians and nurses: causes, consequences and health policy implications. Paris: OECD.

———. 2003. Service providers on the move: mutual recognition agreements. TD/TC/WP(2002)48/FINAL. Paris: OECD.

Ostrovksy, A., R. Speed, and E. Türk. Forthcoming. GATS and water: retaining policy space to serve the poor. In Weiss, E.B., L. B. DeChazournes, and N. Bernasconi-Osterwalder, eds., *Water and international economic law.* Oxford University Press.

Oulton, J. 2004. Applicability of the accountancy disciplines to nursing. Presentation at the WTO Workshop on Domestic Regulation, 29–30 March.

Raghavan, C. 2002. Developing countries and services trade: chasing a black cat in a dark room, blindfolded. Third World Network, Penang, Malaysia.

Sweden. 1994. Schedule of Specific Commitments, GATS/SC/82 (April 15).

Switzerland. 1994. Schedule of Specific Commitments, GATS/SC/83 (April 15).

Türk E., and M. Krajewski. 2003. the right to water and trade in services: assessing the impact of gats negotiations on water regulation. Paper presented at Conference: Moving forward from Cancún, Berlin, October 30–31.

UKCC (United Kingdom Central Council for Nursing, Midwifery and Health Visiting). 2002. *Statistical Analysis of the UKCC Register 1999–2000*, Vol. 2. London: UKCC.

UNCTAD (United Nations Conference on Trade and Development). 2003. Trade in services and development implications. Note by the UNCTAD secretariat. TD/B/COM.1/62.

UNCTAD/WHO. 1998. *International Trade in Health Services, A Development Perspective.* UNCTAD/ITCD/TSB/5, WHO/TFHE, 981.

UNHCHR. (United Nations High Commissioner on Human Rights, Economic, Social, and Cultural Rights). 2002. Liberalization of trade in services and human rights, report of the High Commissioner. E/CN.4/sub.2/2002/9.

———. Press document, 30 March 2004. Special *rapporteurs* on rights to health and education present findings to commission, http://www.ohchr.org/news/commission60th.htm.

United States of America. 1995. Schedule of Specific Commitments, GATS/SC/90 (April 15).

WHO (World Health Organization). 2001. Macroeconomics and health: investing in health for economic development: report for the WHO Commission on Macroeconomics and Health.

———. 2002, Meeting report of the International Consultation on Assessment of Trade in Health Services and GATS, research and monitoring priorities, Geneva, 9–11 January.

———. 2004. Trade and health notes, managing liberalization of trade in service from a health policy perspective.

Winters, L. A. 2003. The economic implications of liberalizing mode 4 trade. Paper prepared for the Joint WTO–World Bank Symposium on The movement of natural persons (mode 4) under the GATS, Geneva, 11–12 April.

World Bank. 2002. *Global economic prospects.* Washington DC: World Bank.

World Bank/IMF (International Monetary Fund). 2004. Data in *International Herald Tribune*, 21–22 February.

WTO (World Trade Organization). 1992. Scheduling of commitments in trade in services: explanatory note. 22 December.

————. 2000a. GATS Article VI.4: Possible disciplines on transparency in domestic regulation. Communication from the United States, Working Party on Domestic Regulation, S/WPDR/W/4, 3 May.

————. 2000b: Informal note by the Secretariat, Working Party on Domestic Regulation; Application of the necessity test: Issues for consideration, Job No. 5929, 19 March.

————. 2001a: Communication from the European Communities and their member states, Working Party on Domestic Regulation; Domestic regulation: necessity and transparency, S/WPDR/W/14, 1 May.

————. 2001b. Communication from the United States, Council for Trade in Services Special Session; Transparency in Domestic Regulation. S/CSS/W/102, 13 July.

————. 2001c. Guidelines and procedures for the negotiations on trade in services, W/L/93, 29 March.

————. 2001d. WTO Ministerial declaration, ministerial conference, fourth session. Doha. WT/MIN(01)/DEC/W/1, 9–14 November.

————. 2002. Summary of the discussions on the checklist of issues for WPDR. JOB(02)/3/Rev.3, 3 December.

————. 2003a. Communication from Japan, WPDR, draft annex on domestic regulation, job(03)/45, 3 March.

————. 2003b. *International Trade Statistics.*

————. 2004. Document S/C/W/236, 15 March.

WTO Secretariat. 1996. The relevance of the disciplines of the agreement on technical barriers to trade (TBT) and on import licensing procedures to article VI.4 of the General Agreement on Trade in Services. Working Party on Professional Services. S/WPPS/W/9, 11 September, pp.2–3.

————. 2003. Necessity tests in the WTO, Note by the Secretariat, WPDR, S/WPDR/W/27, 2 December.

Yan, J. 2002. Caribbean nurses develop strategy for nurse shortages. *International Nursing Review* 49: 132–134.

Zdouc, W.. 2004. WTO dispute settlement practice relating to the general agreement on trade in services. In F. Ortino and E.-U. Petersmann, eds., *The WTO dispute settlement system, 1995–2003.* Kluwer Law International.

ANNEX Addressing Health-Related Services: Excerpts from Selected Initial and Revised Offers

Sector or Sub-sector	Limitations on Market Access	Limitations on National Treatment
Bahrain **TN/S/O/BHR/Rev.1** **2 June 2005**		
1. Business Services		
(h) Medical and dental services (CPC 9312)	(1) Unbound (2) None (3) Unbound (4) Unbound, except as indicated in the horizontal section as well as for specialized surgeons providing specialized medical and dental services.	(1) Unbound (2) None (3) Unbound (4) Unbound, except as indicated in the horizontal section
(i) Veterinary services (CPC 932)	(1) Unbound (2) None (3) None (4) Unbound, except as indicated in the horizontal section	(1) Unbound (2) None (3) Unbound (4) Unbound, except as indicated in the horizontal section
(j) Services provided by midwives, nurses, physiotherapists (CPC 93191)	(1) Unbound (2) None (3) Unbound (4) Unbound, except as indicated in the horizontal section	(1) Unbound (2) None (3) Unbound (4) Unbound, except as indicated in the horizontal section
8. **Health Related and Social Services** (other than those listed under 1. A.h–j.)		
A. Hospital services (CPC 9311)	(1) Unbound (2) None (3) A private hospital may be established by Bahraini doctors with no less than 5 years of continues experience or by organizations, companies and societies established in Bahrain	(1) Unbound (2) None (3) Unbound (4) Unbound, except as indicated in the horizontal section

ANNEX (*Continued*)

Sector or Sub-sector	Limitations on Market Access	Limitations on National Treatment
	(4) Unbound, except as indicated in the horizontal section	
B. Other Human Health Services (CPC 9319, other than 93191)		
Services of medical laboratories (CPC 93199)	(1) None (2) None (3) None (4) Unbound, except as indicated in the horizontal section	(1) Unbound (2) None (3) Unbound (4) Unbound, except as indicated in the horizontal section
E. Social Services (CPC 933)	(1) None (2) None (3) None (4) None	(1) None (2) None (3) None (4) None
Hong Kong, China TN/S/O/HKG/Rev.1 16 June 2005		
1. Business Services A. Professional Services		
Medical and dental services (CPC 9312)	(1) Unbound (2) None (3) Unbound (4) Unbound	(1) Unbound (2) None (3) Unbound (4) Unbound
Veterinary services : limited to laboratory services for animals and birds (Part of CPC 932)	(1) None (2) None (3) Unbound (4) Unbound	(1) None (2) None (3) Unbound (4) Unbound
Services provided by midwives, nurses, physiotherapists and para-medical personnel (CPC 93191)	(1) Unbound (2) None (3) Unbound (4) Unbound	(1) Unbound (2) None (3) Unbound (4) Unbound
8. Health Related and Social Services		
Hospital services (CPC 93110)	(1) Unbound (2) None	(1) Unbound (2) None

(*continued on next page*)

ANNEX (*Continued*)

Sector or Sub-sector	Limitations on Market Access	Limitations on National Treatment
Other human health services not elsewhere classified (CPC 93199)	(3) Unbound (4) Unbound	(3) Unbound (4) Unbound
India, Initial Offer TN/S/O/IND 12 January 2004		
1. Business Services A. Professional Services		
(h) Medical and Dental Services (CPC 9312) (j) Services provided by Midwives, Nurses, Physiotherapists and paramedical personnel (CPC 93191)	(1) None for provision of services on provider to provider basis such that the transaction is between established medical institutions covering areas of second opinion to help in diagnosis of cases or in the field of research. (2) None (3) Only through incorporation with a foreign equity ceiling of 74 per cent subject to the condition that the latest technology for treatment will be brought in and to the condition that in the case of foreign investors having prior collaboration in that specific service sector in India, FIPB approval would be required. (4) Unbound except as indicated in the horizontal section.	(1) None (2) None (3) Publicly funded services may be available only to Indian citizens or may be supplied at differential prices to persons other than Indian citizens. (4) Unbound except as indicated in the horizontal section

ANNEX (*Continued*)

Sector or Sub-sector	Limitations on Market Access	Limitations on National Treatment
8. Health Related and Social Services A. Hospital Services (CPC 9311)	(1) ~~Unbound*~~ None for provision of services on provider to provider basis such that the transaction is between two established medical institutions, covering the areas of second opinion to help in diagnosis of cases or in the field of research. (2) ~~Unbound~~ None. (3) Only through incorporation with a foreign equity ceiling of ~~51~~ 74 per cent and subject to the condition that the latest technology for treatment will be brought in and further subject to the condition that in the case of foreign investors having prior collaboration in that specific service sector in India, FIPB approval would be required. Publicly funded services may be available only to Indian citizens or may be supplied at differential prices to persons other than Indian citizens. (4) Unbound except as indicated in the horizontal section	(1) ~~Unbound*~~ None. (2) ~~Unbound~~ None. (3) None (4) Unbound except as indicated in the horizontal section

(*continued on next page*)

ANNEX (*Continued*)

Sector or Sub-sector	Limitations on Market Access	Limitations on National Treatment
Pakistan **TN/S/O/PAK** **30 May 2005**		
1. Business Services		
(h) *Medical and dental services (CPC No 9312)*	(1) *Unbound* (2) *None* (3) (a) *As in measures applicable to all sectors* (b) *Subject to Pakistan Medical and Dental Council Regulations* (4) *Unbound except as indicated under horizontal ~~measures~~ commitments*	(1) *Unbound* (2) *None* (3) *None* (4) *Unbound except as indicated under horizontal ~~measures~~ commitments*
(i) Veterinary Services (CPC 9320) The offer does not include services provided by public institutions whether owned and operated by federal, provincial, district, Tehsil or municipal Authorities	(1) Unbound (2) None (3) (a) Market Access subject to transparent ENT (b) ENT based on inquiry to gauge if direct or indirect govt. subsidy being provided (4) Unbound, except as indicated in the horizontal commitments	(1) Unbound (2) None (3) (a) Residency requirement essential for natural persons. (b) Subject to fulfillment of all requirements and conditions applicable only to foreign investors/juridical entities (4) Unbound except as indicated in the horizontal commitments 1,2,3,4) Subsidies unbound
(j) Services provided by midwives, nurses, physiotherapists, and Para-medical personnel (CPC 93191)	(1) Unbound (2) None (3) None (4) Unbound except as under horizontal commitments	(1) Unbound (2) None (3) Subject to fulfillment of all requirements and conditions applicable only to foreign entities

ANNEX (*Continued*)

Sector or Sub-sector	Limitations on Market Access	Limitations on National Treatment
The offer does not include services provided by public institutions whether owned and operated by federal, provincial, district, Tehsil or municipal Authorities		(4) Unbound except that qualifications for foreign service suppliers will be set by the Pakistan Nursing Council and any other relevant law for the time being in force
8. Health and Related Social Services		
A. Hospital services (CPC 9311)	(1) Unbound* (2) None ~~(3) (a) As in measures applicable to all sectors (b) Subject to Pakistan Medical and Dental Council Regulations.~~ **None** (4) Unbound except as indicated under horizontal ~~measures~~ *commitments*	(1) Unbound* (2) None (3) None (4) Unbound except as indicated in the under horizontal ~~measures~~ *commitments*
~~Medical and dental services (CPC 9312)~~	~~(1) Unbound*~~ ~~(2) None~~ ~~(3) (a) As in measures applicable to all sectors (b) Subject to Pakistan Medical and Dental Council Regulations. None~~ ~~(4) Unbound except as indicated in the under horizontal measures commitments~~	~~(1) Unbound*~~ ~~(2) None~~ ~~(3) None~~ ~~(4) Unbound except as indicated in the under horizontal measures commitments~~

Note: The excerpts generally inscribe changes in line with the editorial conventions as stipulated in the Secretariat documents JOB(02)/88 and JOB(05)/6. Accordingly, the introduction of new text is reflected in **bold** and the deletion of text in ~~strike-out~~. Modifications to the initial offer are shadowed in grey. *Italics* have been used in order to reflect technical refinements that do not alter the scope or substance of existing or offered commitments.
a. Note that also Hong Kong, China's commitments (and offers) in the distribution sector relate to health (i.e. distribution of pharmaceutical and medical goods, surgical and orthopedic instruments and devices). For sake of brevity, this table does not reflect the relevant rows of this offer.

3

UPDATE ON GATS
COMMITMENTS
AND NEGOTIATIONS

Rudolf Adlung, Antonia Carzaniga

Current Patterns of Access Commitments in Health Services

The number of sectors committed by individual WTO members tends to be positively related to their level of economic development. Developed countries apparently found it easier—or more economically beneficial—than the majority of developing countries to submit relatively extensive schedules. The commitments of 30 percent of WTO members, all developing and least developed countries, are confined to 20 or fewer of the approximately 160 service sectors contained in a standard classification list. About another third of members has scheduled between 21 and 60 sectors, and the remaining group has inscribed up to about 140 sectors. The composition of the latter group is far from uniform: it not only comprises virtually all OECD members, but also several developing and transition economies and even a few least-developed countries (The Gambia, Lesotho, and Sierra Leone). All countries that have joined the WTO since 1997–98 also fall in this group.

The country pattern of specific commitments in health services is even more diffuse. One large member, Canada, has not undertaken commitments in any of the four relevant subsectors (medical and dental services; services provided by midwives, nurses, physiotherapists, and paramedical personnel; hospital services; and other human health services such as ambulance services and residential health facility services), while the United States and Japan have scheduled only one subsector each (see Table 3.1). This contrasts with least developed countries such as Burundi, The Gambia, Lesotho, Malawi, Sierra Leone, and Zambia, which

TABLE 3.1 Specific Commitments of WTO Members on Individual Health Services, June 2003

Members	Medical & dental services	Nurses, midwives, etc	Hospital services	Other human health services
Albania	x	x	x	x
Antigua & Barbuda	x			
Armenia	x	x	x	x
Australia	x			x
Austria	x	x	x	x
Barbados	x			
Belize	x			x
Bolivia			x	
Botswana	x	x		
Brunei Darussalam	x			
Bulgaria	x			
*Burundi	x		x	x
China	x			
Chinese Taipei			x	x
*Congo, Dem. Rep.	x			
Costa Rica	x		x	
Croatia	x	x	x	x
Czech Republic	x			
Dominican Republic	x		x	x
Ecuador			x	
EC (12)	x	x	x	
Estonia	x		x	x
Finland		x		
*Gambia, The	x	x	x	x
Georgia	x		x	x
Guyana	x			
Hungary	x		x	x
India			x	
Jamaica	x	x	x	
Japan			x	
Jordan	x	x	x	x
Kuwait			x	x
Kyrgyz Republic	x	x	x	x
Latvia	x	x	x	
*Lesotho	x	x		x
Lithuania	x	x	x	

TABLE 3.1   (Continued)

Members	Medical & dental services	Nurses, midwives, etc	Hospital services	Other human health services
Macedonia	x	x	x	x
*Malawi	x	x	x	
Malaysia	x		x	x
Mexico	x	x	x	
Moldova	x	x	x	
Norway	x	x		
Oman	x		x	
Pakistan	x		x	
Panama			x	
Poland	x	x	x	
Qatar	x			
*Rwanda	x			
St. Lucia			x	
Senegal	x			
St. Vincent			x	x
*Sierra Leone	x	x	x	
Slovak Republic	x			x
Slovenia	x		x	
South Africa	x	x		
Swaziland	x		x	
Sweden	x	x		
Switzerland	x			
Trinidad & Tobago	x		x	
Turkey			x	
United States			x	
*Zambia	x	x	x	x
Total	54	29	44	17

No commitments: Argentina, Aruba, Bahrain, Brazil, Canada, Chile, Colombia, Cuba, Cyprus, Egypt, Gabon, Ghana, Guinea, Haiti, Honduras, Hong Kong (China), Iceland, Indonesia, Israel, Kenya, Korea (Rep. of), Liechtenstein, Macau, Malta, Mauritius, Morocco, New Zealand, Nicaragua, Nigeria, Paraguay, Peru, Philippines, Romania, Solomon Islands, Sri Lanka, Thailand, Tunisia, United Arab Emirates, República Bolivariana de Venezuela. (EC member states are counted individually.)

In addition to the sectors included above, the definition of medical and health services employed by most WTO members for scheduling purposes also includes veterinary services and a nonspecified category of other health-related and social services.
*Least developed countries.

have each included at least three subsectors. Jordan and a number of Central and Eastern European economies,[1] that have acceded to the WTO since December 1998 also undertook relatively extensive commitments. Nevertheless, education aside, no service sector has drawn fewer bindings among WTO members than the health sector.[2]

Of the four subsectors, medical and dental services are the most heavily committed (62 members), followed by hospital services (52 members), and services provided by midwives, nurses, etc. (34 members). Overall, this pattern suggests that it is politically easier or more economically attractive for administrations to liberalize capital-intensive and skills-intensive sectors than labor-intensive activities (see Table 3.2).

What factors could explain the generally shallow level of commitments on health services? The most obvious reason is the existence of government monopolies, in law or in fact, offering their services free or significantly below cost. There seems to be no point in assuming external policy bindings, at least under Mode 3 (commercial presence), if private activities are either prohibited or rendered commercially unattractive. However, total monopoly situations are likely to be rare. In many countries with a public health sector, there are also private suppliers. The mere fact that commercial providers are able to survive economically suggests that the public and the private segments do not compete directly, which means that they do not provide the same services. For example, there may be differences in terms of waiting periods, quality of equipment, or types of treatment offered. With this in view, five WTO members (Latvia, Malaysia, Mexico, Poland, and Slovenia) explicitly confined their commitments to various parts of the private health sector. Nevertheless, given prevailing policy patterns in many countries, the potential for Mode 3 trade and, consequently, for meaningful commitments, may have been lower in health services than in many other areas.

Requests for liberalization, or liberal policy bindings, in the Uruguay Round might also have been weak in this sector. In the absence of vocal export interests, many governments might have hesitated to request access commitments abroad and reciprocate by way of their own bindings on health services. There were apparently no pacesetters in these negotiations comparable to the role played, owing to strong export interests, by the United States, the European Communities, and other OECD countries in areas such as telecommunications and financial services. Moreover, as noted above, many administrations might have been concerned, rightly or wrongly, about the potential impact of access liberalization on basic social and quality objectives. The commitments ultimately made for Mode 3, possibly the most significant mode for many health services, have possibly been inspired by the intention to overcome shortages of physical and human capital, and to promote efficiency through foreign direct investment and the attendant supplies of skills and expertise.

TABLE 3.2   Numbers of WTO Members with Commitments on Individual Health Services, June 2003

		Medical and dental services	Midwives, nurses, etc.	Hospital services	Other human health services
Total		62	34	52	22
Market Access					
Mode 1	Full	21(–2)	8(–1)	18	11
	Partial	12	6	1	1
	Unbound	29	20	35	10
Mode 2	Full	35(–3)	12(–1)	44	15
	Partial	24	21	5	5
	Unbound	3	1	3	2
Mode 3	Full	29(–8)	7(–2)	18(–8)	12(–5)
	Partial	26	25	31	9
	Unbound	7	2	3	1
Mode 4	Full	0	0	0	0
	Partial	56	32	48	21
	Unbound	6	2	4	1
National Treatment					
Mode 1	Full	24	9	21	12
	Partial	10	6	1	1
	Unbound	28	19	30	9
Mode 2	Full	34	12	44	15
	Partial	23	21	5	5
	Unbound	5	1	3	2
Mode 3	Full	19	10	33(–24)	11(–4)
	Partial	37	22	15	9
	Unbound	6	2	4	2
Mode 4	Full	3	1	3(–1)	1
	Partial	54	31	44	19
	Unbound	5	2	5	2

Note: EC member states are counted individually.

( ) Reduced number of full commitments if horizontal limitations, which apply to all sectors contained in the individual country schedules, are taken into account.

Partial commitments on market access include commitments that carry any of the six limitations specified in Article XVI:2 of GATS as well as commitments subject to limitations in sectoral coverage (e.g., exclusions of small hospitals or public sector entities) or geographical coverage within the member's territory, and any other measures scheduled in the relevant column (including domestic regulatory measures for which Article VI might have provided legal cover). Similarly, partial commitments recorded under national treatment may include cases of "overscheduling" or misinterpretations.

A comparison across all schedules and sectors reveals that trading conditions are considerably more restrictive for Mode 4 than for other modes. Reflecting the political constraints involved, many members have limited the entry of natural persons to intracorporate transferees or to experts with special skills that are not domestically available. This contrasts with the conditions for Mode 2 (consumption abroad), which tend to be the most liberal. In many cases, governments may have felt that it would be pointless to try influencing demand patterns once consumers had left the countries concerned. Nevertheless, such possibilities may exist. Cases in point include the exclusion of health treatment abroad from domestic consumer subsidies or public reimbursement schemes. Consumer movements under Mode 2 may prove economically significant in sectors such as education and health, where they can be viewed as a partial substitute for the movement of personnel under Mode 4 and inward direct investment under Mode 3. Economically advanced developing countries in the vicinity of major export markets, e.g., Mexico, Morocco, and Tunisia, appear to be particularly well placed for developing such trade, i.e., for attracting foreign patients for longer-term health treatment.

Commitments on individual health services largely follow this general pattern. The highest share of full market access commitments is recorded for Mode 2 (consumption abroad), exceeding four-fifths in the hospital sector. From the standpoint of developing countries, which may be competitive suppliers in this area, it is interesting that virtually all relevant commitments scheduled by developed members are without limitation (see Table 3.3; see Mode 2, hospital services), thus amounting to a legally enforceable guarantee not to deter their residents from consuming like services abroad. In other subsectors, however, developed countries have tended to use limitations on Modes 2 and 3 more frequently than developing countries have (see Tables 3.3 and 3.4). Concerning Mode 4, no WTO member has undertaken full commitments in any of the four health subsectors. As in virtually all other services, commitments for this mode are subject to limitations and these are generally highly restrictive.

The high percentage of nonbindings for Mode 1 in some core health sectors, close to half for medical and dental services, and 60 percent and more for nursing and similar services, as well as for hospital services, may reflect the perception that cross-border provision of these services is not technically possible. In particular for hospital services, some schedules contain footnotes explaining that a noncommitment under Mode 1 is due to the unfeasibility of such supplies. The question arises, however, as to whether the administrations involved have considered all conceivable possibilities of combining traditional health services with modern communication technologies (see Box 3.1). Telehealth is a case in point. If applied to inpatients, the electronic provision of medical advice across borders could actually be classified as a hospital service, an interpretation not necessarily anticipated by all

**TABLE 3.3 Numbers of WTO Developed Members with
Commitments on Individual Health Services,
June 2003**

		Medical and dental services	Midwives, nurses, etc.	Hospital services	Other human health services
Total (out of 21 schedules)		18	17	15	2
Market Access					
Mode 1	Full	4(–1)	2(–1)	0	0
	Partial	1	1	0	0
	Unbound	13	14	15	2
Mode 2	Full	5(–1)	2(–1)	14	0
	Partial	13	15	1	2
	Unbound	0	0	0	0
Mode 3	Full	2(–2)	2(–2)	0	0
	Partial	14	15	15	2
	Unbound	2	0	0	0
Mode 4	Full	0	0	0	0
	Partial	16	17	14	2
	Unbound	2	0	1	0
National Treatment					
Mode 1	Full	4	2	0	0
	Partial	1	1	0	0
	Unbound	13	14	15	2
Mode 2	Full	5	2	14	0
	Partial	13	15	1	2
	Unbound	0	0	0	0
Mode 3	Full	1	2	13(–13)	0
	Partial	16	15	2	2
	Unbound	1	0	0	0
Mode 4	Full	0	0	0	0
	Partial	17	17	14	2
	Unbound	1	0	1	0

Note: EC member states are counted individually.
( ) Reduced number of full commitments if horizontal limitations are taken into account.

Box 3.1: Electronic Commerce in the Health Sector: The Relevance of GATS

The Concept of Technological Neutrality

As a general rule, the introduction of new transport or transmission technologies does not affect WTO members' rights and obligations under GATT and GATS. For example, there would be no legal basis in GATT, and no reasonable health- or trade-related justification, to subject pharmaceuticals ordered electronically to border treatment different from that of the same consignments ordered via regular mail. Such treatment may include the examination of content, product verification, tariff collection, or the seizure or refusal of hazardous products. Similarly, GATS ensures in principle that cross-border trade in services is not affected by the transmission processes employed. For example, except for reasons falling under Article XIV (protection of life and health, etc.), countries would find it difficult under GATS to explain why medical advice provided electronically from abroad is not subject to the same rules as advice conveyed by mail. The underlying concept of technological neutrality in the treatment of like services applies both to scheduled and nonscheduled sectors, as departures are likely to fall foul of the basic MFN obligation.

Application of Domestic Regulation to Electronic Supplies

The provision of telehealth services under Mode 1 may raise challenging new issues for health administrations. Imagine a foreign supplier that is significantly less qualified or subject to less rigorous controls than domestically established operators. Could the ensuing risks be contained the same way as risks associated with the use of foreign-produced pharmaceuticals? Possibly not, as there is one important difference: a foreign country's control over its domestic pharmaceutical industry, in application of producer-related and product-related regulations, may be complemented by the importing country's own procedures for the testing and approval of products. Such possibilities do not exist for services; they are not standardized and their quality cannot normally be assessed independently of the production process. However, such process assessment is beyond the importing country's jurisdictional control.

Yet this does not mean that no adequate instruments are available. Possible solutions could consist, for example, of a requirement on domestically established hospitals or doctors to cooperate only with foreign telehealth providers that have been certified by the governments concerned and/or are insured against malpractice with an internationally recognized company. Additional provisions may help to clarify the place of jurisdiction in the event of disputes. Governments in countries operating public health insurance schemes may also make payments contingent on the qualification of the foreign subsuppliers involved. These possibilities also exist vis-à-vis residents seeking reimbursement for health services consumed abroad.

Further Considerations. The implications of electronic commerce for the health sector are multifaceted and they extend beyond the scope of GATT and GATS. They include issues related to the security and privacy of transactions and to contract and liability law.

members at the time of scheduling. From the legal standpoint, this should not be a matter of concern: new technologies do not turn a noncommitment, even if attributed to technical constraints, into a binding access obligation.

Commitments do not have the same importance across all sectors and modes. Their economic value may be high in certain cases, e.g., midwifery services/Mode 4, but not in others, e.g., midwifery services/Mode 1. Likewise, the restrictiveness of similar limitations, e.g., discriminatory subsidies, nationality requirements, or land ownership restrictions, can vary widely between sectors. Uncertainties may remain with regard to the measures scheduled in individual cases. For example, licensing requirements for doctors or hospitals, contained in a number of schedules, may be operated for either quality purposes or for the administration of restrictions on access. In the former case, scheduling is not necessary, as quality-related measures do not fall under either the market access provisions of Article XVI or the national treatment obligations of Article XVII. In contrast, if quantitative restrictions were involved, it would be appropriate to schedule size, time frame, and other relevant features rather than the existence of an implementation mechanism.

Limitations on Trade in Health Services

In order to obtain a full picture of the limitations made by individual members, it is necessary to examine both the horizontal and the sector-specific parts of schedules. Horizontal limitations, which apply across all committed sectors, typically reflect economy-wide policy concerns and objectives. These may include restrictions on the physical presence of foreign suppliers, foreign equity ceilings, restrictions on the legal form of establishment (e.g., joint ventures only), exclusion of foreign-owned entities from certain subsidies and incentives, or limitations on the acquisition of land or real estate. The relationship between horizontal and sector-specific commitments is not straightforward in all cases, however, and there may be conflicting entries in the two sections. For the purpose of this study, the more restrictive or more specific version has been taken into account.

The relatively few limitations applying to health services under Modes 1 and 2 (cross-border trade and consumption abroad) are predominantly sector-specific. In the main, they concern the nonportability of insurance entitlements (see Table 3.5). Horizontal limitations that may prove relevant for health services include the noneligibility of foreign suppliers for subsidies, and restrictions on foreign exchange availability.

The restrictive effects associated with such limitations may be matched by other barriers that are not necessarily recorded in schedules. They include the nonrecognition of foreign licenses, qualifications, or standards. For example, public health insurers may refuse to reimburse the cost of treatment abroad on the

TABLE 3.4 Numbers of WTO Developing Members with Commitments on Individual Health Services, June 2003

	Medical and dental services	Midwives, nurses, etc.	Hospital services	Other human health services
Total (out of 44 schedules)	44	17	37	20
Market Access				
Mode 1: Full	17(−1)	6	18	11
Partial	11	5	1	1
Unbound	16	6	18	8
Mode 2: Full	30(−2)	10	30	15
Partial	11	6	4	3
Unbound	3	1	3	2
Mode 3: Full	16(−3)	5	18(−8)	13(−4)
Partial	23	10	16	7
Unbound	5	21	3	1
Mode 4: Full	0	0	0	0
Partial	40	15	34	19
Unbound	4	2	3	1
National Treatment				
Mode 1: Full	20	7	21	12
Partial	9	5	1	1
Unbound	15	5	15	7
Mode 2: Full	29	10	30	15
Partial	10	6	4	3
Unbound	5	1	3	2
Mode 3: Full	18	8	20(−10)	11(−3)
Partial	21	7	13	7
Unbound	5	2	4	2
Mode 4: Full	3	1	3(−1)	1
Partial	37	14	30	17
Unbound	4	2	4	2

Note: Includes Central and Eastern European transition economies.
( ) Reduced number of full commitments if horizontal limitations are taken into account.

TABLE 3.5   Limitations on Insurance Portability

Member	Sector
Bulgaria	Medical and dental services
Latvia, Lithuania, Poland	Medical and dental services; services provided by midwives, nurses, etc.; hospital services
Moldova	Private medical and dental services; services provided by midwives, nurses, etc.
Slovenia, United States	Hospital services

All limitations relate to Mode 2 trade, except in the case of Poland, which has also included Mode 1 supplies of medical and dental services and the services provided by midwives, nurses, etc.

grounds that the services involved have been of lesser quality than those offered domestically. It could prove difficult to challenge such practices under GATS. Similar measures employed by private commercial insurers would not even fall under the Agreement. While Article VII entitles members to enter into recognition agreements or grant recognition autonomously, notwithstanding the potential tension with the MFN obligation, they are under no obligation to develop a liberal approach in this regard. Under the relevant provisions of Article VII:3, governments are merely required, once they grant recognition, not to do this "in a manner which would constitute a means of discrimination...or a disguised restriction on trade in services." By May 2003, WTO had received 38 notifications of recognition measures under the relevant provisions (Article VII:4 of GATS). Of these notifications, 17 were potentially relevant for health services; they were submitted by Latvia, Macau, Switzerland, and several Latin American countries and concerned the recognition of diplomas.

As noted above, Mode 3 (commercial presence) and, in particular, Mode 4 (presence of natural persons) have drawn the highest share of partial commitments. Most of the limitations scheduled for Mode 4 are horizontal, while relatively many of those for Mode 3 are sector-specific. In limiting their Mode 3 commitments to natural persons, some countries, most of them developed, have reserved the right to restrict the commercial incorporation of foreign health care providers. Frequent market access limitations scheduled under Mode 4 concern quota-type restrictions, mainly setting a ceiling on numbers of foreign employees or denying access to all persons not considered to be specialist doctors, etc. Typical national treatment limitations under Mode 4 relate to training and language requirements.

Economic needs tests (ENTs) have also been frequently referred to in limitations under Modes 3 and 4, mostly for hospital services but also for medical and dental services. There are few cases where members have indicated the relevant criteria underlying such tests, for example population density, age structure, death rates, and the number of existing facilities. However, a recommendation in the guidelines developed for scheduling purposes in the Uruguay Round calls on members to indicate the main criteria on which ENTs are based.[3] For example, if the authority to establish a facility depends on a population criterion, the criterion should be described concisely. Unspecified ENTs have been used in particular by economically advanced countries. Given their potential for discretionary application, such entries may come close to a situation where no commitment exists.

Also of dubious value are the relatively large number of Mode 4 commitments that are limited to trainees or intracorporate transferees. Their significance depends essentially on the ability of a foreign supplier to establish a commercial presence under Mode 3. However, this tends to be more difficult for "exporters" of medical personnel in developing countries than it is for those in developed countries, given current investment patterns, and could prove elusive in those large segments of the health sector where private entrepreneurial activity is either not admitted or commercially unattractive.

Restrictions on foreign equity participation and on permissible types of legal incorporation have been scheduled as market access limitations (Article XVI) for Mode 3 in a few cases. Such restrictions may be intended to encourage transfers of technology, skills, and expertise; they are mostly contained in the horizontal section of the schedules concerned. Some members have also made horizontal national treatment limitations reserving the right to require foreign-owned facilities to train nationals. Other horizontal limitations under the relevant provisions of Article XVII include restrictions on the composition of boards of directors and the acquisition of land or real estate, as well as a requirement to grant more favorable treatment to economically disadvantaged groups or backward regions. The latter requirement may prove to be a potentially powerful instrument for developing countries to reconcile trade with social equity objectives. It may not even have been necessary to provide legal cover by way of scheduled limitations.

General references to national legislation are relatively frequent entries in both the horizontal and the sectoral sections. It is difficult in such cases, however, to identify the restrictive or discriminatory elements that would need to be covered by limitations on market access or national treatment. As noted above, the mere existence of national legislation with adverse impacts on market entry or market participation, such as licensing requirements or training obligations, does not call for scheduling per se.

Somewhat surprisingly, there are no advance commitments in the health sector providing for liberalization from specified later dates. Such precommitments have been used in telecommunications by about half of the approximately 90 members who have undertaken commitments in this sector, in order to map out future paths of liberalization. Precommitments are as legally valid as any other obligations under Articles XVI or XVII, and may thus serve the same purpose. They may be an interesting policy option in any sector, possibly including health, for which governments have developed longer-term reform strategies allowing for increased private participation. In circumscribing and guaranteeing future market access opportunities, precommitments enable potential new entrants as well as incumbent suppliers to adjust in time.

MFN exemptions are quite rare in health services. Three members have listed them specifically for medical, dental, and/or human health services and another four have done so for professional services in general. All exemptions are intended to provide legal cover for reciprocity provisions (e.g., potentially affecting the right of foreign suppliers to exercise the medical profession or their qualification for reimbursement under public health insurance schemes). However, a number of MFN exemptions that are not sector-specific may also be relevant for health services, including guarantees under bilateral investment protection agreements or tax preferences for certain nationalities.

Social and Developmental Implications

The potential for trade in health services has expanded rapidly over recent decades. New telecommunications technologies have reduced the impact of geographical barriers to trade (for example for telediagnosis, teleanalysis, and the like), while rising incomes and enhanced information have tended to increase the mobility of potential patients. At the same time, from the standpoint of domestic health authorities, cost pressures associated with aging or fast-growing populations, new medical developments, and a widening price/productivity gap in the health sector have underscored the importance of efficiency objectives. Such objectives, in turn, tend to be associated with the existence of competition, including competition generated by foreign market entrants. However, while such trade/efficiency links appear appealing to economists, at least within an appropriate regulatory environment, doubts may remain as to the effects of stiffening competition on other core policy concerns in the health sector, such as quality and the alleviation of poverty.

There are limits to the extent to which governments can influence the level and structure of trade in health services through various instruments. For example, while nonportability of insurance cover may deter many residents from seeking treatment abroad, well-to-do persons are not likely to be discouraged. While a monopoly hospital sector, without foreign investment, may be viewed as instrumental in ensuring fair distribution, cross-border mobility of patients may compensate, at least in part, for the absence of alternatives to domestic supply. The traveling of patients abroad also complicates distributional objectives: do they apply only to the nonmobile part of the population or do they include people who are physically *and* financially able to seek treatment in foreign hospitals? Furthermore, while administrative restrictions might prevent publicly controlled facilities from offering telemedical services, private suppliers may be eager to fill any ensuing market niches.

From a wider developmental standpoint, additional considerations come into play. Health is among the relatively few service areas in which, subject to various qualifications, developing countries may prove to be competitive exporters under several modes, including Mode 2. Possibly capitalizing on inward direct investment, which may in turn benefit from Mode 3 commitments, they may be able to attract patients not only from other developing countries (e.g., to Thailand or South Africa from South-East Asia or sub-Saharan Africa) but also from adjacent developed countries (for instance to the Caribbean from North America, and to North Africa from Europe). Such possibilities are particularly relevant for countries endowed with sufficient infrastructural resources, which are able to benefit not only on locational advantages but also from a range of efficient ancillary service industries. However, this is not necessarily the perspective of low-income developing countries. Their interests tend to hinge predominantly on other modes of supply: Mode 3 (i.e., attracting investment inflows) and Mode 4 (i.e., sending medical personnel abroad and receiving remittances).

It might be argued that reliance on foreign investment is a more viable development strategy, since it is associated with resource inflows, while labor movements abroad are tantamount to a loss of human capital. Are the ensuing remittances sufficient compensation? Empirical studies generally confirm that the majority of migrants from developing into industrial countries are better educated than the average workforce remaining behind. This may reflect prevailing policy patterns in the recipient countries, which tend to favor inflows of qualified rather than nonqualified persons, as well as a higher propensity of educated and well-informed persons to move abroad. In any event, it means that existing migration data tend to understate the corresponding transfer of human capital. However, not all movements imply economically significant losses for the home country. The critical factors are whether the persons involved have left permanently and whether they would have found, or would find on returning home, employment matching their qualifications.[4]

Foreign investment in health facilities represents a positive transfer of resources whose ramifications may reach well beyond the health sector. Indirect effects, including those on growth, income, and employment, may occur in related industries such as construction, transport, communication, and, possibly, tourism. The attendant developmental benefits may prove difficult to trace empirically, but this does not mean that they are economically irrelevant. Such benefits may have health-related implications. From the standpoint of public health, it might prove too narrow a view to consider only the direct effects on a population's health status of an increased foreign presence in, for example, a country's hospital sector. Broader routes of causation, leading from the liberalization of trade and investment to development and from development to health, may be equally significant in this connection. Infant mortality is significantly lower and has dropped far more rapidly over the past two decades in Hong Kong (China), the Republic of Korea, and Singapore than in Indonesia, the Philippines, and Thailand. This may have less to do with the organization of public health than with the resources produced in the former group by trade and investment regimes that in general are more open than those in the latter three countries.

Concerns have been voiced that health sector liberalization may turn out to be a two-edged sword for developing countries. Increased trade in the sector may satisfy the interests of hospital operators, health professionals, and an urban economic elite, but how would it affect the economically disadvantaged? Such concerns are understandable but they need to be put in a proper perspective:

First, it is important to bear in mind that GATS does not impose any constraints on the terms and conditions under which a potential host country treats foreign patients. For example, nothing in the Agreement would prevent members from subjecting the services provided to foreigners who have come for treatment to special taxes or charges. The proceeds, in turn, might be used to enhance the quantity and quality of basic domestic supplies.

Second, there are no legal impediments in GATS that would affect the ability of governments to discourage qualified staff from seeking employment in the private sector, whether at home or abroad. Deterrent measures might include deposit requirements or guarantees, which would make it financially unattractive for young professionals to capitalize immediately on taxpayers' investment in their education by seeking higher incomes. In addition, there are positive measures that may limit the risk of brain drain: liberalization under Mode 3, combined with foreign countries' commitments under Modes 2, may help to create domestic employment opportunities and, in turn, dissuade staff from moving abroad.

Third, it is difficult to see any crowding-out effects, to the disadvantage of resident patients, that could not be addressed through adequate regulation. Such regulation would not normally fall foul of GATS provisions, even in sectors that have been committed without limitation. For example, a country might require all private hospitals to reserve a minimum percentage of beds for free treatment for the needy, to offer some basic medical services in remote rural areas, or to train beyond the number required for the purposes of these institutions. Such measures would withstand examination under both Article XVI on market access and Article XVII on national treatment. If only foreign-owned facilities were subject to such public service obligations, the relevant regulation would need to be covered by limitations under Article XVII.

Similar obligations have been discussed at length in the GATS negotiations on basic telecommunications, concluded in February 1997, where social and regional policy considerations also came into play. A reference paper developed in this context protects the right of any government to define the kind of universal service obligation it wishes to maintain and confirms that such measures will not be regarded as anticompetitive per se. Commitments under the reference paper are self-commitments in so far as its content was negotiated in the context of the telecommunications negotiations, while its implementation, through incorporation in schedules, in full or in part, was left to individual members. About 80 percent of the WTO members undertaking commitments on basic telecommunications incorporated the paper. These members are self-committed to administering their universal service obligations in a transparent, nondiscriminatory and competitively neutral manner and to ensuring that they are not more burdensome than necessary for the kinds of services envisaged.

It could be argued that these provisions do not add a lot to what already exists in GATS Article III on transparency, Article VI on domestic regulation, Article XVI on market access, and Article XVII on national treatment. However, the inclusion of relevant obligations in the reference paper might have reassured telecommunications administrators and regulators who, for understandable reasons, were perhaps not entirely familiar with the terms and structure of GATS. A common interpretation of existing rules and, in some cases, specification of additional disciplines should be of particular interest to developing countries, as it would allow them to economize on negotiating resources. It may be worth considering such an approach in health services as well.

Current Negotiations

Given the basic social and infrastructural functions conferred on core services sectors, including health, there is certainly no point in talking policymakers into hasty liberalization. The consequences should be carefully considered, and this may well indicate a need for new regulation to accompany the phasing-in of external competition. In a public monopoly environment the production, financing, regulation, and control of a service tend to go hand in hand, whereas the move toward competitive systems necessarily implies a separation of tasks and functions. Liberalization may therefore presuppose reregulation to meet the multiplicity of legitimate objectives involved. This is a challenging task, not least for developing countries lacking regulatory experience. However, there is nothing to prevent administrations from joining forces to exploit possible synergies and/or mandating competent international organizations to propose model solutions. Regulatory approaches developed for telecommunications in recent years, under the auspices of the International Telecommunication Union, could inspire work in WHO and comparable bodies in other areas as well. The technological and economic forces working toward global market integration are unlikely to leave the health sector unaffected, and timely action by governments would seem to be desirable.

There is virtually no evidence, however, to suggest that the scope and content of current commitments on health services will change significantly as a result of the ongoing negotiations. Health services are the only large services sector that has not generated any negotiating proposals, let alone discussions in relevant WTO bodies, during the early stages of the round (2000–01). While the negotiations have since progressed to request/offer mode, with initial requests scheduled to be circulated by the end of June 2002 and initial offers by the of end March 2003, there has been no indication of any of the relevant sectors moving to the forefront. Of the 39 initial offers (covering 53 WTO members) circulated by mid-November 2003, less than a handful contained new or improved commitments in health-related areas (medical and dental services; services provided by midwives, nurses, etc.; hospital services; other human health services). Moreover, the improvements currently proposed for Mode 4 on a horizontal basis are not likely to generate palpable changes in these sectors. Despite a lot of public excitement, for various reasons, the negotiations may thus prove a nonevent—or even a missed opportunity—for health services in most countries.

Notes

1. Albania, Armenia, Croatia, Estonia, Georgia, the Kyrgyz Republic, Lithuania, Latvia, Macedonia, and Moldova.

2. World Trade Organization, Market Access: Unfinished Business, Special Studies 6, Geneva 2001.

3. See document S/L/92, 28 March 2001

4. WTO document S/C/W/75, 8 December 1998, Background Note on "Presence of Natural Persons (Mode 4)" (via WTO Web site).

References

WTO (World Trade Organization). 2001. S/L/92, 28 March.
———. 1998. Background note on Presence of natural persons (Mode 4) S/C/W/75, 8 December.
———. 2001. Market access: unfinished business. Special Studies 6, Geneva.

4

TEN STEPS TO CONSIDER BEFORE MAKING COMMITMENTS IN HEALTH SERVICES UNDER THE GATS

Julia Nielson

Introduction

The purpose of this paper is to assist policymakers in assessing whether or not to make commitments on health services under the GATS. To this end, it provides a step-by-step outline of the legal obligations under the GATS, with a view to assisting policymakers in assessing their options in the context of the negotiations. This is less a detailed discussion of the legal implications of different provisions of the GATS (which is covered extensively in Chapter 5) than a rough guide to the sequence of questions policymakers might want to ask in terms of understanding what commitments under the GATS mean and what they may or may not be able to do under the agreement.

Note that the paper does not presume to advocate that countries should make—or seek from others—commitments under the GATS. That needs to be a

The author is a senior trade policy analyst at the Organisation for Economic Co-operation and Development (OECD) in Paris. The views expressed in this paper are the author's alone and do not bind the member States of the OECD in any way. The author is grateful to Antonia Carzaniga, Mireille Cossy, and Pierre Latrille of the WTO Secretariat for helpful comments and discussions.

national decision based on careful consideration of the country's specific national circumstances—including the nature of the health system (i.e., the extent of private sector participation) and, crucially, the country's regulatory capacity (including enforcement capacity). This paper merely aims to provide some raw materials to assist policymakers in thinking about the issue and understanding the implications of any decisions they make.

The Threshold Issues

Public, Private, or Both?

A threshold issue for any health system is whether, or the extent to which, the private sector can participate in the provision of health services. In many countries, the past decades have seen a redrawing of the line of public/private participation in health services, in many cases resulting in increased private sector participation in parts of the health sector. In some cases, publicly funded systems permit service provision by private suppliers; in other cases, publicly funded and delivered systems coexist with privately funded and delivered services. The decision about whether, or how, to involve private suppliers in health care funding and provision has been essentially a domestic debate.

Such decisions include consideration of, among other factors, national budget priorities; the desire to increase the available resources; questions about the efficiency of resource use; ensuring that public policy objectives (e.g., universal provision, high quality care) are met; and what government should provide and how costs should be shared among different groups within the society.[1]

Many countries will describe themselves as having a public health system, although these systems range from publicly funded and provided, through publicly funded and publicly and privately provided, to systems that include both publicly and privately funded and provided health services. It is not the purpose of this paper to get into the details of financing and provision arrangements for health services; for our purposes, it is sufficient to note the variety of national choices that exists.

Nationals or Foreigners?

A different, often second, question is whether to allow participation by foreign suppliers. It is only at this stage that the GATS comes into the equation; the GATS only deals with the treatment of foreigners, not nationals; and the GATS has nothing to say on the debate over whether to allow private provision per se.

Debates over whether to allow foreign private suppliers to provide services may involve some of the following considerations: the desire to increase the efficiency of national private providers by exposing them to competition; the use of foreign suppliers to meet key shortages in the short to medium term; the desire to have access to new technologies or skills that may not be available from national suppliers; and the desire to increase the facilities and services available to health care consumers beyond what the domestic suppliers can provide. Equally, consideration must be given to how to ensure the quality of foreign providers and the impact of foreign suppliers on local suppliers and on the system for health care as a whole. Many of the issues that arise in consideration of allowing in foreign suppliers also arise in the context of domestic private providers.

It is only when a country allows foreign suppliers into its market that the GATS comes into play. Countries that are members of the WTO—and thus members of the GATS—are bound by two basic requirements—most favored nation (MFN) treatment (the obligation not to discriminate among WTO members) and some core transparency disciplines (both of these requirements are explained below). These are the main obligations that apply *unless* a country also specifically chooses to make GATS commitments on health services.

Trade vs. Trade Agreements

If a country decides not to make commitments under the GATS on health services, the trade itself will not stop. Indeed, trade in health services has been occurring for some time, and is increasing, largely independently of the GATS. Trade agreements might facilitate or encourage trade, but the existence of trade is rarely initiated by trade agreements (indeed, such agreements tend to be developed in response to trade that is already underway). Thus whether or not a country decides to make GATS commitments on trade in health services, it will still need to deal with many of the issues and challenges that arise from that trade. Many of the policies that may be needed to manage this trade (e.g., avoiding loss of investment in training by requiring doctors to serve a given period in the national system after graduation) are unconnected with, and not affected by, the GATS.

The question could then be asked, why make GATS commitments? GATS commitments provide for predictability and certainty for foreign suppliers. In this way, they can serve to attract foreign investment. However, governments also wish to maintain policy flexibility. While the GATS is a flexible agreement, allowing for governments to calibrate their commitments to allow themselves room to maneuver, some governments may feel that they do not wish to enter into any commitments. This is a judgment that must be made taking into account a full range of national policy objectives and interests.

With an increasing number of countries entering into regional trade agreements, one final consideration may also be whether countries would consider liberalizing trade in health services in the context of a regional trade agreement, but not under the GATS. Whether this is an attractive option will depend upon a country's assessment of, among other things, whether its trade interests are regional or global (e.g., while some countries may feel more comfortable opening up to foreign investment from their neighbors, their export interests—such as in temporary movement of personnel—may be more global in character); the extent to which the key shortages expected to be met by trade can be met from the parties to the regional agreement, as opposed to on a global basis; the relative costs and benefits of negotiating effort; relative negotiating power; and the scope for leveraging the outcome of one process in the context of another. Where countries are involved in deep integration agreements (e.g., the Southern African Development Community), the broader ambitions of these agreements may also be relevant.

Liberalization and Regulation

One final threshold point is that liberalization is not synonymous with deregulation. The liberalization process often necessitates reregulation or regulatory reform. Liberalized markets pose different—and often greater—regulatory challenges and require different kinds of regulatory structures. It is normally easier to regulate a state-owned monopoly than a market with multiple participants, including some foreign participants. Equally, however, while the regulatory challenges may be more complex, regulatory failure is by no means limited to liberalized markets (problems can be encountered in regulating domestic providers or indeed in ensuring that a state-owned monopoly is also subject to appropriate oversight).

It is increasingly recognized that liberalization needs to be underpinned by appropriate regulation, and that this regulation should be in place before market opening. However, it is also increasingly recognized that developing countries face particular challenges in terms of lack of regulatory capacity (including challenges involving enforcement). Decisions about liberalization must take careful account of the regulatory framework needed.

Making Commitments Under The Agreement: A Flow Chart

While the following section aims to present a solid overview of GATS disciplines, it does not go through all elements of the agreement in detail.[2] It aims primarily to cover those provisions and disciplines of most relevance to trade in health services. Equally, while it is written with the implications of making commitments in mind, this part of the paper could also serve as a guide to requesting market opening from other WTO members. That is, in discussing all the options for making a commitment, these same considerations could be used in terms of making a request. Countries should approach the guide as a tool for either making or requesting commitments.

What is Covered by the Agreement?

The GATS is a broad agreement, applying to measures affecting trade in services. Measures can be related to the production, distribution, marketing, sale, and delivery of a service and can take any form, including (but not limited to) laws, regulations, rules, procedures, decisions, administrative actions. The GATS also applies to measures taken by central, regional, or local governments and authorities and to nongovernmental bodies where they are exercising delegated powers.[3]

The Governmental Services Carve-Out The GATS also applies to any service in any sector, with some important exclusions.[4] From the health point of view, the key exclusion is that of governmental services. The exclusion for governmental services means that none of the disciplines of the agreement apply to them, and no commitments on market access or national treatment can be made covering these services.

The relevant Article (I.3) states that the GATS excludes "services in the exercise of governmental authority." This is further defined as being a service that is supplied neither on a commercial basis nor in competition with one or more service suppliers.

There has been much debate about what this actually covers. One view is that it means services provided "not-for-profit," which would not include, for example, free medical treatment at public facilities, or treatment provided at such facilities, where some element of cost recovery is involved. However, given the range of public-private mixes in health systems, some have argued that WTO members should agree on an authoritative interpretation to clarify the meaning of this provision. They argue that such a clarification could specify that, for example, the existence of private providers in the health sector does not automatically mean that all public providers are "in competition" with them and are thus brought under the GATS.

However, others point to the difficulty of finding a definition that would cover the range of health provision models found in all (145-odd) WTO members. They argue that the breadth of the existing definition allows all WTO members to interpret it to cover their systems and that attempts to clarify it might paradoxically have the effect of narrowing the range of systems covered. They argue that members can also define the exact scope of any commitment they wish to make to make on health services, describing within their own system what is covered and what is not covered. Indeed, a number of members who made commitments for health services stipulated that they covered only private or privately funded services. Some members have also indicated in their horizontal commitments that public services are excluded for all sectors listed in the schedule.

While the debate continues about the best way to deal with this in the agreement, all WTO members attach great importance to the principle of excluding their governmental services from the GATS and, none has indicated an interest in narrowing this exclusion.

Monopolies and exclusive service providers The GATS does not prevent members from maintaining monopoly or exclusive suppliers; in fact, it specifically recognizes that these are likely to exist or that members might introduce them. Monopolies are further discussed below.

Unfinished Business The GATS contains a number of areas of unfinished business—issues that were not completed by the end of the Uruguay Round and where it was considered that more time was needed to undertake negotiations to determine whether, or what type of, disciplines were necessary. The main areas of unfinished business are government procurement, subsidies, emergency safeguards and disciplines applying to certain types of domestic regulation. The first two are described here; the latter two are covered later in this paper for reasons of logical flow.

Government procurement A number of important GATS provisions currently do not apply to government procurement. In particular, three key provisions do not apply: WTO members are not bound to treat all other WTO members equally (i.e., the Most Favored Nation—MFN—requirement does not apply) and commitments on market access and national treatment in a sector do not cover government procurement. Government procurement is defined in GATS as "the procurement by governmental agencies of services purchased for governmental purposes and not with a view to commercial resale or with a view to use in the supply of services for commercial sale." Thus, for example, the hiring of temporary foreign nurses by a government department of health to address shortages in public hospitals may not be covered by GATS commitments on Mode 4 in health services.

The GATS mandates negotiations on government procurement in services (Article XIII) within two years of its entry into force. However, there has been limited interest in these negotiations and little progress has been made to date.[5]

Subsidies There are currently no specific disciplines on subsidies under the GATS. However, there is a mandate (Article XV) to enter into negotiations with a view to developing the necessary multilateral disciplines to avoid trade-distortive effects of subsidies. Indeed, the GATS does not condemn subsidies per se, but recognizes that, in certain circumstances, they may have distortive effects on trade.

To date, progress under this mandate has been limited largely to information exchange among members on subsidies applied in services. A questionnaire developed at the request of members in 1996 has had few responses, among other reasons because members have experienced difficulty in identifying what might constitute a subsidy—and a subsidy with trade-distortive effects—in services.[6]

STEP 1: Work Out What is Actually on the Table to Request or Offer

Excluded:
Services supplied in the exercise of governmental authority

- Services supplied neither on a commercial basis (not for profit) nor in competition with one or more service suppliers.
- One view is that the mere coexistence of public and private suppliers in the market does not necessarily render them "in competition."
- But there has been no definitive interpretation.

Nothing at the moment—unfinished business:
Government procurement

- Market opening commitments do not cover government procurement.
- All WTO members do *not* have to be treated equally.

Subsidies

- Recognizes that, in certain circumstances, they may have a distortive effect on trade in services.
- Mandates the development of the necessary disciplines to avoid such trade-distortive effects.

Can I Decide to Leave out Health Services from any Market Opening Commitments? Do Some GATS Disciplines Apply Regardless of Whether or Not I Make Market Opening Commitments?

While all service sectors are covered by the GATS, countries are not obliged to make commitments in all sectors. They can choose to omit a sector entirely from their schedule of commitments.[7] Some WTO members have already indicated that they will neither be requesting, nor offering, health services in the current negotiations.

If I Don't Include Health Services in My Commitments, What Obligations Apply? If a WTO member decides to exclude health services from its schedule, a number of GATS disciplines still apply to the sector. They are:

Most Favored Nation (MFN) Short for "treating all nations as you would your most favored nation," this obligation means that a WTO member cannot discriminate among other WTO members. That is, treatment offered to one member must be offered to all WTO members. There are three exceptions to this:

- If the WTO member in question is party to a regional trade agreement (RTA) notified under Article V of GATS.[8]
- If the WTO member has taken out an MFN exemption for the sector. All WTO members have a one-off opportunity to claim such exemptions at the time they joined the GATS. Some 424 exemptions have been made, of which 78 apply to all sectors and one applies specifically to health services.[9] In principle these exemptions should not last for more than 10 years and are subject to negotiation in subsequent rounds. However, a number of members have listed the duration of their exemptions as "indefinite."
- MFN does not apply to recognition of qualifications.

Transparency Three basic obligations apply. WTO members:

- Must publish promptly, and except in emergency situations, at the latest by the time of their entry into force, all relevant measures of general application that pertain to or affect the operation of the GATS. If publication is not practicable, the information should be made otherwise available.
- Must reply promptly to requests for information from any other member and should establish inquiry points for this purpose (developing countries have longer to do so).

- Can notify the Council for Trade in Services of measures taken by other members that they consider as affecting the operation of the agreement.

However, members are not required to provide confidential information where disclosure would impede law enforcement or otherwise be contrary to the public interest or that would prejudice legitimate commercial interests of particular enterprises, public or private.

Review procedures for administrative decisions   Members should maintain or put in place judicial, arbitral, or administrative tribunals that provide for the prompt review of administrative decisions affecting trade in services. However, they are not required to do so where this would be inconsistent with their constitutional structures or legal system.

Basic competition disciplines Members shall, if requested by another member, enter into consultation with a view to eliminating certain types of business practices (other than monopolies or exclusive suppliers) that may restrain competition. Members are to accord full and sympathetic consideration to such requests and provide relevant nonconfidential information.

STEP 2: Decide If I Want to Exclude Health Services from my GATS Commitments. If I Do, Determine what Basic Obligations Still Apply

A WTO member can decide to exclude health services from market opening commitments under the GATS.

    If the member does so, the following general disciplines still apply:

- *MFN*—the requirement to treat all WTO members equally (unless an MFN exemption has been taken, or a regional trade agreement notified).
- *Transparency*—make information publicly available, respond to requests for information from other members and establish inquiry points.
- *Review of administrative decisions*—provide some tribunals or procedures for the review of administrative decisions, but not where this would conflict with the constitutional structure or nature of the legal system.
- *Basic competition disciplines*—consult one request with a view to eliminating business practices that restrain competition (does not apply to monopolies and exclusive service suppliers).

*If I am Considering Making or Requesting Commitments
on Health Services, How Do I Define Them?*

Defining the Sector   Members can define the scope of the services for which they
are prepared to make a commitment or for which they are requesting access.
Commitments do not have to cover an entire sector; WTO members can commit
make requests or commitments covering only a subsector, or even only part of a
subsector. Members can define the scope of their requests or commitments as
broadly or narrowly as they choose.

In defining the area for which they are making requests or market opening
commitments, WTO members can use their own definitions or make reference
to the *WTO Services Sectoral Classification List,* or to the United Nations Central Product Classification. The WTO Services Sectoral Classification List
(MTS.GNS.W/120, known as "W/120") was developed during the Uruguay
Round to assist members in making commitments. The list covers 12 main service sectors and 160 subsectors and is cross-referenced to the *United Nations Provisional Central Product Classification* (Provisional CPC, which provides more
detailed definitions of particular services). However, use of W/120 was voluntary—while many members have used it in making their commitments, others
have referred simply to the UN Provisional CPC or have used their own definitions.

There are several classifications in W/120 of relevance to health services.
They are: Class 8, Health Related and Social Services, which are broken down
into Hospital Services, Other Human Health Services, Social Services, and
Other). However, health professionals are classified under Class 1, Business
Services, A. Professional Services, (h) Medical and Dental Services and (j)
Services Provided by Midwives, Nurses, Physiotherapists, and Paramedical Per-
sonnel. Also of relevance to health are some types of financial services—namely,
Class 7 Financial Services, A. All Insurance and Insurance Related Services, (a)
Life, Accident, and Health Insurance Services. A detailed breakdown of the defi-
nitions of these activities is in Annex I of this chapter.

As noted above, many WTO members have used the description of the sector
for which they are making commitments to underline the private, commercial—
not public—nature of the services for which access is being offered. For example:

- The United States (which uses it own definition and does not reference either
  W/120 or the UN CPC) makes commitments for "Hospital and other health
  care facilities—direct ownership and management and operation by contract
  of such facilities on a 'for fee' basis";
- Malaysia has referenced the CPC but stated that its commitment refers only to
  private hospitals—the definition used is "Hospital Services, Private Hospital

Services, (93110).*" The asterisk next to the CPC code means "part of" the activities covered by that classification. Mexico has also specified that the services are private in defining the scope of its commitment as "A. Private Hospital Services." Mexico also refers to CPC 9311, but without the asterisk.

- Bulgaria similarly specifies that it intends its commitment to cover only private services, again indicating that this is only part of the relevant CPC code—"C. Social Services, Privately Funded Social Services (part of CPC 933)."

How Else are Services Described in the Agreement? What Do Commitments Cover?

In addition to the definition of the sector outlined in the section above, the GATS also differentiates among four ways (called "modes" of supply) in which services can be supplied. Countries use these modes of supply for making commitments.

Modes of Supply For the purpose of making commitments, the GATS divides the supply of services into four modes. These are:

- Mode 1—cross-border trade (e.g., telemedicine—a Cuban doctor provides diagnostic services over the Internet to a patient in Mexico);
- Mode 2—consumption abroad (e.g., a Mexican patient travels to Cuba for health treatment);

STEP 3: If I Want to Make or Request Commitments, Decide How to Define the Scope of the Health Services I Want Covered by My Request or Commitment.

- WTO members may make commitments or request access for a sector, subsector or only part of a subsector. Countries are free to define the scope of their commitment or request as narrowly as they wish. Commitments only apply to those sectors listed in the schedule and only to the range of services indicated.
- In defining the services for which access is being offered, WTO members can reference the WTO Sectoral Classification List (W/120) or the UN Central Product Classification or both, or can use their own definition.
- In defining the scope of the services for which access is being offered, a number of WTO members have additionally specified that the services are only private, commercial—not public—services.

- Mode 3—commercial presence (e.g., a Chinese clinic establishes in Mexico);
- Mode 4—*temporary* movement of persons as service suppliers (e.g., nurses from the Philippines work temporarily in Japan). Mode 4 covers only temporary movement. While temporary is not defined under the GATS, permanent migration is explicitly excluded.[10]

For each service sector, GATS commitments can be made separately for the four modes of supply. Countries may choose to make commitments or requests for only some modes and not others. For example, a country may wish to allow foreign nurses to operate in its territory (Mode 4), but not foreign clinics (Mode 3). While it may be comfortable with allowing its nationals to consume health services in others countries (Mode 2), it may have concerns about them receiving medical advice over the Internet (Mode 1). Each mode of supply raises quite different regulatory issues and may require quite different frameworks and flanking policies.

Because they involve the movement of people—health consumers or providers—Modes 2 and 4 can be confusing. Mode 2 commitments pertain only to whether a WTO member is prepared to allow its own nationals to go abroad for health treatment; they do not apply to whether a country is prepared to receive foreign patients or what it is prepared to offer them. Equally, Mode 4 commitments apply to the *entry* of foreign health workers into a country, not the export of that country's health professionals to other countries. That is, a country's commitments cover its acceptance of foreign nurses, but not the sending of its own nurses abroad. Under the GATS, countries neither commit to receive foreign patients nor to send their own health workers overseas. They thus remain free to prevent their health workers from going abroad (this may raise human rights issues, but it does not raise GATS ones) and to refuse foreign patients any or all health services.

Horizontal vs. Sectoral Commitments GATS commitments can be made for each sector listed in the schedule (e.g., a country's schedule includes separate commitments for telecommunications, tourism, and health services), or can be made "horizontally," covering a single mode of supply across all service sectors listed in their schedule (e.g., the same country makes a horizontal commitment on Mode 3 applying to telecommunications, tourism, and health services). Horizontal commitments apply to all sectors listed in the schedule unless otherwise clearly specified at the sectoral level (e.g., the country's schedule specifies that the Mode 3 horizontal commitment does not apply to health services). Most commitments for movement of service suppliers (Mode 4) are horizontal, allowing access under certain conditions by "managers, executives, and specialists" for any sector listed in the schedule. Similarly, many WTO members have horizontal commitments for Mode 3 requiring, for example, screening for foreign invest-ment above a certain value in all service sectors listed in its schedule.

Horizontal commitments do not apply to sectors not listed in the schedule. However, if a member is considering adding a new sector to its schedule, then it should also consider the impact of any existing horizontal commitment on that new sector. If a member does not want a particular horizontal commitment to apply to the new sector, it can specifically exclude it at the time it includes the new sector in its schedule (e.g., if an existing Mode 3 horizontal commitment excludes investments under a certain value from screening, but the member concerned wishes to retain the right to screen all investment in health services, that member can specify "excluding health services" for the Mode 3 horizontal commitment at the time it includes health services in its schedule).

Horizontal commitments can also be used to include important conditions that apply to all sectors in the schedule. For example, the European Community (and its member states) includes the following horizontal Mode 3 commitment in its schedule: "In all EC Member States services considered as public utilities at a national or local level may be subject to public monopolies or to exclusive rights granted to private operators." The explanatory note accompanying this text notes that "Public utilities exist in sectors such as related scientific and technical consult-ing services, R&D services on social sciences and humanities, technical testing and analysis services, environmental services, health services, transport services and services auxiliary to all modes of transport. Exclusive rights on such services are often granted to private operators, for instance operators with concessions from public authorities, subject to specific service obligations. Given that public utili-ties often also exist at the subcentral level, detailed and exhaustive sector-specific scheduling is not practical."

What Does a GATS Commitment Involve?

For each service, and for each mode of supply of that service, members must spec-ify whether, and to what extent, market access and national treatment are granted. A commitment is guaranteed *minimum* treatment; foreign service suppliers can-not receive treatment any less favorable than that specified in the commitment appearing in the schedule. More favorable treatment can be extended at any time should a member so wish, provided that it is extended to all members (in line with the MFN rule, described above). GATS commitments are binding; that is, they cannot be changed without paying compensation to other WTO members. This takes the form of a commitment in another area of equal value to the one being changed or withdrawn.

GATS commitments apply on an MFN basis (subject to possible exemptions discussed earlier). That is, the access and treatment offered must be granted to all WTO members (although not all may actually take advantage of it). It is not possible to exclude certain members from the scope of access offered.

In making commitments for each mode of supply, a WTO member has three main choices:

- A commitment to provide full market access and/or national treatment for a particular mode—that is, to maintain no restrictions—indicated in the schedule by "None."
- No commitment at all on national treatment and/or market access for a particular mode, this is indicated by "Unbound" (i.e., no bound commitment undertaken).
- Partial commitments for market access and/or national treatment, with the remaining restrictions listed in the schedule.

STEP 4:   Decide Whether or not I Want to Include all Ways of Delivering Health Services (Cross-Border, Consumption Abroad, Foreign Commercial Presence, Movement of Health Workers) in My Request or Commitment, or Whether Any New or Existing Horizontal Commitments Might be Relevant

- The GATS divides services into four modes of supply: Mode 1—cross-border (e.g., telemedicine); Mode 2—consumption abroad (patient received treatment in another country); Mode 3—commercial presence (a foreign clinic established in a country); and Mode 4—movement of service providers (nurses work temporarily in another country). Commitments can be made separately for each mode.
- Under the GATS, countries neither commit to receive foreign patients nor to send their own health workers overseas. They thus remain free to prevent their health workers from going abroad and to refuse foreign patients any or all health services.
- Commitments can also be horizontal, applying to a mode of supply across all sectors listed in the schedule. Horizontal commitments can be used to place a general condition on access to all services in the schedule, including in relation to public services that may appear in a number of sectors. If a member wishes to exclude a newly added sector from the scope of its existing horizontal commitments it can do so by clearly indicating this in its schedule.

Read together, market access and national treatment commitments inform a foreign supplier about the access they will have to the WTO members' market and any special conditions that will apply to them as foreigners.

What Does Market Access Mean? Market access commitments set out the conditions under that foreign suppliers are allowed to enter the market. Countries can choose to place no restrictions on market access ("None") or to make no commitment ("Unbound") or to allow access subject to limitations and conditions (partial commitment).

In the case of a partial commitment, there are six types of restrictions that members can *only* maintain for sectors where they have chosen to make commitments *if* they list them in their schedule. These are basically quantitative restrictions, either in the form of numerical quotas or economic needs tests.[11] These six restrictions cover:

- Restrictions on the number of service suppliers, including in the form of monopolies or exclusive service suppliers (e.g., the number of hospitals);
- Restrictions on the total value of service transactions or assets (e.g., foreign private clinics must not have assets worth more than US$50 million[12]);
- Restrictions on the total number of service operations or the total quantity of service output (e.g., number of surgical operations or hospital beds);
- Restrictions on the total number of natural persons that may be employed in a particular service sector or that a service supplier may employ (e.g., numbers of doctors and nurses employed);
- Restrictions on or requirements for certain types of legal entity or joint venture for the supply of a service (e.g., a foreign private clinic must enter into a joint venture with a local clinic to enter the market);
- Limitations on the participation of foreign capital in terms of maximum percentage limit on foreign shareholding or the total value of individual or aggregate foreign investment (e.g., that foreign private clinic is limited to 30 percent of the equity in the newly established private clinic).

All of these types of restrictions can be maintained if a country so chooses *but* it must list them in its schedule of commitments. These restrictions can be either discriminatory (applying only to foreigners) or nondiscriminatory (applying to both foreign and domestic suppliers); in either case, they only need to be listed in the market access column of the schedule of commitments. If a restriction is discriminatory, the country should, on a best endeavors basis, indicate the discriminatory elements.

What if I have a monopoly or exclusive supplier for a service? As noted in at the beginning of this chapter, the GATS does not prohibit monopolies—rather, it acknowledges that they may continue to exist. The main disciplines that apply to monopolies and exclusive service providers are that they do not act inconsistently with either the MFN requirement or the market opening commitments that a country has made.

If a monopoly or exclusive service supplier exists for a service where a country is making some sort of commitment, it can remain, but needs to be listed in the schedule as a market access limitation. If a country wants to introduce new monopoly rights in an area in which it had previously made market opening commitments, it can renegotiate those commitments and compensate affected trading partners.

Finally, if a monopoly competes (either directly or via an affiliated company) in the supply of services other than those for which it has a monopoly, and those are services for which the country concerned has made market opening commitments, that country must ensure that the monopoly does not abuse its monopoly position to act in a manner inconsistent with those commitments.

What Does National Treatment Mean? National treatment means that foreign services and service suppliers are granted treatment no less favorable than that accorded to like national services and service suppliers. This can mean formally identical or formally different treatment—the key requirement is that it does not modify the conditions of competition in favor of services or service suppliers who are nationals instead of foreigners. National treatment can also cover both de jure and de facto discrimination; that is, even if a measure applies to both foreigners and nationals it may still be discriminatory if its effect is to discriminate against foreign suppliers. However, national treatment does not require a member to compensate for any inherent competitive disadvantage that results from the foreign character of the relevant service or service suppliers, i.e., if a country takes a full national treatment commitment on Mode 4 nursing it is not obliged to provide local language training for foreign nurses.

A key consideration in national treatment is whether the services or service suppliers are "like." The GATS, like other WTO Agreements, does not define "like" and panels under the WTO dispute settlement system have tended to approach the issue of "likeness" on a case-by-case basis, taking into account, among other things, consumer perceptions of the degree to which a particular good is like, and its substitutability.

WTO members are free to make no commitment on national treatment, or to provide partial national treatment, provided they list the measures they maintain that discriminate in favor of nationals in their schedule. Unlike the case of market access, there is no specific list of the types of measures that have to be scheduled; members must judge whether a measure breaches national treatment and therefore should be scheduled. A measure may not be considered discriminatory if it is genuinely open to both nationals and foreigners to fulfill it—e.g., a requirement for a degree of proficiency in a certain language need not be discriminatory if it is

---

Box 4.1 Foreign Investment in Private Hospitals: the Careful Approach of Indonesia

The Indonesian government has identified areas where foreign investment could contribute to strengthening the health sector, i.e., investment for private wings in teaching hospitals and in tertiary-care hospitals, especially in cities other than Jakarta. The government hopes that such investment will not only benefit the higher income groups, which desire access to sophisticated and expensive equipment, but also the population as a whole. For instance, the private wings will improve services in government teaching hospitals as a whole, as the revenues generated by services offered to richer patients can cross-subsidize services offered by the same highly qualified health professionals working in teaching hospitals to the general population.

Indonesia has not made any commitments on health services at the WTO and has not made offers on health services in the current GATS negotiations. However, its current investment rules allows for foreign investment in: (a) hospitals; (b) medical checkups; (c) evacuation and transportation; (d) mental rehabilitation centers; (e) clinical laboratories; (f) hospital management; and (g) maintenance and calibrations for medical equipment. The domestic rules specify that the foreign companies have to be in joint venture with Indonesian companies. There have been few measures to actively promote investment in these sectors. However, as the government strives to attract health care investors in islands other than Java and the major cities (such as the Nusa Tenggara Isles, which include Timor Island, Mollucas, Sumatra, and Papua), it imposes fewer regulatory requirements on foreign investors in regions with weak public health infrastructures.

We do not have exact figures regarding foreign investment in the Indonesian health sector but, for the moment, it seem to be still quite limited. Thus, about 12 out of 500 hospitals are actually under private enterprise or limited foreign company. Investment in the health sector is mainly done by Singaporean, Malaysian, and Australian companies. The government is very cautious in opening its market or making commitments on health services at the GATS, as it wants to ensure that regulations are in place before completing liberalization. For now, the main concern is the regulation of the health professions. Many regulations for licensing, standardization, competency testing, and competency-based education are still being constructed. The government will consider further gradual liberalization only once a solid regulatory framework is in place.

Source: Untung Suseno Sutarjo, 2003.

genuinely possible for foreigners to be able to learn the language and achieve the required level of proficiency. Some examples of the types of measures that would need to be listed in the schedule as limitations on national treatment include: eligibility for subsidies reserved for nationals; the ability to lease or own land is reserved to nationals; and citizenship requirements for certain health professions.

What about subsidies for national suppliers? Many WTO members have indicated in their schedules that they are making no commitments regarding subsidies for foreign suppliers for any service sector (i.e., a horizontal commitment of "Unbound" under national treatment with regard to subsidies). Others have chosen to schedule limitations on the availability of subsidies to foreign suppliers as national treatment restrictions in their schedules. Others have taken the view that, as there are currently no GATS disciplines on subsidies that they do not need to schedule such measures as restrictions on national treatment. While the GATS (Article XVII) does not provide specific guidance on this point, it is understood that a full commitment on national treatment (i.e., a scheduled commitment of "None," or no restrictions) would prevent, for example, foreign-owned hospitals from being excluded from subsidies or other benefits under domestic policy schemes.

What Does a Commitment Mean? Is it Necessarily Liberalization? In making GATS commitments, WTO members have three choices. They can choose to bind (i.e., commit to providing): the current level of access; new and more liberal access; or access less than they currently offer in reality. For example, where a country allows foreign private clinics to operate in its territory, but only as a minority partner (maximum equity 49 percent) in a joint venture with a local private clinic, that member's GATS commitments could be:

- the existing level of access to the market (e.g., foreign private clinics can enter but only in a joint venture with a local private clinic and with a maximum shareholding of 49 percent);
- new, more liberal level of access to the market (e.g., foreign private clinics to enter the market *without* forming a joint venture with a local private clinic);
- access that is less than the status quo (e.g., foreign private clinics can enter the market but only in joint ventures with local private clinics and with a maximum shareholding of 20 percent).

At present, many WTO members' GATS commitments represent the *status quo* at the time of the Uruguay Round (i.e., the situation in around 1993–1994) and, in many cases, less than that. Many GATS commitments thus do not represent the existing level of openness—for example, the actual migration regimes for temporary entrants to both the United States and Australia are much more liberal than their GATS commitments on Mode 4 indicate, and both feature special visa programs for health professionals that also do not appear in their GATS commitments. Indeed, WTO members may choose to maintain a level of openness to foreign suppliers without making the relevant GATS commitments. Or, as many WTO members have done in their initial offers in the current round of negotiations, they can offer to bind liberalization that they undertook unilaterally three or four years ago. Many GATS commitments thus do not represent actual new market opening; indeed, many current commitments represent significantly less openness than actually exists in the country concerned.

Do Commitments Have to Take Effect Immediately? The GATS also allows members to commit to liberalizing in the future; that is, to make commitments to liberalize within a certain time frame, but not immediately. For example, a WTO member can commit to allowing foreign private clinics to enter into joint ventures with local private clinics, effective 1 January 2015. These "precommitments" can be useful in allowing the committing member to indicate that foreign suppliers will enter the market but to give the local suppliers time to prepare themselves for the competition (or new partnerships) and the government time to ensure that the necessary regulatory framework is in place. Precommitments were widely used in the telecommunications sector by developing countries.

As a Developing Country, Do I Have to Liberalize? The GATS states that the process of liberalization shall take place with due respect for national policy objectives and the level of development of individual members, both overall and in individual sectors. Developing countries have appropriate flexibility to open fewer sectors, liberalize fewer types of transactions, progressively extend market access in line with their development situation, and attach conditions to the access they offer (Article XIX).

Furthermore, the participation of developing countries in trade should be facilitated by, among other things, the liberalization of market access in modes and sectors of interest to them (Article IV). Developed countries should also establish dedicated inquiry points that developing country service suppliers can approach for information, including about the granting, registration, and recognition of professional qualifications.

*Now That I've Made a Commitment, Are There Any Other
General Obligations that Now Apply?*

There are several additional obligations that apply once a commitment has been
made. All of them concern the process, rather than the substance, of regulation.
These are:

- *Transparency*: notify the WTO Council for Trade in Services annually about
  any new or changed measures significantly affecting trade in services covered
  by commitments;
- *Timely authorizations*: where authorization is required to supply a service for
  which a commitment has been made, decisions should be made within a reasonable period of time;

**STEP 5: Decide What Kind of Commitments I Want
to Make, and What Sort of Conditions I Want
to Place on Foreign Suppliers**

GATS commitments allow WTO members to:

- Exclude health services entirely, or only make commitments for certain
  types of health services;
- Exclude certain modes of supply of health services (e.g., not permit foreign
  investment via Mode 3 or telemedicine via Mode 1) or maintain a restriction on a particular mode for all sectors;
- Limit market access for health services (i.e., restrict the number and type of
  foreign suppliers and the activities in which they can engage);
- Discriminate against foreign suppliers of health services in favor of nationals
  (e.g., by placing additional conditions or requirements on foreign suppliers, or restricting some activities or benefits to nationals);
- Discriminate among foreign suppliers (i.e., give better treatment to suppliers from some countries) if they have an MFN exemption or are party to a
  regional trade agreement notified under Article V
- Commit to a less open market than currently exists;
- Commit to liberalize at a chosen future date to give themselves time to
  ensure that the necessary regulatory frameworks are in place.

Note: Developing countries have additional flexibility to liberalize fewer sectors
and to attach conditions to access offered. Additionally, other members should
facilitate their participation in trade, including by liberalizing modes and sectors of interest to them, and should establish special contact points to provide
information to developing country service suppliers.

Annex II of this chapter contains an example of a specific commitment on
health services, illustrating these options.

- *Administration of measures*: Where commitments are made all measures of general application affecting trade in services must be administered in a reasonable, objective, and impartial manner;
- *Recognition*: for professional services where a commitment has been made there must be adequate procedures to verify the competence of professionals of any other member (see also below).

What Impact Does the GATS Have on my Ability to Regulate Health Services?

The GATS recognizes the right to regulate and to introduce new regulations on the supply of services. Disciplines apply to certain types of regulatory measures; which disciplines apply depends upon whether commitments have been made in the relevant sector and whether the measures in question apply to both domestic and foreign suppliers (nondiscriminatory) or apply only to foreign suppliers (discriminatory).

As noted above, if a country has made no commitments for a specific sector, only the general obligations outlined in II above—MFN, transparency, review of administrative decisions, and basis competition disciplines—apply. Where a country has made commitments in a sector, some additional procedural—but not substantive—obligations related to transparency, timely authorizations to supply a service, how measures are administered, and recognition apply.

STEP 6: Some Other General GATS Obligations are Triggered Once Commitments Have Been Made for Health Services

Transparency: notify the WTO Council for Trade in Services annually about any new or changed measures significantly affecting trade in services covered by commitments.

Timely authorizations: where authorization is required to supply a service for which a commitment has been made, decisions should be made within a reasonable period of time.

Administration of measures: Where commitments are made, all measures of general application affecting trade in services must be administered in a reasonable, objective, and impartial manner.

Recognition: for professional services where a commitment has been made, there must be adequate procedures to verify the competence of professionals of any other member.

What Other Obligations Might Apply to How I Regulate Services? *What are my options for regulating foreign suppliers in my country?* Foreign suppliers operating in a country (e.g., a foreign clinic established under Mode 3, or a foreign doctor practicing temporarily under Mode 4) are subject to the general legal and regulatory framework governing the supply of the service in that country. Furthermore, under the GATS, foreign suppliers can be subject to additional, or more stringent conditions—e.g., foreign doctors can be required to undertake an additional year's training before being permitted to practice in the country.[13] It is up to each individual country to determine whether health policy outcomes would be served by discriminating against foreign suppliers, or subjecting them to additional conditions.

In GATS terms, there are two scenarios under which countries can apply additional, less favorable conditions to foreign suppliers:

- If a country has *not* made any commitment for the relevant health service, it is free to maintain whatever discriminatory measures it likes. The main obligations that apply are MFN—that is, that whatever regulations it applies should be the same for suppliers from all other WTO members—and basic transparency obligations.
- If a country *has* made a commitment for the relevant health service, and wants to have regulations that result in less favorable treatment for foreigners as compared to nationals, it can do so, but it must list these regulations in its schedule of commitments as restrictions on national treatment. Because a commitment is guaranteed minimum treatment, the country cannot add new or additional restrictions once a commitment is made.

The only situation where a country *cannot* maintain any regulations applying only to, and resulting in less favorable treatment for, foreigners is where it has made an explicit commitment *not* to discriminate in favor of its nationals (i.e., a commitment of "None" under national treatment for the health sector).

Even where a country has made a commitment not to discriminate against foreign providers, it is still free to regulate the sector as it sees fit, provided that the measures that apply (e.g., forbidding certain treatments, requiring certain standards) apply to both foreign and domestic providers.

So what about the general conditions that apply to both foreign and national suppliers, are there any disciplines applying to them? General measures that apply to both foreign and national suppliers (nondiscriminatory measures) are subject to some disciplines under the GATS.

For these nondiscriminatory measures, the first question to ask is whether a particular measure would actually be considered a market access restriction under the GATS. For example, a requirement that any new physiotherapy clinics will only be permitted where there are less than 10 such clinics per 1,000 people can apply to both new foreign and new domestic clinics. But this requirement would be considered a market access restriction for GATS purposes (it is a restriction on the number of service suppliers). Measures that are market access restrictions can be maintained in two circumstances:

- If a country has *not* made any commitment for the relevant health service, it is free to maintain whatever measures it likes. The main obligations that apply are MFN; that is, that whatever measure it applies should be the same for suppliers from all other WTO members and basic transparency obligations.
- If a country *has* made a commitment on the relevant health service, and wants to maintain market access restrictions, it can do so, but it must list these regulations in its schedule of commitments. As a commitment is guaranteed minimum treatment, the country cannot add new or additional restrictions once a commitment is made.

But for nondiscriminatory measures (applying to both foreigners and nationals) that are *not* market access restrictions, other GATS disciplines apply. In addition to the general disciplines that always apply (MFN and transparency), for certain types of measures in this category, there is a negotiating mandate to develop additional disciplines. This is the mandate under Article VI.4, which contains the famous "necessity test."

Negotiations Under Article VI.4 Article VI.4 mandates the development of any necessary disciplines to ensure that nondiscriminatory measures relating to qualification requirements and procedures, technical standards and licensing requirements do not constitute unnecessary barriers to trade in services. There is a general understanding that this excludes measures that would be considered limitations on market access and those that would be considered limitations on national treatment.[14] These measures should be:

- based on objective and transparent criteria, such as competence and ability to supply the service;
- no more burdensome than necessary to ensure the quality of the service;
- in the case of licensing procedures, these measures should not in themselves be a restriction on the supply of a service.

As yet, these disciplines *do not* exist. In the interim, disciplines under Article VI.5 apply; however, Article VI.5 disciplines will cease to apply once any disciplines developed under Article VI.4 enter into force. Article VI.5 disciplines apply only in sectors where commitments have been made. They require that WTO members *not* apply measures relating to licensing and qualification requirements and technical standards that nullify or impair specific commitments in a manner that does not meet the three criteria set out in the preceding paragraph. However, all existing—or reasonably foreseeable—measures that nullify or impair specific commitments and do not meet these three criteria are excluded. In effect, because all such measures that a country already had in place, or that it could have reasonably been expected to introduce, are excluded, these disciplines are not seen as having any force. So the real focus is on what might be developed in the negotiations on Article VI.4.

Progress on Article VI.4 has been very slow and there are different views among WTO members on what sorts of disciplines should be developed. The most controversial provision has been the requirement that any measures relating to qualification and licensing requirements and procedures and technical standards be not be more burdensome than necessary to ensure the quality of the service. A number of arguments have been raised about this provision, including:

- Some members argue that any disciplines should only focus on increasing transparency, and that any "necessity test" in itself is not necessary. The argument goes that, because these are measures that also apply to nationals, a country should be free to set its standards as it sees fit—even if they might not seem to be a good idea to others. For example, if a country wishes to require that all taxi drivers be trained intensive care nurses (in the interests of having quality medical care close at hand should passengers give birth, have heart attacks, etc.) then it should be free to do so even though this is clearly a burdensome, trade-restrictive (and perhaps rather silly) requirement.
- Others argue that, in this situation, other WTO members should be free to challenge such requirements as they are also affected by them. Other WTO members should, they argue, be able to suggest other—equally effective and reasonably available but less trade-restrictive—ways of achieving the same objective. For example, they could suggest that all taxi drivers be required to be trained in First Aid, rather than be highly qualified medical personnel. This, it is argued, would result in a better outcome, not just for trade, but also for the country concerned in terms of better, more efficient regulation (and, in this case, a better use of the skills of highly trained personnel—and an increase in the number of taxi drivers).
- Essentially, some members have expressed concern that a necessity test could allow other WTO members to "second-guess" the decisions of national regulators;

while others argue that a necessity test would only look at whether there were other, equally effective and reasonably available but less trade-restrictive, ways to achieve the same objective. That is, they would not question the objective itself, nor a country's right to see that objective fully achieved; they could only comment on the particular instrument or means chosen to achieve the objective.

- In any event, a number of WTO members have argued that "ensuring the quality of the service" is too narrow and that the full range of policy objectives that countries might want to pursue should be acknowledged (e.g., a licensing requirement for clinics related to disposal facilities for medical waste might be aimed at environmental protection).

- A further argument has been about whether any disciplines should only apply in sectors where commitments are made, rather than across all sectors. While no final decision has been made on this issue, the presumption created by the Accountancy Disciplines[15] and by Article VI.5 (both of which only apply where specific commitments have been made) is that any Article VI.4 disciplines would have the same scope of application. Equally, logic of the agreement would tend to suggest that such disciplines could only apply to sectors where specific commitments had been made.[16]

While Article VI.4 is still a work in progress, from a health policy point of view, policymakers could perhaps usefully focus on identifying which sorts of measures they currently apply that might be subject to any possible disciplines under Article VI.4—that is, measures that are qualification requirements and procedures, technical standards, and licensing requirements; are not market access restrictions; and are nondiscriminatory. Identifying these measures can form the basis of consideration of the extent to which possible disciplines might impact on the way that health services are regulated and the types of measures that a country might wish to implement. Such an exercise underlines again the need for close cooperation and ongoing dialogue between health and trade policymakers.

Additional Commitments on Regulatory Practices The GATS also gives countries the opportunity to make commitments on good regulatory practices. These can be done unilaterally by a country or, as happened in telecommunications, a group of WTO members can agree on a set of good regulatory practices for a sector that they then can choose to include, in whole or in part, in their commitments.

Additionally, other WTO members can request that countries make commitments on specific regulatory practices under the "additional commitments" part of their schedule. For example, countries can be requested to provide national and foreign suppliers with the opportunity to comment upon any proposed new regulations affecting health services before they are brought into effect.[17] A commitment to do so would appear in the additional commitments column next to a commitment on health services (see the example in Annex II).

What About Recognition of Qualification of Health Professionals? The GATS does not require recognition of the professional qualifications of other members, nor does it require any particular standards to be applied. The GATS simply allows members to recognize the qualifications of some WTO members and not others (i.e., it permits countries to break the MFN rule in relation to recognition). The only requirement is that members entering into recognition arrangements among themselves notify the WTO of the arrangements and give other interested members the opportunity to demonstrate that they also meet the required standards.

Given the variety of approaches taken (reflecting particular societal choices), and the important policy objectives involved, there are no requirements in the GATS regarding the *substance* of recognition (i.e., the particular standards to be applied). Members are free to set whatever standards they like for the professions; the only requirement is that they apply the same standards to all WTO members (i.e., that they do not apply lower standards to some members). Recognition can be achieved through any means, but use of international standards is encouraged, as is cooperation with relevant nongovernmental and intergovernmental organizations.

Where commitments have been made for a particular professional service, such as for health professionals, WTO members are required to have adequate procedures in place to verify the competence of professionals from other WTO members. "Adequate procedures" is not further defined. In practice, countries that receive health professionals from other countries—as either temporary entrants or permanent migrants—tend to have these procedures in place already.

What If I Change my Mind? What If I No Longer Want to Keep a Commitment?

Renegotiating Commitments A WTO member can withdraw or modify its GATS commitments three years after their entry into force but must pay compensation to other members. This is because WTO commitments are obligations owed to other WTO members. Compensation is negotiated between the country wishing to change its commitments and other WTO members who are affected by the change, and takes the form of additional access being granted in another area. The aim is to reach agreement on maintaining a general level of mutually advantageous commitments not less favorable to trade than the previous commitments.

Access offered as compensation is, like the original commitment, offered to all WTO members on an MFN basis.

Balance of Payments Members can also restrict their commitments in the event of serious balance of payments and external financial difficulties. These restrictions must: apply to all members on an MFN basis; be consistent with the Articles of Agreement of the International Monetary Fund (IMF); avoid unnecessary damage to the interests of other members; not exceed those necessary to deal with the problem; and be temporary and phased out as the situation improves.

STEP 7: What Regulatory Issues Do I Need to Consider? Are there Any GATS Disciplines Related to How I Regulate?

- Foreign suppliers only receive access to provide the range of services permitted in the territory, e.g., a commitment on Mode 3 market access for foreign clinics does not enable that clinic to provide services that are generally forbidden by law in the country.
- Commitments do not interfere with a member's ability to regulate health services; foreign entrants to the market remain subject to the national regulatory framework; GATS commitments also allow a country to impose stricter regulation or special conditions on foreign suppliers, provided a national treatment limitation is scheduled.
- Where no commitments are made for a sector, only the general obligations (e.g., MFN and transparency) apply. Where specific commitments are made, some additional procedural obligations apply (related to transparency, administration of measures, decisions regarding authorizations to supply a service, and recognition) apply.
- Certain types of regulatory measures—those relating to qualification and licensing requirements and procedures and technical standards that are nondiscriminatory and that are not market access restrictions—may be subject to some further disciplines to be developed under Article VI.4.
- WTO members can also make commitments to apply good regulatory practices (e.g., providing all suppliers—national and foreign—with the opportunity to comment on new regulations before they are introduced), either for a particular sector or across all sectors.
- WTO members are free to recognize the qualifications of some members and not others. However, they must notify any recognition agreements they are negotiating and give other interested WTO members the opportunity to prove that they meet the same standards. Where a commitment to provide access to health service professionals is made, there must be adequate procedures in place to verify their competence.

Safeguards A safeguard is a mechanism that allows WTO members to temporarily suspend their commitments in the event of unforeseen and negative consequences for domestic suppliers. While such mechanisms exist for goods trade, there is currently no safeguard for services. The GATS has a mandate for negotiations on the question of an emergency safeguard (Article X). Negotiations have been underway since 1996, with a deadline of 15 March 2004. Progress has been slow, both because of differences of opinion among WTO members on the desirability of a safeguard, and because of technical and conceptual difficulties in developing a safeguard for services. The nature and coverage of any safeguard mechanism are still to be determined.

Exceptions WTO commitments are owed to other WTO members. For a dispute to take place, a WTO member not only has to be in breach of its commitments, but another member has to make a complaint and claim that it has suffered a nullification or impairment of the benefits it expected to get under the agreement because of the action of the member breaking its commitments.

If a WTO member breaks its commitments, and is challenged by another WTO member, it can rely on the exceptions provisions in the GATS to justify and defend its actions. These provisions enable members to take measures, among other things:

- necessary to protect public morals or to maintain public order;
- necessary to protect human, animal, or plant life and health;
- necessary to secure compliance with laws or regulations that are not inconsistent with the GATS, including those related to: the prevention of deceptive and fraudulent practices, the handling of the effects of a default on services contracts, the protection of the privacy of individuals in relation to the processing and dissemination of personal data, and the protection of confidentiality of individual records and accounts; and safety.[18]

These are, however, subject to some provisos. Any measures taken must not be applied in a manner that would constitute a means of arbitrary or unjustifiable discrimination between countries where like conditions prevail; further, they must not be a disguised restriction on trade in services. For example, a country can ban the performance of a certain medical procedure on the basis that such a ban is necessary to protect human health, but it cannot ban the performance of the procedure by doctors from some countries but not others unless it can establish that conditions between those countries are not "like."

A Word of Caution It should be recalled that many issues will arise if a country wants to stop an existing trade, regardless of whether they have made GATS commitments covering that trade. For example, even in the absence of GATS commitments, if a country decided that it wanted to revert to a health system that was entirely publicly provided (i.e., no private providers at all, domestic or foreign) the constitutions of many countries would require some form of compensation to be paid by the government to domestic private providers who had lost their livelihood. In this case, the question would be whether to extend such compensation to foreign private providers also; in many cases, if these providers were locally incorporated they might well be considered as domestic providers under national law in any case. In the case of Mode 4, issues would arise about whether and in what circumstances (and with what right of appeal etc) existing holders of medical practitioner visas could be fired and deported, regardless of whether GATS commitments had been made on Mode 4 for health services.

> ## STEP 8: What if I Change My Mind? What if I No Longer Want to Keep a Commitment?
>
> *Renegotiation of commitments*: a WTO member may withdraw or modify its GATS commitments three years after their entry into force but must pay compensation to all other members. Compensation takes the form additional access being granted in another area.
>
> *Balance of payments*: members may also restrict their commitments in the event of serious balance of payments or external financial difficulties. These restrictions must: be MFN; be consistent with the Articles of Agreement of the IMF; avoid unnecessary damage to the interests of other members; not be excessive to what is necessary to deal with the problem; and be phased out as the situation improves.
>
> *Exceptions*: a country can be in breach of its commitments if it can justify what it has done under one of the exceptions provisions. These relate to, among other things, public morals; human, animal, or plant life and health; protection of individual privacy and security. These are subject to the proviso that any measures taken do not arbitrarily or unjustifiably discriminate between countries where like conditions prevail or that the measures are not disguised restrictions on trade in services.
>
> *Emergency safeguards*: negotiations are underway for a mechanism to enable members to suspend their commitments in the event of unforeseen damage to the local industry. However, these negotiations are difficult and the nature and coverage of any final mechanisms are yet to be determined.
>
> *A word of caution*: many issues will arise if a country wants to stop an existing trade, regardless of whether they have made GATS commitments covering that trade. Deporting persons holding temporary medical practitioner visas or ceasing the activities of companies operating in a country involve a range of issues for the domestic legal system, regardless of GATS commitments.

STEP 9: What About the Future?

The GATS provides for progressive rounds of negotiations to liberalize trade in services. However, this does not mean the inexorable march to the free market for all services; WTO members remain free not to make commitments in a given service sector should they so wish.

The guidelines for the negotiations reaffirm the flexibility in the GATS for developing countries to open fewer sectors, liberalize fewer types of transactions, extend market access progressively in line with their development situation, and, when granting market access, attach conditions to fulfilling development objectives.

What Happens Next?

The GATS provides for the progressive liberalization of services. This does not necessarily imply an inexorable march towards a completely free market for all service sectors. Rather, it signals that, in recognition of the complexity and variety of service sectors, liberalization under the GATS will be a gradual process. While successive rounds of negotiations with a view to achieving a progressively higher level of liberalization are foreseen, the purpose of these negotiations is to promote the interests of all participants on a mutually advantageous basis and to secure an overall balance of rights and obligations. Equally, while the negotiations are directed toward increasing the general level of commitments and no sector is a priori excluded from the negotiations, WTO members remain free to keep particular service sectors closed to foreign supply if they so wish.

Finally, the negotiating guidelines agreed by WTO members on March 31, 2001[19] reaffirmed the flexibility in the GATS for developing countries to open fewer sectors, liberalize fewer types of transactions, extend market access progressively in line with their development situation, and, when granting market access, attach conditions to fulfilling development objectives.

STEP 10: A Final Thought

- Dialogue, consultation, and coordination are essential to answer to two questions regarding the GATS and trade in health services:
- Can the GATS help us to achieve any of the health policy outcomes we are seeking?
- How might we need to regulate this trade to ensure that our objectives are met and what is our capacity to do so?

A Final Thought

Trade in health services raises many complex issues, and whether or not to make GATS commitments on that trade adds another dimension to this complexity. The expertise and active involvement of a range of players—health policymakers and professionals, patients' groups, and trade negotiators—is essential, at the national and international levels.

At the national level, two fundamental questions underlie this dialogue: (1) what, if anything, do we want out of the GATS process for health services—i.e., can GATS help us to achieve any of the health policy outcomes we are seeking; and (2) how might we regulate this trade to achieve the best health outcomes and what is our capacity to do so?

Notes

1. Public services are often referred to as "free," when they are free to the consumer. Of course, free to the consumer does a not mean free; someone is paying. The question is how a society chooses to allocate costs, e.g., via the general tax system, via consumer contribution, by use of means-testing, etc. While beyond the scope of this paper, consideration of the role of public services needs also to take into account the structure of the tax base in service provision, which can vary considerably between countries. For example, it is not always the case that the cost of public services is shared equitably over a large tax base and the benefits similarly distributed; in some countries, the tax burden can fall disproportionately on lower-income groups, while public services are consumed disproportionately by the higher-income groups.

2. More detailed information about the entirety of the agreement is available from www.wto.org.

3. While the agreement covers measures taken by these subnational and nongovernmental bodies, it is recognized—as in other WTO agreements—that countries may face constitutional limitations on the extent to which they can actually compel adherence by subnational entities. Thus, the GATS requires that, in fulfilling its commitments under the agreement, "each member shall take such reasonable measures as may be available to it to ensure their observance by regional and local governments and authorities and nongovernmental bodies within its territory."

4. Other exclusions include air traffic rights and services directly related to the exercise of traffic rights.

5. A number of documents and proposals from members related to government procurement are publicly available via the WTO Web site (www.wto.org).

6. Documents relating to the subsidies work—including background notes by the WTO Secretariat on information on subsidies from WTO Trade Policy Reviews and responses to the questionnaire by a number of WTO members—are publicly available via the WTO Web site (www.wto.org).

7. A "schedule of commitments" is the technical term for the document in which countries list the undertakings they are making to other WTO members in terms of the access they are providing to their services markets. The schedules list the service sectors that the country has decided to open and the conditions under which that opening is being granted.

8. Article V (Regional Integration Agreements) requires that: these agreements have substantial sectoral coverage; do not a priori exclude any mode of supply; and provide for the elimination of substantially all discrimination between the parties. Flexibility on these conditions applies to agreements between developing countries. While a number of regional trade agreements have been reviewed by the WTO members in the Committee on Regional Trade Agreements, no consensus has been reached on the compliance of any agreement with GATS Article V or GATT Article XXIV (the parallel provision for trade in goods).

9. The majority of these exemptions are in transport (151 exemptions, or 35 percent of the total) and communications (104, or 25 percent of the total, of which 85 are audiovisual services).

10. In practice, most WTO members' commitments under Mode 4 range from a couple of days (e.g., for business visitors) to up to five years. The length of time varies with the type of entrant: while, in most cases, business visitors are limited to stays of up to three months, intracorporate transferees can stay for several years.

11. An economic needs test is a provision in national regulation, legislation, or administrative guidelines that restricts the entry of service suppliers based on an assessment of the needs in the market. They can restrict the entry of both foreigners and nationals to a market, or only foreigners—e.g., a country may restrict the number of pharmacies or hospital beds to a given number per head of population (one pharmacy per 500 persons; 100 hospital beds per 1,000 persons).

12. This is a strange example and, indeed, it is difficult to find an example of this type of market access restriction in health services. These types of restrictions are much more common in, for example, financial services.

13. Countries are free to provide more favorable treatment to foreigners than nationals if they wish; the GATS is only concerned with less favorable treatment.

14. See WTO, 1998a.

15. The Accountancy Disciplines were developed pursuant to the Article VI.4 mandate. They are a range of additional disciplines that apply only to trade in accountancy services and only where a member has made commitments to allow trade in accountancy services. The disciplines were agreed in 1998 but are yet to enter into force; they are due to do so at the end of the current round of negotiations. See WTO, 1998b.

16. This argument rests on the idea that the purpose of possible Article VI.4 disciplines is to prevent frustration of trade by the "back door." Given that if a country's real aim is to exclude foreign suppliers or to discriminate against them, it is free to do so anyway under the GATS, introducing these disciplines only makes sense if there is some commitment made to allow foreign supply under some conditions in the first place. If no opportunity for foreign supply is promised, it is argued that the need to develop disciplines to prevent the use of other measures to undermine that promise disappears.

17. A number of countries operate prior consultation for various types of regulation at the national level, some including foreign suppliers in the consultation process. However, some countries have expressed concern that any such obligation in their commitments to provide prior consultation for services could be administratively burdensome. It should also be stressed that provision of an opportunity for comment on proposed regulations does not guarantee that those comments will be reflected in the final decision; it is merely an opportunity for those affected by the regulation to put forward their views.

18. Two other exceptions refer to taxation. A further exception provision, Article XIVbis, provides for exceptions related to security.

19. WTO, 2001.

References

WTO (World Trade Organization). 1998a. "Report to the Council for Trade in Services on the Development of Disciplines on Domestic Regulation in the Accountancy Sector." S/WPPS/4, 10 December.

———. 1998b. "WTO Adopts Disciplines on Domestic Regulation for the Accountancy Sector." Press Release dated 14 December (available at www.wto.org/wto/new).

———. 2001. "Guidelines and Procedures for the Negotiations on Trade in Services," adopted by the Special Session of the Council for Trade in Services on 28 March 2001, S/L/93.

ANNEX I: Detailed Definitions

W/120 sector	Corresponding CPC code	CPC definition
8. Health related and social services		
A. Hospital services	CPC 9311	*Includes:* —surgical services delivered under the direction of medical doctors chiefly to inpatients, aimed at curing, restoring, and/or maintaining the health of a patient; —medical services delivered under the direction of medical doctors chiefly to inpatients, aimed at curing, restoring, and/or maintaining the health of a patient —gynecological and obstetrical services delivered under the direction of medical doctors chiefly to inpatients, aimed at curing, restoring, and/or maintaining the health of a patient —rehabilitation services delivered under the direction of medical doctors chiefly to inpatients, aimed at curing, restoring, and/or maintaining the health of a patient —psychiatric services delivered under the direction of medical doctors chiefly to inpatients, aimed at curing, restoring, and/or maintaining the health of a patient —other hospital services delivered under the direction of medical doctors chiefly to inpatients, aimed at curing, restoring, and/or maintaining the health of a patient. These services comprise medical, pharmaceutical, and paramedical services; nursing services; laboratory and technical services, including radiological and anesthesiological services, etc. —military hospital services —prison hospital services *Does not include:* —services delivered by hospital outpatient clinics, cf. 9312

ANNEX I: Detailed Definitions

W/120 sector	Corresponding CPC code	CPC definition
		—dental services, cf. 93123
		—ambulance services, cf. 93192
B. Other human health services	CPC 9319 (other than 93191)	**Ambulance services** *Includes:* —services involving transport of patients by ambulance, with or without resuscitation equipment or medical personnel
		Residential health facilities services other than hospital services *Includes:* —combined lodging and medical services provided without the supervision of a medical doctor located on the premises
		Other human health services *Includes:* —services provided by medical laboratories —services provided by blood, sperm, and transplant organ banks —dental testing services —medical analysis and testing services —other human health services n.e.c.
C. Social services	CPC 933	**Welfare services delivered through residential institutions to elderly persons and persons with disabilities** *Includes:* —social assistance services involving round-the-clock care services by residential institutions for elderly persons —social assistance services involving round-the-clock care services by residential institutions for persons with physical or intellectual disabilities, including those having disabilities in seeing, hearing, or speaking *Does not include:* —education services, cf. 92 —combined lodging and medical services, cf. 93110 (hospital services) if under the direction of medical doctors, and 93193 if without supervision by a medical doctor

ANNEX I: Detailed Definitions

W/120 sector	Corresponding CPC code	CPC definition
		Other social services with accommodation *Includes:* —residential social assistance services involving round-the-clock care services to children, e.g., social services for orphanages, homes for children in need of protection, homes for children with emotional impairments —residential social assistance services involving round-the-clock care services to other clients, e.g.: —homes for single mothers —juvenile correction homes —rehabilitation services (not including medical treatment) for persons with impairments such as alcohol or drug dependence —other social rehabilitation services
D. Other		
1. Business services		
A. Professional services		
h. Medical and dental services	CPC 9312	**General medical services** *Includes:* —services consisting of the prevention, diagnosis, and treatment by doctors of medicine of physical and/or mental diseases of a general nature, such as: — consultations
		—physical checkups, etc. These services are not limited to specified or particular conditions, diseases or anatomical regions. They can be provided in general practitioners' practices and also delivered by outpatient clinics, clinics attached to firms, schools, etc. **Specialized medical services** *Includes:* —consultation services in pediatrics, gynecology-obstetrics, neurology and psychiatry, and various medical services

ANNEX I: Detailed Definitions

W/120 sector	Corresponding CPC code	CPC definition
		—surgical consultation services —treatment services in outpatients clinics, such as dialysis, chemotherapy, insulin therapy, respirator treatment, X-ray treatment, and the like —functional exploration and interpreting of medical images (X-ray photographs, electrocardiograms, endoscopies, and the like) *Does not include:* —services of medical laboratories, cf. 93199 **Dental services** *Includes:* —orthodontic services, e.g., treatment of protruding teeth, cross bite, overbite, etc., including dental surgery even when given in hospitals to inpatients —services in the field of oral surgery —other specialized dental services, e.g., in the field of periodontics, pedodontics, endodontics, and reconstruction —diagnosis and treatment services of diseases affecting the patient or aberrations in the cavity of the mouth, and services aimed at the prevention of dental diseases *Note:* these dental services can be delivered in health clinics, such as those attached to schools, firms, homes for the aged, etc., as well as in own consulting rooms. They cover services in the field of general dentistry, such as routine dental examinations, preventive dental care, treatment of caries, etc.
j. Services provided by midwives, nurses, physiotherapists and paramedical personnel	CPC93191	*Includes:* —services such as supervision during pregnancy and childbirth —supervision of the mother after birth —services in a field of nursing care (without admission), advice and prevention for patients at home, the provision of maternity care, children's hygiene, etc. —services provided by physiotherapists and other paramedical persons (including homeopathological and similar services)

ANNEX I: Detailed Definitions

W/120 sector	Corresponding CPC code	CPC definition
		—physiotherapy and paramedical services are services in the field of physiotherapy, ergotherapy, occupational therapy, speech therapy, homeopathy, acupuncture, nutrition, etc. These services are provided by authorized persons, other than medical doctors
7. Financial services		
A. All insurance and insurance-related services		
(a) Life, accident, and health insurance services	CPC 8121	**Accident and health insurance services** *Includes:* —underwriting services of insurance policies that provide protection for hospital and medical expenses not covered by government programs and usually other health care expenses such as prescribed drugs, medical appliances, ambulance, private duty nursing, etc. — underwriting services of insurance policies that provide protection for dental expenses — underwriting services of insurance policies that provide protection for medical expenses incurred when traveling outside a certain geographic area — underwriting services of insurance policies that provide periodic payments when the insured is unable to work as a result of a disability due to illness or injury — underwriting services of insurance policies that provide accidental death and dis-memberment insurance, that is, payment in the event that an accident results in death or loss of one or more bodily members (such as hands or feet) or the sight of one or both eyes

ANNEX II: Example of Commitments on Health Services Under GATS

Horizontal commitments	Limitations on market access	Limitations on national treatment	Additional commitments
	(4) Stays limited to 6 months; and subject to labor market testing	(4) Unbound	Prior comment procedures exist for all new regulations introduced at the national level. Such procedures do not apply to services regulated at the state level, including health services.
Sectoral commitments			
8. Health and related social services Surgical consultation services (part of CPC 9312), excluding those services supplied in public hospitals	(1) None	(1) Only private surgical con-sultation services supplied by nationals can be reimbursed under national health plan.	
	(2) None	(2) None	
	(3) From 1 January 2005, the following conditions will apply: — Surgical consulta-tion services subject to an economic needs test. Estab-lishment will only be permitted where there is no existing service within a 500 km radius.	(3) Unbound	

ANNEX II: Example of Commitments on Health Services Under GATS

Horizontal commitments	Limitations on market access	Limitations on national treatment	Additional commitments
	— Foreign providers must form joint ventures with national providers, with a maximum foreign equity of 50 percent.		
	(4) Unbound except as indicated in the horizontal section	(4) Unbound except as indicated in the horizontal section	

MAKING COMMITMENTS IN HEALTH SERVICES UNDER THE GATS: LEGAL DIMENSIONS

David P. Fidler, Nick Drager,
Carlos Correa, Obijiofor Aginam

Introduction: GATS, Health Policy, and International Law

The GATS is one of the most important multilateral trade agreements to emerge from the Uruguay Round negotiations that created the World Trade Organization (WTO). GATS constitutes the legal framework through which WTO members will progressively liberalize trade in services, including health-related services. Health policy is an important social endeavor that faces both opportunities and challenges in GATS. Many factors, including the complexity of GATS, the lack of empirical data on the level of international trade in health-related services and on the health effects of liberalized trade in services, and inequalities in resources and position in negotiations between developed and developing countries, create a difficult environment for people in public health and health care who want to understand the actual and potential impact of GATS on their activities.

David Fidler, Carlos Correa, and Obijiofor Aginam are members of the GATS Legal Review Team. Nick Drager is Senior Advisor, Globalisation, Trade and Health, Department of Ethics, Trade, Human Rights, and Health Law, World Health Organization, and Project Director of the *Legal Review of the General Agreement on Trade in Services (GATS) from a Health Policy Perspective.*

One particularly difficult aspect of the GATS challenge involves understanding the international legal implications of GATS for health policy. Controversies have arisen about the legal impact of GATS on public services, such as health and education, and a debate has developed on the relationship between GATS and health that underlines the importance of discerning how health policy communities should handle this WTO agreement. This debate centers on whether GATS hurts or helps WTO members in exercising their respective abilities to protect health and provide health services.

States have long used international law to create disciplines on the exercise of sovereignty for health policy purposes. Two examples are the International Health Regulations (IHR) and international human rights law. Member states of the World Health Organization (WHO) who are bound by the IHR are required, among other things, to notify the WHO of outbreaks of diseases subject to the regulations and limit health measures taken against the trade and travel of a country suffering a disease outbreak to the measures prescribed in the IHR.[1] The human right to health under international law requires bound countries to achieve, progressively, the highest attainable standard of physical and mental health, which includes protecting populations from health threats and providing health services to the people.[2]

Neither the IHR nor the right to health have historically represented significant limitations on health policy. As the recent outbreak of Severe Acute Respiratory Syndrome (SARS) illustrated, the IHR, in their present form, are inadequate for the threats the world faces today from infectious diseases.[3] Although the right to health is normatively powerful, according to the UN's Special Rapporteur on the Right to Health, it has been historically neglected, leaving its actual legal content not well established.[4] Generally speaking, health policy has been relatively unfettered by these areas of international law.

More significant, international legal disciplines affecting health policy have developed in international trade law, most prominently through the General Agreement on Tariffs and Trade (GATT) and the WTO Agreement on Trade-Related Aspects of Intellectual Property Rights (TRIPS). The international legal controversies concerning the scope and meaning of provisions in TRIPS that affect health policy demonstrate the importance of health policy communities possessing a sophisticated understanding of the law created by WTO agreements and their ability to promote health policy objectives within the framework of this law.

GATS is also an international trade agreement that contains legal rules that may affect health policy more than the existing IHR and international law on human rights. Understanding GATS' legal implications for health policy is difficult, given the immense scope and complexity of the agreement. This chapter undertakes a brief analytical overview of the international legal implications of GATS, in order to provide health policymakers with a tool for navigating the international legal waters through which health policy must now traverse with respect to trade in services.

The "Tale of Two Treaties" Problem

The health policy community has been exposed to analyses and controversies about GATS' potential impact on health. These controversies reveal the existence of a debate about the meaning of GATS provisions and their implications for health policy. The following paragraphs provide a glimpse of the GATS and health debate.

A considerable body of literature has raised concerns about how GATS might affect a WTO member's ability to pursue public policies, such as health. This literature expresses fears that GATS threatens to constrict policy flexibility for health procedurally, structurally, and substantively. Procedurally, concerns exist that GATS creates a fundamentally new and difficult process through which WTO members will have to organize their health policies. Structurally, the worry is that the GATS duty to liberalize trade in services progressively will force WTO members to privatize public health and heath care services currently provided by governments and "lock in" policy experiments with privatization, preventing returns to publicly operated and funded services.

Substantively, concerns have arisen that GATS erodes a WTO member's ability to regulate health-related services adequately because of limitations the treaty places on the ability of a WTO member to regulate for health protection and promotion purposes. According to this view, the interdependence of the procedural, structural, and substantive effects of GATS constrains health policy and brings about a revolution in how states use international law to regulate sovereignty in connection with public services such as health.

The opposite view stresses the flexibility of GATS, which allows WTO members to shape how they wish to liberalize international trade in services. From the flexibility perspective, GATS respects—rather than threatens—health policy. The inclusion of health-related services in the scope of GATS means that GATS will affect certain aspects of health policy; but, under this position, how GATS affects health policy, and what aspects of health policy GATS will affect, remain largely sovereign decisions not imposed by the WTO or any of its agreements.

The GATS and health debate often reads like a "tale of two treaties"—it is the best of treaties, it is the worst of treaties. Even though more nuanced legal interpretations of GATS exist, health policymakers often do not have the time or the training to monitor the evolving debate on what the law of GATS means for them. This context makes it difficult for people working in the public health and health care sectors to understand how the law of GATS may or may not affect their work.

Undertaking International Legal Analysis of GATS

International lawyers use principles of treaty interpretation found in general international law to discern the meaning of treaty provisions. Both critics and defenders of GATS have used these principles in their work. The conflicting interpretations given by experts engaged in this debate, however, often cannot be reconciled. This reality forces analysis back to first principles—in this case, principles of treaty interpretation in international law as codified in the Vienna Convention on the Law of Treaties of 1969.

Another important factor in treaty interpretation in the context of GATS concerns cases decided by dispute settlement bodies under the old GATT system (e.g., *Thailand—Cigarettes*[5]) and the existing WTO (e.g., *EC—Asbestos*[6]). The dispute settlement bodies deciding these cases apply the principles of treaty interpretation found in the Vienna Convention on the Law of Treaties, and the decisions in these cases may constitute nonbinding precedents that affect how treaties will be interpreted in future disputes. GATT and WTO cases will, wherever relevant, play important roles for interpreting GATS.

Utilizing these tools of international legal analysis, certain provisions of GATS stand out as the most relevant parts of the Agreement for health policy. These provisions are summarized in Box 5.1. The chapter then reviews these provisions from a health policy perspective.

The Threshold Question: Is a Health-Related Service within the Scope of GATS?

Broad Scope of GATS and Health Policy

Legal analysis of GATS begins with understanding how the scope of GATS overlaps with the scope of health policy. Because the scopes of both GATS and health policy are broad, the overlap is significant, making GATS an important treaty in terms of its potential effect on health policy.

GATS' scope is very broad. Article I:1 of GATS provides that "[t]his Agreement applies to measures by Members affecting trade in services." GATS defines each of the key terms in this provision—"trade in services," "measures by Members," "affecting"—broadly. For example, GATS covers all possible ways in which services are provided (Box 5.2). "Measures by Members" covers any rule or action by any level of government, and "affecting" means merely having an effect on trade in services, whether or not the WTO member intended such effect.

The extensive coverage of GATS becomes important when the broad scope of health policy is taken into account. The exercise of sovereign powers to protect and promote health extends across a vast range of governmental activities, economic sectors, and social objectives. Threats to health arise in a multitude of contexts in which governments seek to protect and promote health. Health-related services can be found in many sectors—business, communications, distribution, educational, environmental, financial, and health and social services—further underscoring the significant overlap between GATS and health policy.

**Box 5.1:   Articles of GATS of Greatest Relevance
to Health Policy**

Topic (GATS article)	Substance of the GATS Provision (Note that a number of articles contain further details that are spelled out in GATS)
Scope of GATS (Part I)	
Scope and definitions (Article I)	GATS applies to measures by WTO members affecting trade in services.
	Trade in services is defined as the supply of a service: (1) from the territory of one WTO member into the territory of any other WTO member; (2) in the territory of one WTO member to the service consumer of any other WTO member; (3) by a service supplier of one WTO member through commercial presence in the territory of any other WTO member; and (4) by a service supplier of one WTO member through presence of natural persons of a WTO member in the territory of any other WTO member.
	"Services" includes any service in any sector except services supplied in the exercise of governmental authority.
	A "service supplied in the exercise of governmental authority" means any service that is supplied neither on a commercial basis nor in competition with one or more service suppliers.
General obligations and disciplines (Part II)	
Most-favored-nation treatment (Article II)	With respect to any measure covered by GATS, each WTO member shall accord immediately and unconditionally to services and service suppliers of any other WTO member treatment no less favorable than that it accords to like services and service suppliers of any other country.
Domestic regulation (Article VI)	The Council for Trade in Services shall develop any necessary disciplines on measures relating to qualification requirements, technical standards, and licensing requirements to ensure that such measures do not constitute unnecessary barriers to trade in services. Such disciplines shall aim to ensure that such requirements are, among other things, not more burdensome than necessary to ensure the quality of the service.

(Continued)

Box 5.1: Articles of GATS of Greatest Relevance to Health Policy (Continued)

Monopolies and exclusive service suppliers (Article VIII)	If a WTO member grants monopoly or exclusive service rights regarding the supply of a service covered by specific commitments, then that WTO member must make compensatory arrangements with any WTO member adversely affected by such granting of monopoly or exclusive service rights.
General exceptions (Article XIV)	WTO members may restrict trade in health-related services in violation of general obligations or specific commitments when such restrictive measures are necessary to protect human, animal, or plant life or health, and the application of which does not constitute a means of arbitrary or unjustifiable discrimination or a disguised restriction on trade in services.

Specific commitments (Part III)

Market access (Article XVI)	With respect to market access through the modes of supply identified in Article I, each WTO member shall accord services and service suppliers of any other WTO member treatment no less favorable than that provided for under the terms, limitations, and conditions agreed and specified in its Schedule of Specific Commitments. WTO members must list measures restricting market access they wish to maintain in sectors subject to market access commitments.
National treatment (Article XVII)	In the sectors inscribed in its Schedule of Specific Commitments, and subject to any conditions and qualifications set out therein, each WTO member shall accord to services and service suppliers of any other WTO member, in respect of all measures affecting the supply of services, treatment no less favorable than that it accords to its own like services and service suppliers.

Progressive liberalization (Part IV)

Negotiation of specific commitments (Article XIX)	WTO members shall enter into successive rounds of negotiations with a view to achieving a progressively higher level of liberalization in trade in services.
Modification of schedules (Article XXI)	To withdraw or modify a Schedule of Specific Commitments, a WTO member must make compensatory arrangements for WTO members adversely affected by such withdrawal or modification; and such compensatory arrangements are then available to all WTO members on a most-favored-nation basis.

(Continued)

**Box 5.1: Articles of GATS of Greatest Relevance
to Health Policy (Continued)**

Institutional provisions (Part V)

Dispute settlement   Disputes that arise under GATS are subject to the WTO
and enforcement   Dispute Settlement Understanding.
(Article XXIII)

Council for Trade in   The Council for Trade in Services shall facilitate the
Services (Article   operation of GATS and advance its objectives.
XXIV)

Box 5.2: Scope of "Trade in Services" under GATS

Mode	Supply of a service	Health-related example
1	*Cross-border supply of health services*: From the territory of one member into the territory of any other member (Article I:2(a))	Telemedicine; cross-border supply of health insurance
2	*Consumption of health services abroad:* In the territory of one member to the service consumer of any other member (Article I:2(b))	Consumption of medical services by a patient from one WTO member in the territory of another WTO member
3	*Commercial presence:* By a service supplier of one member, through commercial presence in the territory of any other member (Article I:2(c))	Foreign direct investment in another WTO member by, for example, health insurance, hospital, water, and/or waste disposal companies
4	*Movement of natural persons:* By a service supplier of one member, through the presence of natural persons of a member in the territory of any other member (Article I:2(d))	Nurses or doctors supplying medical services while present in another WTO member state

*Exclusion for "Services Provided Pursuant to the Exercise
of Governmental Authority"*

In the overlapping scopes of GATS and health policy, the key controversy is the provision that excludes "services supplied in the exercise of governmental authority" (GATS, Article I:3(b)). GATS defines such services as "any service that is supplied neither on a commercial basis, nor in competition with one or more service suppliers" (GATS, Article I:3(c)). Some experts assert that this exclusion is narrow, bringing government-supplied health-related services inside GATS. Others argue that this provision of the treaty excludes government services, which puts government-supplied health-related services outside of GATS. The debate is, therefore, about the breadth of the exclusion.

To benefit from this exclusion, a service has to satisfy three tests: the service: (1) has to be provided pursuant to governmental authority; (2) cannot be supplied on a commercial basis; and (3) cannot be supplied in competition with one or more service suppliers. Figure 5.1 provides a step-by-step guide through these rules.

The meanings of the "commercial basis" and "in competition" tests remain unclear, which is a concern for government-provided health-related services. Although many legal experts expect the exclusion to be interpreted and applied narrowly, the ambiguity provides an opportunity for the health policy community to influence the interpretation of this provision in a way that is sensitive to health policy concerns. For example, WTO members can clarify what "commercial basis" and "in competition" mean in a way that excludes the provision of most government-provided health-related services.

In addition, this provision raises issues about which WTO member has the burden of proof as to whether a government-supplied service benefits from the exclusion. From a health policy perspective, the burden of proof should fall on

FIGURE 5.1 Threshold Question: Does GATS Apply?

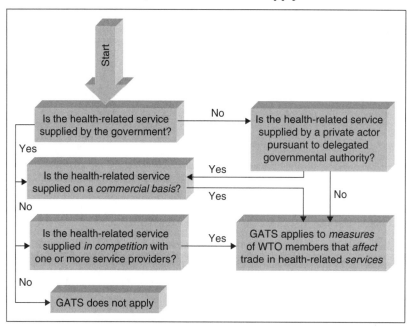

the WTO member claiming that the exclusion does not cover a government-supplied service. In other words, a WTO member complaining about a possible GATS violation has the initial burden of establishing that a government-supplied service does not meet the criteria found in Article I:1(c). Thus, government-provided services should be presumed to be outside GATS unless a WTO member establishes that such services do not meet the tests provided in Article I:1(c). The WTO Secretariat's position that government-provided services are excluded from GATS supports this approach.[7]

Even when a government-provided service falls within the scope of GATS because it does not satisfy the Article I:1(c) tests, the implications of this outcome for health policy depend on two further aspects of GATS: (1) the impact of the general obligations, such as the most-favored-nation principle; and (2) the extent of market access and national treatment commitments made by the relevant WTO member. In other words, determination that a service is within GATS is the beginning rather than the end of the analysis of how GATS affects government-provided health-related services.

Four Pillars of GATS' Legal Architecture

When a health-related service falls within GATS, the next analytical step involves examining the rules that GATS applies to measures that affect trade in services. GATS contains four sets of obligations for WTO members with respect to trade in services (Figure 5.2). The first set of rules involves the general obligations that apply to all measures affecting trade in services. GATS literature often refers to these obligations as "horizontal" or "top-down" disciplines because they apply to all service sectors and measures affecting trade in services.

The second set of rules governs the making of specific market access and national treatment commitments by WTO members. In contrast to the mandatory general obligations, the specific commitments on market access and national treatment: (1) arise from voluntary undertakings by WTO members; and (2) apply only to the service sectors specified in the commitments. WTO

FIGURE 5.2 Four Legal Pillars of GATS

members bind themselves to their specific commitments by detailing them on schedules that become part of the binding treaty. The rules on specific commitments are often called "bottom-up" rules because the commitments originate with WTO members rather than with GATS itself.

The third set of rules lays out the obligation of WTO members to engage in successive rounds of negotiations with a view to achieving a progressively higher level of liberalization in trade in services. These rules envision GATS as a dynamic process that continually involves negotiations to further liberalize trade in services.

The fourth set of rules establishes the institutional framework for GATS. Most important are the application of the WTO's dispute settlement machinery to GATS disputes and the creation of the Council for Trade in Services to oversee the implementation and progressive development of the agreement.

General Obligations That Apply to All Measures Affecting Trade in Services

Part of the GATS and health debate centers on how the general obligations and disciplines of GATS affect health policy. The general obligations divide into substantive and procedural duties (Figure 5.3). The substantive duties have been the source of controversy because they potentially affect the content of measures affecting trade in services. Procedural duties require WTO members to participate in certain processes deemed important to the functioning of the agreement but do not touch the substantive content of domestic regulation.

Substantive Duties

GATS' substantive duties divide into two categories: the most-favored-nation obligation and obligations that relate to domestic regulatory powers. The duties that relate to domestic regulatory powers further divide into obligations that

FIGURE 5.3 General Obligations and Disciplines

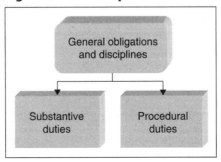

FIGURE 5.4 Substantive Duties

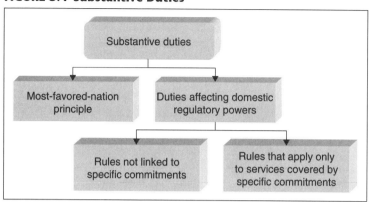

apply to all measures affecting trade in services and those that only apply to services subject to specific commitments (Figure 5.4).

Most-Favored-Nation Principle   One of the most important substantive general obligations is the most-favored-nation principle, under which each WTO member has to accord immediately and unconditionally to service and service suppliers of any other WTO member treatment no less favorable than it accords to like services and service suppliers of any other country (GATS, Article II:1). Figure 5.5 provides a guide to the application of the MFN principle.

FIGURE 5.5 Has the MFN Principle Been Violated?

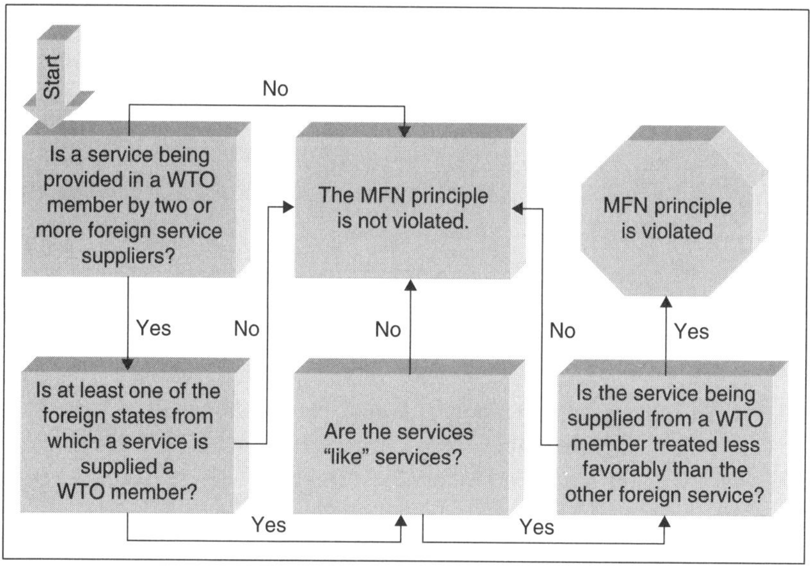

Box 5.3: Possible Problematic Scenarios under the MFN Principle in GATS

MFN and the "Brain Drain" Problem

State A allows nurses, doctors, and other health professionals from States B and C to provide services within its territory under Mode 4 (Movement of Natural Persons) of GATS. State A begins to restrict Mode 4 access to health professionals from State B but not State C in order to help State B address a brain drain problem in its health care system. Technically, State A's action violates the MFN principle because this action treats Mode 4 services from State B less favorably than like Mode 4 services from State C. However, the violation of the MFN principle would only be a concern if State B wanted to pursue a claim against State A under GATS. In this scenario, State B probably would not oppose State A's action because such action was taken to assist State B in dealing with a brain drain problem.

MFN and a Preference for NGO Service Suppliers

State A wants to increase the supply of a particular health-related service and seeks foreign service suppliers to help achieve this increase in supply. However, because of the nature of the service to be supplied (e.g., health clinics in rural communities), State A prefers to have the service supplied by not-for-profit service suppliers from foreign countries rather than for-profit suppliers. Thus, State A treats NGO service suppliers from State B more favorably than it treats like for-profit service suppliers from State C in connection with increasing the supply of the relevant service in its territory. State C could claim that State A's behavior violates the MFN principle of GATS by discriminating against its service suppliers.

Article II:1 of GATS is a serious substantive discipline for WTO members, as it is in other WTO agreements, such as GATT. The MFN principle prohibits discrimination, whether it is intentional or unintentional, and thus has broad application. Despite the reach of the MFN principle, it probably does not affect health policy significantly. The ability of a WTO member to discriminate as between foreign services or service suppliers does not seem to be important to the protection and promotion of health. Some cases may arise, however, in which the MFN principle may have problematic implications (Box 5.3).

Rules Affecting Domestic Regulatory Powers Linked to Specific Commitments

A second category of general obligations involves duties affecting domestic regulatory powers. A significant aspect of the GATS and health debate revolves around whether GATS interferes with the ability of a WTO member to regulate services domestically. Because many experts have noted the importance of strong domestic regulation of health-related services, the differing positions on the general obligations affecting domestic regulatory powers create a critical area of GATS interpretation.

Many of the general obligations on domestic regulatory power only affect domestic regulations in sectors covered by market access or national treatment commitments. The potential effect of these provisions on health policy depends on the level and nature of specific commitments made by WTO members in health-related sectors. The most controversial of these provisions have been Article VI:5(a) on domestic regulations and Article VIII on monopoly service suppliers.

Article VI:5(a) of GATS regulates licensing and qualification requirements and technical standards implemented in sectors subject to specific commitments. This provision obliges a WTO member not to apply such requirements and standards in a manner that is not transparent, is more burdensome than necessary to ensure the quality of the service, and could not have reasonably been expected at the time the WTO member in question made the relevant specific commitments (GATS, Article VI:5(a)). Article VI:5(a) is a weak discipline on the domestic regulation of trade in services because, as commentators have noted, its requirements would make it difficult for WTO members to successfully challenge domestic regulations on services. Nevertheless, Article VI:5 should be monitored in case it is used in ways that affect health policy.

Article VIII addresses the domestic regulation of monopoly service suppliers. Criticism of Article VIII has focused on Article VIII:4, which imposes rules that apply if a WTO member grants monopoly or exclusive rights regarding the supply of a service covered by specific commitments (GATS, Article VIII:4). These rules require the WTO member granting such rights to provide affected WTO members with compensation or face trade sanctions (Figure 5.6).

Concerns have been raised that this compensation requirement illegitimately restricts a WTO member's ability to expand monopoly or exclusive service supply rights for public interest purposes. Article VIII:4 does impose a constraint on health policy in that it increases the political, economic, and diplomatic costs of using monopoly and exclusive service rights as a health policy tool in service sectors covered by specific commitments (Box 5.4). Other international legal agreements, such as bilateral investment agreements, may pose additional constraints because they regulate the treatment of foreign direct investment more substantively than GATS does, especially with respect to compensation for expropriations (Box 5.4).

Rules Affecting Domestic Regulatory Powers Not Linked to Specific Commitments   In terms of general substantive obligations on domestic regulation not linked to specific commitments, one set of these rules contains provisions contingent on certain factual settings and thus does not apply to all measures affecting

FIGURE 5.6 Granting Monopoly or Exclusive Rights

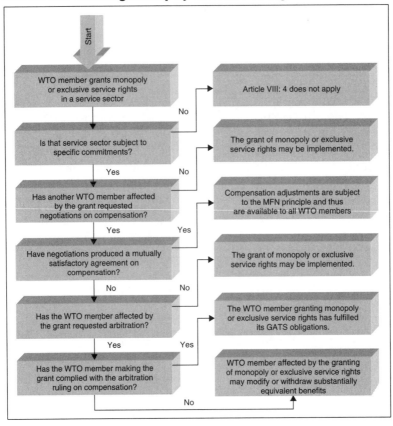

trade in services (e.g., GATS, Articles VII:3, VIII:1, and VIII:5). These rules do not pose significant problems for health policy. The only substantive obligation on domestic regulation that is not connected with specific commitments or contingent on the existence of certain facts is a duty to maintain judicial, arbitral, or administrative tribunals that provide for prompt review of decisions affecting trade in services (GATS, Article VI:2). This obligation is not problematical for health policy.

Procedural Duties

Procedural duties under GATS divide into two categories: (1) duties to provide information or to establish certain government procedures, which further break into generally applicable rules and rules that apply only when specific commitments exist; and (2) duties to participate in negotiations or consultations (Figure 5.7).

> ## Box 5.4: Granting Monopoly or Exclusive Service Rights in Sectors Covered by a Specific Commitment: An Example under GATS and Bilateral Investment Treaties
>
> *GATS*
>
> State A makes a specific commitment to increase market access for foreign suppliers of water distribution services. This specific commitment forms part of State A's plan to privatize government-owned water distribution networks and assets. The privatization strategy proves, however, to increase water tariffs and decrease water supplies to poor and vulnerable populations. To control water tariffs and increase equity in water distribution, State A decides to grant monopoly rights for water distribution to a government-supported enterprise. To effect this grant of monopoly rights in compliance with GATS, State A will have to enter into negotiations for compensation (probably in the form of liberalization commitments in other service sectors) with, and provide compensation to, WTO members the service suppliers of which are adversely affected by State A's grant of monopoly rights in the water distribution sector.
>
> *Bilateral Investment Treaty*
>
> If State A is a state party to bilateral investment treaties with the countries the service suppliers of which are affected by State A's granting of monopoly rights in the water distribution section, State A will, in all likelihood, be subject to rules on the expropriation of foreign direct investment in connection with the granting of monopoly rights. Thus, under such treaties, State A will have to provide the foreign service suppliers affected with prompt, adequate, and effective compensation for the assets and investments rendered unprofitable by the granting of the monopoly rights. This outcome holds whether or not State A made specific commitments under GATS for the service sector affected.

The generally applicable procedural duties in GATS require providing information, establishing governmental procedures, negotiating, consulting, and cooperating in specified circumstances. The most important of these procedural duties for health policy are the duties to engage in multilateral negotiations on disciplines for domestic regulations (Article VI:4), emergency safeguards (Article X:1), government procurement of services (Article XIII:2), and subsidies for service suppliers (Article XV).

Among these provisions, Article VI:4 has been the most controversial. Article VI:4 obliges WTO members to engage in negotiations in the Council for Trade in Services to develop disciplines on licensing, qualification, and technical standard regulations. Such disciplines shall aim to ensure that regulations are: (1) based on objective and transparent criteria; (2) not more burdensome than necessary to

FIGURE 5.7 Procedural Duties

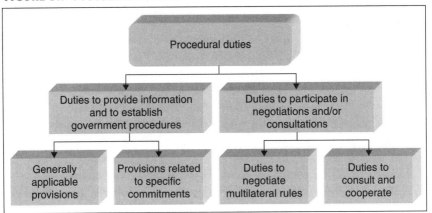

ensure the quality of the service; and (3) in the case of licensing procedures, not in themselves a restriction on the supply of a service (Article VI:4). The requirement that domestic regulations be no more burdensome than necessary to ensure the quality of the service raises public health concerns because it may limit WTO members' freedom to establish regulations to attain other legitimate objectives, such as equity in access to health-relates services.

At present, Article VI:4 poses no direct threat to health policy because no discussions on adopting such disciplines for a health-related service have occurred or, to our knowledge, been proposed. Health ministries of WTO members should be vigilant, however, about the Article VI:4 process because health-related services could be affected by the development of disciplines under this provision. The same vigilance is in order in connection with negotiations to formulate multilateral disciplines on government procurement, subsidies, and emergency safeguards.

Conclusion on General Obligations under GATS

Overall, in terms of the general obligations and disciplines of GATS, their present impact on health policy is not particularly troubling. The general obligations that are universally binding are not large in number or particularly worrying for health policy. The low level of specific commitments made in health-related sectors to date mitigates the effect of the general obligations linked to specific commitments. More concerns are likely to arise in the future, however, as the level and nature of specific commitments in health-related sectors increases and as WTO members negotiate additional multilateral disciplines on trade in services.

The Rules on Specific Commitments and Progressive Liberalization

The Relationship between the Second Pillar and the First and Third Pillars of GATS' Legal Architecture

The second pillar of GATS' architecture contains the rules governing the making of specific commitments on market access and national treatment. Market access commitments represent undertakings by a WTO member to remove barriers to foreign participation in domestic markets for services. National treatment commitments constitute pledges that a WTO member state will treat like foreign and domestic services and service suppliers the same.

For many experts, the rules on specific commitments reflect the flexibility and discretion that GATS allows WTO members to retain in calibrating where and how much to liberalize trade in services. However, this perspective obscures the fact that the freedom and flexibility WTO members have to make specific commitments change once specific commitments are made, perhaps locking WTO members into liberalization commitments that may turn out to be bad policy moves.

Specific commitments made concerning market access and national treatment connect to the first pillar of GATS—the general obligations—because, under the MFN principle, the treatment provided for in specific commitments must be accorded to all WTO members on a nondiscriminatory basis (Box 5.5). Thus, even though a WTO member makes a specific commitment in response to a request from one WTO member, the MFN principle makes that specific commitment apply to all WTO members.

Box 5.5: Link between the MFN Principle and Specific Commitments

Market access	National treatment
A specific commitment on market access means that all other WTO members can attempt to take advantage of the market access opportunities provided in the specific commitment on a nondiscriminatory basis.	A specific commitment on national treatment means that the WTO member making the commitment must treat all services and service suppliers from WTO members in the committed sector no less favorably than like domestic services or service suppliers.

Further, the flexibility of the specific commitment provisions cannot be isolated from the duty to participate in successive negotiating rounds to progressively liberalize trade in services—the third pillar of GATS' architecture. Although the legal duty to enter into successive negotiating rounds contains nothing directly threatening to health policy, this duty will feed into the politics of progressive liberalization efforts. The political dynamic created by the duty to negotiate progressive liberalization may, over time, be detrimental to a government's ability to provide and regulate public-interest services such as health.

Health ministries have not historically been influential actors in the process of making trade policy in developed or developing countries. The danger that trade ministries insufficiently aware of the complexities of health policy could make specific commitments in health-related services is significant. The present low level of specific commitments on health-related services and the lack of sustained interest in the liberalization of trade in such services to date on the part of WTO members provide no guarantee that future negotiating rounds will not increase pressure on WTO members to make more specific commitments on health-related services.

The Challenge of the "List It or Lose It" Process in Making Specific Commitments

For these reasons, understanding the rules on the making of market access and national treatment commitments is important from a health policy perspective. Of central concern are tensions these rules create between the freedom to make specific commitments and the disciplines applied to specific commitments made.

For example, if a WTO member makes a market access commitment in a service sector, the entire sector is opened to foreign participation except with regard to market access restrictions the WTO member lists in its schedule of specific commitments (GATS, Article XVI:1-2). Thus, when making market access commitments, a WTO member must list any measures restricting market access that it wishes to apply in the future in that sector.

The same "list it or lose it" process exists in the rules on making national treatment commitments: a WTO member must list on its schedule any measures that violate the national treatment principle that the member wants to use in that sector in the future (GATS, Article XVII). Box 5.6 describes the measures that a WTO member must list on its schedule when making specific commitments on market access or national treatment.

Box 5.6: Measures to "List or Lose" in Making Specific Commitments	
Specific Commitment Area	**Measures**
Market access commitments (exhaustive list)	1. Limitations on: • the number of service suppliers • the total value of service transactions or assets • the total number of service operations or on the total quantity of service output • the total number of natural persons that may be employed in a service • the participation of foreign capital 2. Measures that restrict or require specific types of legal entity or joint venture through which a service supplier may supply a service.
National treatment commitments (nonexhaustive list)	Subsidy measures, tax measures, national requirements, residency requirements, licensing and qualification requirements, registration requirements, authorization requirements, technology transfer requirements, local content requirements, ownership of property or land.

Modifying a Schedule of Specific Commitments

A WTO member that makes a specific commitment and later wishes to change or withdraw such commitment must generally provide compensation to the WTO members who would be affected by such modifications (Figure 5.8). The compensation would most likely be in the form of liberalized specific commitments in other service sectors. The compensation requirement may chill legitimate regulatory changes in sectors subject to specific commitments and freeze in place policies that have not proven beneficial.

The Challenges Created by the Specific Commitment Rules and Process

The GATS rules on making specific commitments require that WTO members exercise great care and foresight in listing the types of access restrictions or

FIGURE 5.8 Modifying Specific Commitments

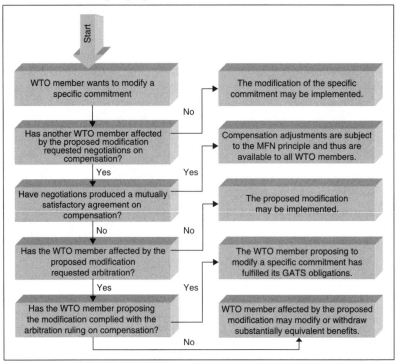

national-treatment restrictions they want to maintain or adopt in the future. The broad scopes of GATS and health policy combine to create challenges for WTO members seeking to appropriately calibrate moves to increase market access and/or national treatment in health-related services while retaining needed regulatory tools and policy flexibility.

Market Access and Health Policy

From a health policy perspective, measures that restrict market access may be more important than measures that restrict national treatment, which gives the market access rules particular importance for health policy. Restricting market access may serve legitimate health policy objectives, such as limitations on the number of service suppliers in a geographical area based on an economic needs test.

Caution is also in order concerning specific commitments on national treatment. On the one hand, the ability to discriminate as between a foreign service supplier and a like domestic service supplier in violation of the national treatment principle does not appear to be a regulatory power required for robust and effective health policy. On the other hand, experience under other international trade agreements liberalizing trade in services indicates that countries have explicitly excluded health services from the national treatment principle (e.g., Canada's exclusion of health services from NAFTA's national treatment principle).

The Scheduling of Specific Commitments

Dangers for health policy also arise in the complex process of scheduling market access and national treatment commitments. The schedules form part of the binding rules of the treaty and, as noted above, GATS offers little flexibility to modify schedules of specific commitments. These rules increase the pressure on WTO members to undertake the complex and difficult scheduling process with little margin for error.

Although the heart of the scheduling process involves decisions about whether to make binding liberalization commitments, the complicated scheduling process poses its own difficulties about which health ministries must be aware and vigilant if specific commitments in health-related services are made. Key to such awareness and vigilance will be formulating for health-related services potentially subject to specific commitments a clear understanding of: (1) the regulatory "footprint" for such services; (2) the demographic, economic, and technological trends affecting such services; and (3) the potential social and equity implications of making the proposed commitments.

The Unilateral Liberalization Option

WTO members can liberalize trade in health-related services unilaterally, if they wish, without accepting binding commitments in their national GATS schedules of specific commitments. Such unilateral liberalization would allow WTO members to experiment with such policies in a way that permits them to reverse course on market access or national treatment if the experiment produces unsatisfactory results. The reversal of a unilateral liberalization of trade in health-related services would not be subject to GATS rules on providing compensation to WTO members affected by the change in market access or national treatment. For WTO members also bound by bilateral or regional treaties affecting trade in services, unilateral liberalization policies may have greater legal significance than under GATS.

Exceptions to General Obligations and Specific Commitments

GATS provides general and specific exceptions to general obligations and specific commitments (Figure 5.9). If their conditions are met, such exceptions would justify a violation of a WTO member's general obligations or specific commitments.

FIGURE 5.9 Exceptions to General Obligations and Specific Commitments

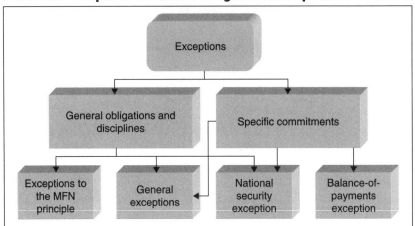

From a health policy perspective, the most important exception is Article XIV(b), the general exception for measures related to the protection of health. Article XIV(b) justifies measures that violate a GATS obligation if such measures are "necessary to protect human, animal, or plant life or health." In addition, measures that satisfy Article XIV(b) must also pass the tests contained in the introductory paragraph of Article XIV: the measure cannot be "applied in a manner which would constitute a means of arbitrary or unjustifiable discrimination between countries where like conditions prevail, or a disguised restriction on trade in services." Figure 5.10 describes the process through which a measure would be analyzed under Article XIV(b).

The burdens imposed by the necessity test of Article XIV(b) and the introductory paragraph of Article XIV on WTO members who seek to justify violations are substantial. The necessity test requires that the measure in question be the least trade-restrictive measure reasonably available to the WTO member. In *EC— Asbestos*, the WTO Appellate Body held that, in cases involving measures designed to protect human health—a value that "is both vital and important in the highest degree," the potential effectiveness of less trade-restrictive alternative measures will be strictly scrutinized because of the significance of protecting human health.[8] This strict scrutiny doctrine provides a basis for defending noncompliant measures that seek to protect human health. The strict scrutiny doctrine may not, however, be sufficient to bring noncompliant health measures within the ambit of Article XIV(b) in all circumstances.[9]

The tests imposed by the introductory paragraph of Article XIV create another least-trade restrictive test: the noncompliant measure must be applied in a manner that is the least-trade restrictive way to apply the measure reasonably available

FIGURE 5.10 Article XIV(b) Process

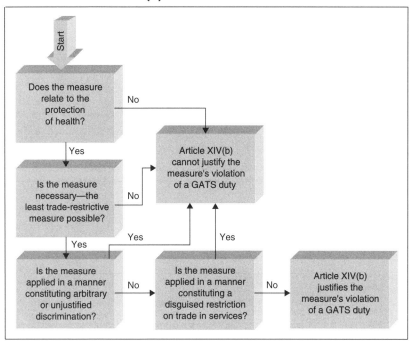

to the WTO member. The necessity test in Article XIV(b) focuses on the substance of the noncompliant measure in question, while the introductory paragraph evaluates the way in which the WTO member applies such measure.

Current Status of Specific Commitments in Health-Related Service Sectors and Current Negotiations

Concerns about GATS' complexity raise questions about the extent to which WTO members have made specific commitments in health-related services. Published literature indicates that the level of specific market access and national treatment commitments in health-related services has been, to date, quite low (see Chapters 4 and 11). WTO and WHO jointly concluded, for example, that "all information to date suggests that current patterns and levels of health services trade are occurring irrespective of GATS.... The overall effect of GATS on trade in health services is thus likely to have remained negligible to date."[10]

Data on aggregate levels of specific commitments in key health-related services demonstrate that the level of commitment is low. Aggregate data on specific commitments in connection with health-related services are not, however, very useful.

First, such aggregate data do not reflect how any given WTO member has shaped its commitments in a service sector. Second, the absence of specific commitments under GATS tells one nothing about whether a WTO member is or is not open to foreign services and service suppliers. Many countries that have made no specific commitments in health-related services already engage in extensive international trade in such services; they simply have not bound themselves under GATS in connection with such trade.

These observations about the limitations of aggregate analysis of specific commitments in health-related services reveal again the complexity created by the structure and dynamics of the process of scheduling specific commitments. Focused and detailed analysis of a WTO member's specific commitments in health-related service sectors would be required to make informed judgments about whether and how such commitments affect that WTO member's health policy.

The fourth pillar of GATS' architecture is its institutional framework. This framework involves the Council on Trade in Services and the WTO dispute settlement mechanism. The Council on Trade in Services is important because it is the forum for the implementation of the treaty and its future development. The WTO dispute settlement mechanism enhances the importance of WTO rules in every field of policy they touch, including the relationship between GATS and health. The actual impact of the WTO dispute settlement process on health policy depends, however, on many factors, including the facts of the case, what GATS principles are under review, and how the parties to the dispute argue their legal positions.

Rulings in other contexts demonstrate that the WTO dispute settlement mechanism will not adopt a deferential attitude toward WTO members, arguing that their behavior protects human health. At the same time, these rulings suggest that the WTO dispute settlement process is capable of producing rulings that recognize the importance of protecting human health within a system designed to liberalize international trade. Health policy is subject to WTO disciplines across many different agreements. The WTO dispute settlement mechanism, and its application to GATS, heightens the importance of GATS from the perspective of health policy, making familiarity with WTO jurisprudence on GATS critical to health policy in the future.

In addition to the text of GATS, health policy experts have to address the ongoing "GATS 2000" round of negotiations on further liberalization of trade in services. At the date of this writing, WTO members were formulating positions on the GATS 2000 negotiations, which are anticipated to accelerate in the coming months. The Council for Trade in Services' guidelines for the GATS 2000 negotiations are, thus, important for health policy's management of this process. The guidelines provide, for example, that "[t]here shall be no a priori exclusion of any service sector or mode of supply"[11] from the GATS 2000 negotiations, meaning that all health-related services are in play in these negotiations. The GATS 2000 negotiations, and parallel negotiations on disciplines for domestic regulation, emergency safeguards, government procurement, and subsidies, may more significantly shape the relationship between GATS and health policy than the existing GATS general obligations and specific commitments made to date.

Making the Health Policy Voice Heard: Lessons from Other WTO Agreements

The importance of the GATS 2000 negotiations in determining the future relationship of GATS and health policy raises questions on identifying the most effective ways of balancing the GATS project of liberalization of trade in services with the need for sufficient space and flexibility for health policy. Lessons learned from the health policy experience with other WTO agreements, especially TRIPS, may be helpful in answering these questions.

Experience in other WTO contexts demonstrates that raising the profile of health policy in international trade law has not been an easy or harmonious project. Cases establishing the health-related jurisprudence of the WTO dispute settlement process, such as *EC—Asbestos* and *EC—Hormones*,[12] were controversial disputes in which panels and the Appellate Body confronted difficult interpretive issues. The debate over TRIPS between and among state and nonstate actors was intense even in a context where the treaty in question allowed WTO members to use, for example, the safeguards of compulsory licensing and parallel importing for health policy purposes.

The extent to which health policy has been recognized as important in WTO agreements relates to the level of legal, health policy, and political mobilization that occurred in these cases and diplomatic disputes. Those interested in health policy's future in the face of globalization and trade liberalization face the challenge of mobilizing their efforts in a sophisticated manner on a sustained basis within multiple WTO contexts. The TRIPS controversy involves the successful mobilization of legal, health policy, and political resources, arguments, and personnel by governments and NGOs to confront perceived threats to the public-health safeguards of compulsory licensing and parallel importing. Similar mobilization in the context of GATS may be required for health policy to have and maintain a sustainable, influential voice in the process of liberalization of trade in health-related services.

In addition to GATS, health experts concerned about the impact of the liberalization in trade in health-related services should also analyze the impact on health policy of other international trade and investment agreements. Although GATS has been the subject of much attention, in many respects regional, subregional, and bilateral trade and investment agreements that cover services contain more aggressive liberalization provisions than does GATS. From this perspective, GATS is not at the cutting edge of liberalization of trade in services either substantively or in dispute-settlement procedures. More attention should be paid to the impact on health policy of these regional, subregional, and bilateral trade and investment agreements that liberalize trade in services. The acceleration of the negotiation and conclusion of bilateral and regional trade agreements expected in the wake of the failed WTO ministerial meeting at Cancún reinforces the importance of focusing more attention on these kinds of agreements.

International legal analysis of GATS from a health policy perspective demonstrates that the relationship between the agreement and health policy may be most significantly shaped by: (1) the ongoing and subsequent efforts to progressively liberalize trade in health-related services; and (2) the negotiation of further multilateral disciplines on domestic regulatory powers. The challenge for health policy communities is to manage this international legal process in an informed and sophisticated manner in order to ensure that the evolving law of GATS recognizes and respects WTO members' rights to promote and protect health.

Notes

The chapter is based on *Legal Review of the General Agreement on Trade in Services (GATS) from a Health Policy Perspective* (Geneva: WHO, 2005, in press), prepared by the GATS Legal Review Team for the World Health Organization. The views expressed in this chapter are those of the authors only and do not represent the views or positions of the World Health Organization or any of its presonnel.

1. See WHO, 1983, Article 3 (disease notification requirements) and Article 23 (health measures prescribed in IHR are the maximum measures WHO members may take for protecting their territories against the diseases subject to the IHR). After this chapter was completed for publication, the WHO adopted the new International Health Regulations. See WHO, 2005b.

2. See U.N., 1966, International Covenant on Economic, Social, and Cultural Rights, United Nations Treaty Series 3, Article 12 (the right of everyone to the enjoyment of the highest attainable standard of physical and mental health); U.N. Committee on Economic, Social and Cultural Rights, 2000, General Comment 14, The Right to the Highest Attainable Standard of Health.

3. WHO, 2003, p. 7. As of this writing, the WHO-led effort to revise the IHR to make them more effective against global disease threats was continuing.

4. U.N. Special Rapporteur, 2003, ¶39.

5. GATT, 1990.

6. EC, 2001.

7. WTO, 2002 (quoting WTO Director-General and Chairman of the WTO Services Negotiations as asserting that government services were excluded from the GATS negotiations).

8. EC, 2001 ¶¶172–175.

9. The panel ruling in *US—Gambling* supports this observation. In this GATS case, the panel acknowledged that the interests and values the United States was trying to protect with a measure not in compliance with GATS were "vital and important in the highest degree"; but the panel held that the noncompliant measure was not necessary under GATS Articles XIV(a) and (c) because the United States had not exhausted alternative measures that would have been GATS compliant (¶¶6.533–6.534, 6.564–6.565). United States, 2004 (unadopted as of the time of this writing).

10. WHO/WTO, 2002.

11. WTO Council for Trade in Services, 2001, ¶5.

12. EC, 1998.

References and Further Reading

Adlung, R., and A. Carzaniga. 2001. Health services under the General Agreement on Trade in Services. *Bulletin of the World Health Organization* 79(4): 352–364.

Chandra, R. 2002. Trade in health services. *Bulletin of the World Health Organization* 80(2): 158–361.

EC (European Communities). 1998. European communities—measures concerning meat and meat products (hormones), Appellate Body Report, WT/DS26/AB/R and WT/DS48/AB/R, Feb. 13, 1998.

———. 2001.European Communities—Measures affecting asbestos and asbestos-containing products, Appellate Body Report, WTO Doc. WT/DS135/AB/R (*EC—Asbestos*), Mar. 12, 2001.

Fidler, D.P., and C. Correa. 2005. "GATS and health-related services: The WTO decision in *US—Gambling:* Implications for health policy. *Trade and Health Notes,* WHO (June).

Fidler, D.P., C. Correa, and O. Aginam. 2005. *Legal review of the General Agreement on Trade in Services (GATS) from a health policy perspective.* Geneva: World Health Organization, in press.

GATT (General Agreement on Tariffs and Trade.) 1990. Thailand—restrictions on importation of and internal taxes on cigarettes, GATT Doc. DS10/R, BISD 37S/200, Nov. 7, 1990.

Hilary, J. 2001. *The wrong model: GATS, liberalization and children's right to health.* London: Save the Children.

Krajewski, M. 2003. Public services and trade liberalization: Mapping the legal framework. *Journal of international economic law* 6(2): 341–367.

PAHO/WHO (Pan American Health Organization/World Health Organization). 2002. *Trade in health services: Global, regional, and country perspectives.* Washington, D.C.

Sinclair, S., and J. Grieshaber-Otto. 2002. *Facing the facts: A guide to the GATS debate.* Ottawa: Canadian Centre for Policy Alternatives.

U.N. (United Nations). 1966. International covenant on economic, social, and cultural rights. U.N. Doc. A/6316 (1966), 993 UNTS 3, Jan. 3, 1976.

U.N. Committee on Economic, Social and Cultural Rights. 2000. General comment 14, The right to the highest attainable standard of health, U.N. Doc. E/C.12/2000/4 (2000), May 11, 2000.

U.N. Special Rapporteur. 2003. Report of the Special Rapporteur on the right of everyone to the enjoyment of the highest attainable standard of physical and mental health. E/CN.4/2003/58, Feb. 13, 2003, ¶ 39.

United States. 2004. United States—measures affecting cross-border supply of gambling and betting services, panel report, issued Nov. 10, 2004. WT/DS285/R.

Woodruffe, J., and C. Joy. 2002. *Out of service: The development dangers of the General Agreement on Trade in Services.* London: World Development Movement.

WHO (World Health Organization). 1983. *International health regulations (1969),* 3rd ann. ed. Geneva.

———. 2003. *Severe acute respiratory syndrome (SARS): Status of the outbreak and lessons for the future.* Geneva.

WHO/WTO. 2002. *WTO agreements and public health—a joint study by the WHO and the WTO Secretariat.* Geneva.

WTO (World Trade Organization). 2001. *GATS fact and fiction.* Geneva.

———. 2002. Director-General of WTO and Chairman of WTO services negotiations reject misguided claims that public services are under threat. Press release 299, June 28.

———. 2005a. United States—Measures affecting the cross-border supply of gambling and betting services, AB-2005-1, appellate body report. WTO Doc. WT/DS285/AB/R, Apr. 7.

———. 2005b. Revision of the international health regulations, World Healthy Assembly resolution. WHA58.3, May 23.

WTO Council for Trade in Services. 2001.Guidelines and procedures for the negotiations on trade in services. WTO Doc. S/L/93, Mar. 2001, para. 5.

6

ECONOMIC DIMENSIONS AND IMPACT ASSESSMENT OF GATS TO PROMOTE AND PROTECT HEALTH

Chantal Blouin

Impact Assessment of Trade Liberalization in Health Services

The existing theoretical and empirical literature on trade in services generally points at the positive economic impact of decreasing and eliminating barriers to foreign services suppliers. Indeed, available empirical studies tend to confirm that there are net welfare gains achieved through liberalization in services (Hoekman and Primo Braga, 1997; Dee and Hanslow, 2001; Brown et al., 2002). The largest welfare gains to be made from liberalization seem to be focused in finance, business services, and telecommunications, as these are key inputs into all sectors of the economy (Konan and Maskus, 2004). Moreover, the economic benefits of trade liberalization are not limited to the short-term allocative efficiency gain of removing barriers for foreign services providers. The long-term impacts of trade liberalization on economic growth are believed to be much larger than the static ones. While there are few empirical studies on the impact of services liberalization on economic growth, recent works on liberalization in telecommunications and

Chantal Blouin is a senior researcher at the North-South Institute. The author would like to thank Aadytia Mattoo, Richard Smith, Nick Drager, and Ron Labonte for their useful comments, and Kristina Maud Bergeron for her research assistance in the preparation of this chapter financial services supported the view that openness in services influences long-run growth performance (Mattoo et al., 2001).

The question, then, for policymakers is to what extent the conclusions and policy recommendations derived from the general findings on the benefits of liberalization in services are applicable to health services and insurance. Indeed, the health sector is usually considered distinct from other service sectors, not only because of the several market failures peculiar to it, but also because of the strong equity consideration linked to health. This revealed preference places health as a constraint on the objective of policy reform; when considering ways of maximizing economic welfare, such as trade liberalization in services, policymakers have to ensure they at least do not decrease access or provision of health services.[1] However, it can be difficult for policymakers to assess whether or not liberalization in health services will improve access to health services and to what extent it will contribute to economic welfare. This chapter presents a framework to use in assessing the impact of such policy reforms.

How can policymakers weigh their policy options? One possibility is to conduct an impact assessment of the reform under consideration. In recent years, the European Commission hired consultants to develop a methodology to conduct a sustainability impact assessment (SIA) of trade negotiations (Kirkpatrick and Lee, 2002; see also Bisset et al., 2003 for application). We present this methodology and how it can be applied in health services.

The sustainability impact assessment developed by Kirkpatrick and Lee includes four stages:

1. **Screening and scoping:** Which trade measures are under assessment? What are the trade policy scenarios to be investigated? Is the analysis to be undertaken at the country level or regional level or by other groupings of countries? This stage also identifies the key sustainability (economic, social, and environmental) issues associated with the trade measures. These indicators include core and second-tier indicators; the latter are components or possible measurements of the core indicators. They are presented in the Annex at the end of this chapter.
2. **Impact assessment:** This stage traces analytically and empirically the main causal effects of a trade reform. Causal chain analysis (CCA) is used to identify the links between the proposed reform and its eventual impacts. The explanation of the causal chain analysis is based on theoretical reasoning and interpretation of the existing evidence. Available evidence to be used includes quantitative and qualitative assessment tools.
3. **Assessment of flanking measures**: This stage identifies alternative measures that might be adopted to avoid or minimize adverse impacts and enhance beneficial impacts.

4. **Monitoring and post-evaluation**: This stage identifies how the outcomes of the trade reform will be monitored and evaluated. They recommend that monitoring engage key stakeholders, that it be focused and strategic in nature to avoid unnecessary data collection and analysis, and that it be "sufficiently independent and transparent to ensure the objectivity and credibility of its findings" (Kirkpatrick and Lee, 2002, p.18).

The remainder of this chapter examines how policymakers in developing countries can use this impact assessment methodology to guide their decisions in the health sector. It applies this methodology by focusing on the economic and health impacts of trade liberalization in health services and insurance.

Screening and Scoping

Measures under Assessment

Based on the classification used at the WTO, liberalization in health services mainly affects five subsectors: (1) medical and dental services, (2) services provided by midwives, nurses, physiotherapists, and paramedical personnel (both under the professional services category), (3) hospital services, (4) other health services (under the category of health-related services), and (5) health insurance (under the life, accident, and health insurance services in the financial services category).

International transactions in each of these subsectors can be subjected to a variety of restrictions. National governments can limit the practice of foreign physicians and nurses in their territory. They can forbid foreign investors to own a hospital or a clinic. The list below identifies the main trade barriers found in health services for each mode of supply that a government can consider liberalizing, as well as some of the general restrictions on trade that can directly affect the sector.

Mode 1—Cross-border Supply With the growth of information and communications technologies, the cross-border supply of health services is made increasingly feasible and convenient. For instance, telemedical services such as diagnostic or advisory services can be offered using communications networks without the physical movement of the patients or the provider. Currently, some of the principal areas of application are e-education in health, health information such as databases of medical literature, and health information websites for physicians and the general public (Singh, 2002). However, the electronic supply of health-related services is only beginning in developing countries, except for medical transcription, medical insurance and claims processing, and back-office services, which are becoming an increasingly large export industry in India and the Philippines (Singh, 2003). We should note that, in the GATS, these health education and health data processing and storage services are not classified under health services, but under education and computer-related services, respectively.

Measures under assessment in trade reforms affecting the cross-border supply of health services could be measures that would ban cross-border supply (market access) or would treat foreign health providers differently than national providers (national treatment). For instance, the public health insurance system could agree to reimburse telemedical services provided by physicians in the same country, but not services provided by physicians located abroad. We should note that some of the important obstacles to this type of trade are not linked to trade policy per se but to other issues, such as the legal uncertainty concerning the recognition of the contractual transactions taking place electronically or related to consumer protection against malpractice (Singh, 2003).

Mode 2—Consumption Abroad The key restrictions on consumption abroad in health services are the restrictions governments can place on the movement of their own nationals, more specifically, rules regarding public health insurance portability. Can patients get reimbursement from their health insurer for services received abroad? If their insurer is a private actor, the question is not covered by the GATS. But if the government provides health insurance to its citizens and does not allow payment for services received outside the country, this can be construed as a barrier to international transactions in health services and will be covered by the GATS. As we can see in the Annex at the end of this chapter, many OECD countries limit the portability of their public insurance to emergency situations occurring during foreign travel and do not cover elective care their citizens receive abroad.

The key concern for developing countries interested in attracting patients from abroad is to negotiate and gain commitments from other WTO members, especially industrial countries, regarding cross-border portability of insurance. In this case, the decision for the policymakers is not to remove their own restrictions to trade, but whether to invest political capital in the negotiations of such concessions by others.

Mode 3—Commercial Presence There are a number of general and sector-specific restrictions that can be placed on foreign investment in health services. Some of the most common horizontal restrictions on investment identified by the OECD are listed below (OECD, 2000, p. 39).

- Full foreign ownership not permitted, joint venture with local partner mandatory
- Foreign ownership approval based on policy guidelines and overall national interest considerations
- Foreign investment approval based on economic needs test or "net national benefit" criteria
- Foreign investment approval subject to agreeing to specific performance requirements, e.g., export achievements; use of local goods, services, or personnel; transfer of technology
- Only acquisition of existing companies permitted, with foreign equity limited to minority stake
- Reservation of some sectors or activities, for investment only by nationals
- Restrictions on acquisition of land
- Restrictions on composition of boards of directors
- Requirement to grant more favorable treatment to economically disadvantaged groups or regions.

In their analysis of WTO members' commitments in health services, Adlung and Carzaniga have noted that Mode 3 and Mode 4 are where most of the restrictions to trade services can be found in the GATS schedule of commitments (Drager and Vieira, 2002, p.28). One can find a number of health sector-specific restrictions on foreign investment:

- Economic needs test for foreign investment in hospital services
- The right to restrict the commercial incorporation of foreign health care providers to natural persons
- Restrictions on foreign equity participation and on permissible types of legal incorporation
- The right to require foreign-owned facilities to train nationals
- Restrictions on foreign investment in insurance services.

Mode 4—Presence of Natural Persons In Mode 4, as in Mode 2, the measures under assessment are mostly restrictions in the markets of export of interest to developing countries, especially industrialized markets. Generally, in Mode 4, these restrictions on cross-border movement are horizontal restrictions, derived from general immigration and labor market policies. "Common examples are specific conditions of approval for entry of service suppliers including: labour market testing, residency requirements for intra-corporate transferees, and requirement that the foreign company employ specific numbers of local staff; authorization subject to non-availability of locals or to performance requirements" (Bisset et al., 2003, p.10).

Other restrictions that are especially relevant to health professionals are related to the registration and certification of skilled workers. These restrictions are usually based on legitimate concerns about the qualifications of professionals, but can also be seen as obstacles to the freer flow of services providers.

Trade Policy Scenarios

The GATS provided that new negotiations on services would start in 2000, with the view of achieving progressive liberalization and gradual improvement of market access in services. No sectors are a priori excluded from the negotiations, but the agreement acknowledges that liberalization shall take place with due respect for national policy objectives and the level of development of each member. Thus, developing countries are expected to open fewer sectors, liberalize fewer types of transactions, and, when gradually opening their markets to foreign suppliers, attach conditions aimed at strengthening their domestic services capacity (Article 19 of GATS). Developing countries are not obligated to liberalize the health sector, as their liberalization effort can concentrate on other sectors. The base scenario is that the national governments would maintain the existing restrictions on international trade in health services, these restrictions varying from one country to another. The preceding list of measures under assessment provided an overview of their diversity. The trade policy scenario under consideration is the removal of the main restrictions on trade in health services and the adoption of GATS commitments reflecting these reforms.

Key Impact Indicators

The SIA methodology developed by Kirkpatrick and Lee identifies nine core indicators to assess the significance of the likely impacts of trade reforms on sustainable development (see the list in the Annex). The indicators focus on the following criteria to assess impact: the direction of change to baseline conditions; the nature, order of magnitude, geographical extent, and reversible duration of changes; and the regulatory and institutional capacity to implement mitigation and enhancing measures. In Table 6.1, we adapt their list of indicators to the health sector, focusing on the social impact indicators and on health indicators. These are the indicators discussed in the causal chain analysis. We should note that, in the case of the health impact indicators, national policymakers are best positioned to identify which particular indicators are the most relevant to their specific situations. For instance, if the measure under assessment has the potential to trigger an exodus of health professionals from rural areas to urban private hospitals, it will be crucial for the authorities to monitor this specific indicator of access to services.

TABLE 6.1 Impact Indicators

Impact	Indicators
Economic impact indicators	Income generated by foreign patients (*Mode 2*)
	Additional resources generated by foreign investment in health services and insurance (*Mode 3*)
	Remittances generated by the temporary movement of health professionals (*Mode 4*)
Health impact indicators	Indicators to monitor access to health services for the local population (e.g., percentage of population covered by private insurance, number of health facilities per region, number of consultations for pre- and postnatal care)
	Indicator to monitor access to health services for the poor (e.g., number of health professionals per capita in rural areas, number of births with skilled attendants in low-income households)
	Indicator of population health status (e.g., infant mortality rate, disability-adjusted life expectancy)
Process impact	Regulatory capacity

Causal Chain Analysis

The causal chain analysis used in the SIA methodology does not require original research; rather, it is based on reviewing the existing evidence and analysis on the impact of reform in the sector under assessment. The following analysis provides a general overview of the potential impacts of liberalization in health services, based on available research and knowledge as well as the country studies commissioned for this project. It attempts to provide a more detailed overview of the existing research relevant to liberalization through commercial presence (Mode 3).[2]

Mode 1—Cross-Border Supply

Telemedicine can offer many benefits to patients in developing countries. Patients, in particular in remote and regional areas, gain access to a wider range of services, including specialized services that may not be available in their own country. However, decisionmakers have to assess whether the investment in technologies necessary to build the physical infrastructure for such imports of services is done at the expense of more cost-effective health interventions.

In addition to removing measures that impede imports of health services through Mode 1, policymakers can also promote the exports of services, such as data entry of health records and health insurance claims, as a way to generate income and employment in their country, as has been done in India (Singh, 2003). (These services are classified under computer-related services.)

Mode 2—Consumption Abroad

Mode 2 covers consumers who travel abroad to receive medical care, tourists who incidentally need medical care while abroad, retirees abroad, temporary workers, cross-border commuters who may have multinational coverage options, and residents of multinational areas with integrated health systems. For the sake of this assessment, we focus on consumers who travel to developing countries expressly to receive care. Assuming that developing countries would spend negotiating capital on receiving commitments from industrial countries on health insurance portability (for example, in exchange for liberalization on foreign investment), what would be some of the potential impact on the national economy and health system of increased health tourism?

Health tourism is sometimes hailed as one sector where developing countries have services export potential. Their comparative advantage is based on a combination of lower costs and availability of qualified personnel, and, in some cases, natural settings (e.g., for convalescent care in resort centers). We still have limited information on what levels of revenue have been generated from these activities and no information on whether these incomes have been reallocated toward the public sector. Thus, we know that in Cuba, health tourism generated US$25 million of revenues in 1995–96 (Chanda, 2001). In Thailand, the government has been actively promoting the export of health services and encouraging foreigners to receive treatment and services in Thailand (see Box 6.1). It is estimated that the country received about one million foreign patients in public and private facilities in 2001 (see Pachanee and Suwit, 2003). It is also estimated that health tourism could bring an additional US$1.1 to 2.2 billion in annual revenue to India by 2012 (*The Economist*, 2004). Singapore hopes to generate US$3 billion a year of additional revenue by the same year (HSWG, 2003a). In addition to their impact on growth, these additional incomes can also have a more direct impact on health, as they can be harnessed to benefit the health system of the country in general and the poor in particular. For instance, they can be taxed and allocated to improve the supply and quality of services in the public sector. In theory, it is entirely possible to redistribute these resources in such a manner, as the GATS does not prevent taxation, even discriminatory taxation, i.e., additional taxation of facilities offering services to foreign patients, if there is no national treatment commitment made in this area.

Box 6.1: Foreign Hospitals and Foreign Patients in Thailand

In Thailand, in the early 1990s (until the economic crisis in 1997), one witnessed a mushrooming of urban private hospitals. Indeed, since the late 1980s, the government has had a policy of promoting trade in health services, even though Thailand has not committed to an open health services market in the GATS. This promotion policy has been implemented through the Board of Investment's (BOI) providing tax incentives to investment in private hospitals; as of 2002, 199 private hospitals in the country had benefited from this program.

Nevertheless, very few of these hospitals are under foreign ownership. Foreign investors can make a request to the Ministry of Commerce to be the major shareholders of health service facilities, but there have been no requests to that effect so far. The data on foreign investment in hospitals in Thailand is limited. A study by Janjaroen and Supakankunti (2002) found data available on six large hospitals (with ≥300 beds); the foreign direct investment in these hospitals accounted for only three percent of the total investment in these hospitals. A survey by the National Statistical Office in 2001 found that there were 24 hospitals nationwide (7.36 percent), mainly in Bangkok, having foreign shares (see table below). The countries of origin were Japan, followed by Singapore, China, Europe, and the United States. Moreover, there are 13 private Thai hospitals in the stock market currently open for foreign investment.

Trade in hospital services under Mode 3 may be very limited, but trade through the movement of patients to Thailand is in great expansion. The Thai health care system is attractive to foreign patients because of its high quality, its hospitable atmosphere, and lower prices. In the year 2001, the Department

Current Foreign Investment in Private Hospitals in Thailand

Location/ Region	Without foreign investment		With foreign investment				
				Hospital size (beds)			
	Number	Percent	Total	<50	51–100	101–200	>200
Bangkok	48	77.2	14	1	5	3	5
Central	117	95.90	5	—	2	1	2
Northeast	42	93.33	3	—	3	—	—
North	59	96.71	2	—	—	1	1
South	36	100.00	—	—	—	—	—
Total	302	92.64	24	1	10	5	8

Source: National Statistical Office in Buddhasri, 2003.

(Continued)

> **Box 6.1: Foreign Hospitals and Foreign Patients in Thailand (Continued)**
>
> of Export Promotion, Ministry of Commerce, carried out a survey of 20 private hospitals that were known to cater to foreign patients (Pachanee and Wibulpolprasert, 2003). For the seven hospitals that responded, it was found that there were 470,000 foreign patients, a 38 percent increase from 2000. Most patients come from Japan, the United States, Taiwan, the United Kingdom, and Australia. Moreover, there is an increasing trend from the Middle East and other Asian countries. It is estimated that in 2001, foreign patients in all public and private facilities amounted to about one million.
>
> The current government is pursuing a policy of further promoting the export of health services to foreigners, targeting a 15 percent increase in 2003. To reach this target, improvement of service quality is highly needed. The hospital accreditation given by the Institute of Hospital Quality Improvement and Accreditation (HA-Thailand) is one of the measures for ensuring standard health care quality. To date, there are 50 hospitals accredited nationwide, of which 10 are private hospitals. In addition, the government also promotes other health-related services that are regarded as niche areas in this sector, for instances, health spas, long stays, and Thai traditional medicine (including Thai traditional massage). For health spas, the government and the Spa Association will provide accreditation to the spa facilities that meet all required standards to ensure adequate quality of services. For the long-stay program, Thai Longstay Management Corporation Ltd. was established in September 2002. Foreigners, particularly the elderly, are encouraged to visit Thailand, stay for a longer period, and participate in several activities, such as medical examinations, sports and recreation, and Thai cooking classes.
>
> What are the direct consequences of the growing influx of foreign patients? The resources used to service one foreigner may be equivalent to those used to service four or five Thais. Thus, the workload is equivalent to three to four million Thai patients. This was equivalent to about three percent of the total workload of the system in 2001. If growth continues at the current rate, the workload for servicing foreign patients may go up to 12 percent of the total workload in five years. This means a requirement of about an additional 3,000 full-time equivalent doctors for urban private hospitals. It also raises the problem of the shift of human resources from the rural public to the urban private service sectors.
>
> *Source:* Pachanee and Wibulpolprasert, 2003.

Another potential benefit of health tourism is to improve the range and the quality of services offered in a country. Indeed, in order to attract foreign patients, developing countries have to offer quality services, which often involve an upgrading of human and physical resources (Adams and Kinnon, 1998, p.42). If these service providers and facilities are available to local patients as well as foreign patients, an improvement in the quality of care in the country in general can be achieved. Moreover, the creation of centers of medical excellence to attract foreign patients may also help limit the brain drain of qualified medical personnel abroad.

The potential benefits of exporting health services have to be weighed against the potential risks of liberalizing this sector. Thus, health tourism can lead to a dual market structure within the health care system, with one higher quality, expensive segment catering to wealthy nationals and foreigners and a lower quality segment with limited resources offering services to the rest of the population (Chanda, 2001). For instance, the growth of health tourism in Singapore may exacerbate the existing disparity in the distribution of medical personnel and expertise between the public and the private sectors. About 48 percent of the physicians work in the public sector and admit almost 80 percent of all inpatients, whereas the private sector admits only about a quarter of the inpatients with more doctors (HSWP, 2003b, p. 8). One way to remedy the problems linked to the dual structure is to facilitate the use of private hospitals by nationals by making the government's health care subsidy portable, to be used in the hospital of the patient's choice.

Another key concern with exports of health services from developing countries is the problem of internal brain drain, where physicians and nurses from the public sector or offering services to rural areas move to the facilities offering care to foreign patients. The case of Thailand provides an example of such a problem. If the influx of foreign patients continues at the current rate, the workload for servicing foreign patients may go up to 12 percent of the total workload in five years. This will require an additional 3,000 full-time equivalent doctors for urban private hospitals, further exacerbating the shortage of health professionals in the rural areas.

Mode 3—Commercial Presence

Trade in health services in developing countries can take the form of inflows of foreign investment in hospital services, management, or insurance. Such imports of health services, based on the establishment of the foreign providers in the country, can have a number of potential positive consequences. First, this inflow of foreign capital provides additional resources to invest in the health care infrastructure and services of the country. The most direct beneficiaries of liberalization are the households who can afford the services offered by foreign suppliers. But the benefits go beyond the direct impact for patients receiving the services from the foreign providers, and can have systemwide impacts. They can take the form of access to new technologies and services, information, and management techniques.

In Chile, competition among public and private providers of health services led to the rapid growth of the supply of new high-technology services (See Box 6.2). Competition coming from foreign actors can also lead to similar positive outcomes. In Indonesia, revenues coming from private wings supported by foreign investment in teaching hospitals cross-subsidize specialized services offered to the general population (see Box 4.1 in Chapter 4). Foreign investors can also bring with them new health management techniques and approaches, which can have a national impact through imitation and competitive pressures (as illustrated in Box 6.3).

As an indirect effect, the inflow of foreign capital to certain parts of the health system may reduce the burden on government resources and allow the public sector to reallocate its resources toward patients with less ability to pay. For instance, when individuals with higher incomes receive care from foreign-owned private hospitals, the public sector does not have to provide services to them. Similarly, if these individuals buy their health insurance from foreign insurance companies, the state does not have to cover the health expenses accrued by these individuals.

Box 6.2: The Positive Impact of Competition among Health Providers on Investment in Equipment and Health Education in Chile

Numerous and far-reaching changes in the Chilean health system between 1983–2003 transformed the dominant public sector model that had prevailed since the 1950s into a heterogeneous model. The emerging model is neither complete nor consolidated, and there are very diverse proposals regarding its future development. From a trade perspective, the most important changes have been those in the rules regarding service providers and their impact on investment in equipment and health training (Leon, 2003). Those changes introduced competition between the public and private sectors and among all actors in each subsector. Competition made modernization necessary for economic survival and to conform to public expectations, e.g., public and private organizations (insurers and health care providers) had to improve the quality of their services to attract clients. Modernization focused at first on investing in infrastructures and importing equipment rather than improving health care practices. Given the competition for resources among private providers, these were inclined to expand their clientele with more visible investments, especially through the importation of medical supplies and equipment (see figure below).

Under the pressure of this modernization process, the need for personnel to operate this new equipment grew and, in turn, the demand for foreign centers and university training grew, both for graduate studies and for short-term training. The number of students and specialists was not enough to supply the

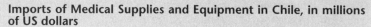

Box 6.2: The Positive Impact of Competition among Health Providers on Investment in Equipment and Health Education in Chile (Continued)

Imports of Medical Supplies and Equipment in Chile, in millions of US dollars

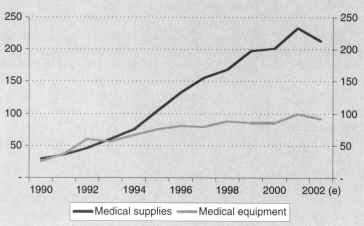

growing requirements of the health services sector. A general shortage in the health professions, from medical specialists to assistant nurses, was emerging. Under these conditions, a significant increase in the training of health professionals abroad and in Chile was observed, followed by growth in the domestic capacity for training, to the extent that Chile can now export these services. During the late 1980s and the 1990s, the problem of inadequate supply of medical specialists was addressed by short-term courses and internships in which professionals and technicians received training in new techniques or methods of care. The demand for short-term training steadily increased and was partially satisfied by training offered abroad, which was made easier by the reduction of international travel costs during the 1990s. The trend toward seeking training abroad of three months or longer, including formal courses and practice periods in specialized centers, also grew in the 1990s.

However, at the end of the 1990s, a reversal in this trade of health training services was observed. This shift originated from institutions of higher education in medical, nursing, and other health professions in order to respond to growing needs in health education. Until then only two departments of medicine, one in a public university (Santiago) and the other in a private university (Los Andes) and both in the Santiago Metropolitan region, were authorized by the Rectors Council, both in 1992. In the period 1999–2002, seven new universities, six private and one public, were authorized and established medical schools and related professional departments. The number of graduates has already increased and continues to accelerate.

(Continued)

Box 6.2: The Positive Impact of Competition among Health Providers on Investment in Equipment and Health Education in Chile (Continued)

At the same time, centers of excellence, both in the public and private sectors, and new departments of medicine started to work together. The establishment of such associations is highly competitive. In 2002, one of the leading private centers of excellence associated with a dynamic private university's department of medicine to form a training center for undergraduate and graduate students. Only a year later, one of its competitors for leadership in excellence joined one of the major traditional centers, the University of Chile, an emblematic Latin American public health institution and Chilean public sector training center.

Such initiatives are linked to the growing interest in short-term training, and in national and international symposia and conferences to serve such purposes. The frequency of such events has been growing and has been financed on a cost-sharing basis with specialists from the United States or Europe. The symposia and conferences proposed by centers of excellence and university departments of medicine and by health professionals' and technicians' associations have changed the availability of places for graduate students and specialized training. This has led to a strengthening of Chilean competitiveness vis-à-vis foreign centers and professional events in developed countries, mostly in Europe and the United States, for short-term training and graduate studies. More than two-thirds of students in the leading departments of medicine in Chile and in Chilean Catholic universities are now foreign students. Chileans interested in graduate or specialized studies for entering the national labor market are also aware that most of the department heads at private and public health services centers of excellence are professors or equivalent-level authorities in national departments of medicine and, more generally, in departments of the health professions. Thus, the probabilities of success in their job-seeking strategies indicate that specialized or graduate students, after evaluating foreign and national centers options, would prefer national centers.

The Chilean case sheds light on the potential positive effects of increased competition, whether this competition comes from domestic or foreign providers. The need to improve services to attract patients led many providers to acquire new technologies. The demand for trained operators of these new types of equipment in turn put pressure on the improvement of health education in the country.

Source: Leon, 2003.

Thus, resources are freed up and can be used for other patients. As observed in a study of a chain of private clinics in South Africa, "the arrival of clinic networks and the growing taste for affordable private health care among the employed but low-income segment of the population could be an opportunity to encourage this group of people using the public sector to use this model, while the public sector concentrates on its role as regulator and in providing services to the poorest. Potentially, this could remove some of the burden on the public sector" (Palmer et al., 2003, page 295). In Vietnam, since the private provision of health services was legalized in 1989, private providers have become the main providers of health services; their services serve all income groups, in both urban and rural areas (Thi Hong Ha et al., 2002).

However, there are some qualifications to the potential of foreign investors injecting new resources and offering services that were previously unavailable. First, the empirical evidence from country studies points out that the expansion of private providers has not always meant offering services that were not offered by the public sector. A survey of Chinese hospitals in the context of this project (see Box 6.3) showed that the great majority of foreign hospitals are established in urban areas and not in the rural areas where the health infrastructure is still very weak. A study of private clinics in Tanzania also pointed to similar results (Benson, 2001). Moreover, a study of private clinics in South Africa highlighted that these establishments did not offer comprehensive services, i.e., no emergency services, weak preventive care and chronic care services. Therefore, the authors of the study stated that "it is doubtful how much of a burden they can remove from the public sector" (Palmer et al., 2003, p. 295).

Another element to keep in mind when considering the liberalization of the health sector is how it will affect the political economy of the public system. For instance, in countries with relatively well-developed public sectors offering broad access to health services, such reforms can break or weaken the political coalitions that support the public system. When politically powerful groups benefit from a social program, they will see it as in their best interest to defend the quality and the funding of the program. If the public program is universal (or offers broad coverage), the poor and groups with little political power also benefit from this program. When powerful groups opt out of a public system, the political support to improve coverage and quality is diminished. The impact of allowing foreign providers of health services and insurance can be to weaken the political configuration in support of the public health system. On the other hand, in many developing countries, the existing public health system is not offering equal access and services to all citizens. Often, public spending on health concentrates on the richer groups of the population (World Bank, 2003, page 39[3]). For instance, in Ghana in 1994, the poorest fifth of the population received 12 percent of public spending on health whereas the richest fifth received 33 percent. In India in 1995–96, the poorest fifth of the population received 10 percent of public spending on health whereas the richest fifth received 32 percent (Filmer, 2003). In these situations, national policymakers have to consider that opening the system to foreign providers may create an opportunity to rebalance the system by reducing

> ## Box 6.3: Foreign Investment in Health Facilities in China: Mostly Limited to Some Urban Areas, but Already Having Positive Demonstration Effects
>
> Between 1989 and 2000, several policies and regulations to facilitate foreign investment and trade in health services in China through joint ventures were adopted. In 2003, the Ministry of Health conducted a national survey on health trade and investment in China (Shi, 2003). Of the 46 Sino-foreign health facilities surveyed, 56.5 percent were specialized hospitals or clinics, such as ophthalmology hospitals, reproductive health centers, tumor hospitals, and dentistry clinics. The total foreign investment was relatively small: for 41.3 percent of the surveyed health facilities, the foreign investment was less than US$600,000, and only six establishments received investments above US$12 million. The joint ventures usually brought together Chinese public hospitals with private investors from the United States or Hong Kong.
>
> The survey revealed an unbalanced distribution of the Sino-foreign health facilities in China. Almost 80 percent (78.3 percent) of the Sino-foreign health facilities were located in large cities in the costal areas rather than in the Central and Western provinces, where the health infrastructure, health manpower, and technical capacity are insufficient to meet the health needs of the population.
>
> Despite their small number, joint venture establishments contribute new concepts of health management and services, advanced medical technology, and good hospital environment. They bring competition pressures on the public hospitals and benefits to the development of the health market in China. Even though they mainly target the foreigners working in China or other high-income groups, a few of them also provide essential health care services to the community. They provide basic health services to the ordinary population, and they have their own strategy for attracting patients. For instance, they set the service charges according to the market environment, taking into account the level of user fees charged by the public hospitals. More and more public hospitals learn from the Sino-foreign joint-venture hospitals, and the quality and management of health services have been improved through imitation and learning.
>
> *Source:* Shi, 2003.

public health spending on richer groups, who can afford the services of the foreign providers and insurers, and by increasing the resources available to the poorest groups.

One potential benefit of allowing foreign providers is their capacity to offer more-efficient and better-quality services than those already in existence. However, the literature on the increased role of private providers in the health sector of developing countries offers ambiguous evidence to this effect. In a review of the implementation of contracting with private providers in developing countries, Mills and Broomberg (1998) observed "limited and contradictory evidence on the impact of selective contracting on efficiency and equity at the facility or health system level (p. 28)." A study of contracting in South African hospitals showed that contractors were successful at delivering services at lower costs than public providers, through lower staff levels and higher productivity, without a strong negative impact on quality (Broomberg, Masobe, and Mills, 1997); on successful contracting in Cambodia, see Soeters and Griffiths (2003).[4] More recently, Palmer et al. (2003) examined a new model of private primary-care provision in South Africa, based on the commercial model of the franchised chain. They observed good quality and relatively low costs at the private clinics, in comparison with the public clinics. But the experiences of contracting clinical services in Thailand offer examples where contracted services were more expensive than services provided by the public sector (Mills, 1998).

The inflows of foreign investment in health services or insurance can also have certain negative impacts. In terms of equity of access, it can lead to a two-tier health care system, with foreign-owned establishments offering sophisticated, high-quality services only to higher-income patients.[5] Indeed, only patients with private or social insurance covering the expenses incurred, or patients able to disburse an out-of-pocket payment, can gain access to these services. The literature on user fees provides us with evidence on the impact of such out-of-pocket cost recovery mechanisms on access to services. Most of the studies are based on African examples, as most Sub-Saharan African countries have introduced user fees in the health sector in order to raise revenues for the public sector.

One of the early measures attempting to do so was the Bamako Initiative, which began in 1987 with support from UNICEF and the World Health Organization as an effort to finance the expansion of access to primary care in Africa using revenues from newly introduced user charges for essential drugs. The presumption was that decentralizing management and allowing for local control of locally generated revenues would provide a way of addressing the persistent problem of insufficient supplies of drugs from government sources. In some instances, it appears that the approach was successful in raising revenues and improving access and quality of care (Audibert and Mathonnat, 2000, on Mauritania; Diop et al., 1995; Wouters 1995; Chawla and Ellis, 2000, on Niger); Bratt et al., 2000 on Ecuador; Mehrotra and Jarrett, 2002 referenced in WB, 2003, p. 76).

Nevertheless, the most persistent finding of this literature is the negative impact of user fees on access to services. "In virtually all cases where user fees were increased or introduced there has been a concurrent decrease in service utilisation. The magnitude of this drop in utilisation was frequently larger, and the effect of a longer duration, amongst the poor part of the population" (Bennett and

Gilson, 2001, p. 11). Numerous case studies and comparative studies document this impact; in some cases the reduction in utilization reached 50 percent (Yoder, 1989; Creese, 1991 and 1997; Moses et al., 1992; McPake, Hanson, and Mills, 1993; Mwabu et al., 1995; Haddad and Fournier, 1995; Gertler and Hammer, 1997; Kipp et al., 2001; Meuwissen, 2002; Nanda, 2002; Ridde, 2003). A survey conducted by the World Bank in 37 African countries also confirmed that the introduction of user fees led to a reduction in service utilization (Nolan and Turbat, 1995). As a result of these fees, lower-income households' access to health services was decreased (on the higher price elasticity of demand for health care services for poorer persons, see Gertler and van der Gaag, 1988).

In principle, such inequitable outcomes could be addressed by regulatory measures. However, empirical evidence points at the difficulty of implementing measures to address this problem. The literature on the introduction of user fees shows that, in most cases, exemptions from fees were in principle available to the poor, but the implementation of these exemptions was ineffective (Gilson et al., 2001; Gilson, 1997; Gilson and Mills, 1995; Mills, 1998; Meuwissen, 2002). Nevertheless, experiences in Cambodia with an earmarked fund entrusted to an independent third party show that institutional solutions to the problem of access for the poor caused by cost-recovery can be found (Hardeman et al., 2004).

Trade in health services can also take the form of foreign investment in health insurance. Expansion of private health insurance through foreign investment offers a way to decrease the heavy reliance on out-of-pocket payment, which is one of the worst problems affecting health systems in developing countries (WHO, 2000). Health insurance not only shelters people from large out-of-pocket payments, but also allows for pooling, i.e., spreading financial risks among the group of participants. However, the evidence from Latin America shows that private insurers, whether foreign or domestic, will tend to serve the higher-income and low-risk groups, who can pay relatively high financial contributions to receive coverage (Baeza and Cabezas, 1999; Barrientos and Lloyd-Sherlock, 2000). In Chile, elderly people and women of fertile age were facing much higher premiums (Sanhueza and Ruiz-Tagle, 2002). Regulation can be introduced to reduce such behaviors by insurers (see Box 6.4 on Argentina), but the expansion of private health insurance through foreign involvement also poses the risk of fragmenting the pool.

A limited number of large pools or a single pool are better than small pools, as they allow better spread of the risks and take advantage of economies of scale in administration. "Health system policy with regards to pooling needs to focus on creating conditions for the development of the largest possible pooling arrangements. When a particular country lacks the organizational and institutional

Box 6.4: The Need for a Regulatory Framework: The Example of Health Insurance in Argentina

One central point highlighted by country studies on the policy implications of trade in health services is the importance of a regulatory framework. Indeed, regulations are recognized as key when it comes to mitigating the potential negative impacts of liberalization and to taking full advantage of the potential benefits. For instance, in their study of trade in health services in Argentina, Salvador and Quiliconi (2003) brought together a diverse group of representatives from the public and private sector. The participants of that roundtable all highlighted the weaknesses in the regulatory framework and in its enforcement in Argentina, especially regarding the regulation of the private sector. They pointed out the need to, first, "put the house in order," and then evaluate the costs and benefits of liberalization in the multilateral negotiations.

The need for a stronger regulatory framework was seen as especially clear in the health insurance sector. In Argentina, about 50 percent of citizens have health insurance coverage through the social security sector, which consists of a large number of institutions that vary greatly in terms of the type of population to whom they offer services, the coverage they offer, their financial resources, and their forms of operation (see table below). Historically, these funds were managed by the *Obras sociales* (OSs) under the responsibility of trade unions, and membership was mandatory. In 1993, in order to reduce the number of OSs and improve the quality of services through competition, the government adopted a reform that allowed beneficiaries to choose their OSs. In order to ensure equity in the provision of health care services, a Compulsory Medical Plan (PMO) was also adopted; it established a standardized basket of benefits for all beneficiaries and controlled the cost of copayment. The quality of heath care and facilities provided by OSs is also regulated by a program called the National Program of Quality Guarantee of Medical Care (PNGCAM).

However, the private insurers and providers are not under the same level of regulation as are the OSs. In 2000, the government went further in the reforms of the social security sector and allowed other entities such as private insurers to become competitors in the system. This implied that these companies, often called "Prepaids," were subject to the same obligations as the OSs regarding minimum coverage and quality. Because private health insurance companies considered these obligations too high, few entered the market. However, many of them have contracts with OSs as managers of the plans.

As we can see in table below, about 10 percent of Argentinians have some coverage from a voluntary subscription plan. This private sector is mostly unregulated, which leads to a number of problems. For instance, when the private health plans go bankrupt, there is no protection for consumers, who suddenly lose their prepaid benefits. "As the Prepaids strive for commercial viability in this market, they are also increasingly looking for ways to avoid the

(Continued)

Box 6.4: The Need for a Regulatory Framework: The Example of Health Insurance in Argentina (Continued)

worst health risks by excluding preexisting conditions and certain expensive treatments such as drug therapies for AIDS" (World Bank/IDB, 1997). With this in mind, the World Bank suggested a set of minimum regulations needed to ensure financial soundness and stability, protect basic consumer rights, and make fund managers accountable for their actions. These regulations typically cover: minimum capital and liquidity to operate, financial accounting standards and independent audits, definitions of standard benefits packages, norms for specifying benefits in contracts, public disclosure of information on financial and health-related performance, and procedures for handling complaints. Moreover, as there is no regulation regarding coverage, selection of beneficiaries, or rates for private insurance, these plans offer little to the poor, the sick, or to workers in the informal sector in general who are not covered by social security plans. For now, those without coverage have to rely on the underresourced public hospitals. Therefore, there was a strong sense from the Argentinian case study that, before further opening the system to private providers, including foreign providers, there was a need to focus on the regulatory framework necessary to deal with these issues.

Medical Care Coverage in Argentina by Type, 2000 (in percentages)

Type of coverage	Total
No coverage	38.04
Obras sociales plans	51.19
Voluntary subscription	6.29
Obras sociales plans and voluntary subscription	3.21
Emergency coverage	1.00
Other coverage	0.13
No answer	0.13

Source: PAHO (2002) and ACR and Asociados based on ENGH and INDEC data; Salvador and Quiliconi, 2003.

capacity to have a single pool or large pools for all citizens, [...] policymakers should promote pooling arrangements whenever it is possible, as a transitional stage towards the future aggregation of pools. Even small pools or pools for segments of the populations are better than pure out-of-pocket financing for all" (WHO, 2000, p. 103). Adopting this pragmatic approach, policymakers have to consider whether private insurers (foreign or domestic) or community-based pooling organizations are most likely to support such a transition.

The available evidence regarding the introduction of user fees and private health insurance in developing countries highlights that the cost-recovery requirement of private providers and insurers usually makes access to care more difficult for poorer groups. It also stresses the difficulty of implementing flanking measures targeted at the poor. Policymakers have to weight this evidence against the potential benefits of expanding the private sector through trade liberalization.

Another potential negative impact of imports through Mode 3 is the possible diversion of resources if public funds are allocated to attract foreign direct investment (FDI) in the health sector. Developing countries' governments often offer a number of financial incentives to attract foreign investment in their territory (UNCTAD, 1995). Whether they take the form of direct subsidies to purchase land for the facilities, tax breaks, or other incentives, there are several direct and indirect ways through which public funding can be channeled to support foreign-owned hospitals or clinics that would only serve high-income patients. This diversion of resources is especially critical if the public funds were used in the creation of superspecialty establishments, with high investment in sophisticated medical technologies. Such a trend goes against the need of developing countries' health systems to focus on cost-effective services.

Mode 4—Presence of Natural Persons

One area that has been highlighted as a key area of interest for developing countries is the temporary movement of their health professionals abroad. Indeed, exports of health services can also take place through the temporary movement of nurses, physicians, and other health professionals. However, GATS commitments apply on letting foreign workers into one's national market, not on letting your workers go. Therefore, as in the case of Mode 2, the key interest of developing countries in Mode 4 lies in extracting commitments from their trade partners.

One potential benefit of such exports is the remittances that the professionals send back to their home countries. We know from the literature on remittances from migrants that the volume of such financial transfers can be very large and can have macroeconomic impact by providing a significant source of foreign currency, increasing national income, financing imports, and contributing to the balance of payments (for a review of the literature, see Meyers, 1998). We also know that the vast majority of remittances are used for consumption purposes, not spent on savings and "productive investment," such as buying land and tools or starting a business. However, the literature does not reach any consensus on the development impact of remittances. On the one hand, they are seen as improving the standard of living of the recipients and as a potential source of savings and investment capital for development. On the other hand, other development specialists do not consider them as a force for development, as they are usually spent on consumer goods, especially imported goods, which can increase inflation and/or create balance of payment problems, and are not invested in capital-generating activities. Moreover, research also tells us that short-term migrants remit more than long-term migrants (Lozano-Ascencio, 1993). In the case of the temporary movement of health professionals, the question is how to harness the private flows of remittances for the development of the health system. How can we ensure that the income sent from physicians and nurses to their families, often higher-income families, can contribute to the development of their communities? In their review of the literature, Puri and Ritzema (2000) note that some labor-exporting countries have adopted mandatory or incentive schemes to influence the choice of the remittance channels adopted by migrant workers, but few measures were adopted to influence the use of the remittances.

Another potential benefit of trade through the movement of persons is the impact on knowledge and skills. When health professionals temporarily work in another country, this can be an occasion for them to upgrade and expand their skills. When the professionals return to their country, this human capital can be added to the resources of the national health system. Some countries have adopted measures to support returned migrants in using their new skills to establish their own businesses and build on these new skills, and also on the savings accumulated by the workers during their stay abroad.

However, when the movement of health professionals is not temporary but permanent, such gains cannot be achieved by the sending country. The latter is often characterized as the "brain drain" and the former, as "brain gain." The danger that the temporary movement of professionals will become permanent migration is a key concern with exports of health services from developing countries. This brain drain through large international migration of highly skilled workers is experienced in many sectors. The cost of such migration not only includes the public investments in the education of these professionals and the loss of human capital and slower economic growth, but also the direct impact in terms of access to health services. (Long-term migration of high-skilled workers can also have a beneficial impact on the sending countries through certain feedback effects such as return migration and technology transfer; see Lowell, 2001 and Commander et al., 2002)

In the health sector, the migration of professionals appears to be the starkest and most persistent form of brain drain (Commander et al., 2002). Most developing countries do not experience an oversupply of health professionals, but rather shortages of them. Therefore, the relevance of exports of health services through Mode 4 is limited to countries that have a surplus of health care workers. For the majority of developing countries, such exports can exacerbate existing human resources problems. Indeed, where skilled personnel are in short supply, even short-term loss can result in considerable loss of health services to nationals.

Additional Benefits and Costs of GATS Commitments

This causal chain analysis focuses on the costs and benefits of opening health services and the insurance sector to foreign providers. Once this question has been explored, and if liberalization reforms are adopted, the next question for policymakers is whether these reforms should be included in the GATS or other trade agreements. What are the advantages of making commitments at the multilateral forum?

The first advantage is the possibility of using this commitment as a bargaining chip in the negotiations. One country could decide to offer this commitment in order to gain better market access or achieve other goals with its trading partners. From a political economy perspective, the cross-sectoral links made during multilateral negotiations can also help policymakers build domestic coalitions in support of their reforms. For instance, if a commitment in health services was offered in exchange for a reduction in agricultural subsidies from other members of the WTO, this could rally many domestic actors such as farmers and consumers. Another perceived advantage of binding trade reforms in international treaties is that they will be seen by investors as an insurance policy that their entry to a market and their nondiscriminatory treatment are guaranteed. For the government making these commitments, the benefit lies in the hope that such an insurance policy increases investor confidence and leads to greater foreign investment in the sector where the commitments were made. (However, there is little empirical evidence to support this.) Finally, making commitments can also have the benefit of increasing the transparency and clarity of the rules and remaining restrictions relating to entry of foreign providers, as they have to be made explicit in the schedules of commitment.

On the other hand, one major disadvantage of making commitments under GATS is the difficulty of policy reversal. By definition, is it not easy to withdraw commitments made in the GATS. As mentioned in Chapter 5, the Agreement allows a member to withdraw a commitment, but only provided that compensation—usually in the form of liberalization commitments in other sectors—is offered. For example, if a member country has made market access commitments in hospital services but judges that the results of a reform allowing private (domestic and foreign) providers have yielded more negative than positive impacts, it can change this policy and remove its GATS commitments after negotiating compensation with WTO members. Therefore, the space for policy experimentation is reduced, as the costs for policy reversal can be very high.

Assessment of Flanking Measures

The causal chain analysis has identified several potential negative impacts of liberalization in health services.[6] These potential impacts can, however, be prevented or mitigated if the government adopts flanking measures. The list below identifies a number of these mitigating measures. National policymakers need to assess the domestic capacity to adopt and implement such measures. Indeed, the regulatory capacity of developing countries varies greatly, and realistic expectations of the effectiveness of flanking measures have to be adapted accordingly. For instance, middle-income countries may more frequently have the regulatory capacity than poorer countries to harness the potential of trade in health services to benefit the whole population. Regulatory capacity is also one of the impact indicators included in our list of indicators above. Indeed, policymakers also need to assess whether and to what extent their liberalization policy will limit their flexibility to adopt and implement flanking measures.

Mitigating Measures

Mode 1—Cross-border Supply One of the concerns related to the cross-border supply of health services is the need to control the quality of the services provided to nationals. One way to address this issue is to require all providers of telemedicine to register with a ministry or to have an alliance arrangement with a local hospital. For instance, such supply could be allowed only within the framework of special arrangements between registered hospitals nationally and overseas, subject to government approval of the supply agreement. Such a regulatory framework could also ensure that the development of telemedicine would not lead to an overinvestment in high technology at the expense of more cost-effective health interventions.

Mode 2—Consumption abroad To reduce the risk that health tourism diverts resources from the public health sector, authorities can restrict the number of beds in public hospitals that can be made available to foreigners and limit the range of services that can be provided to them. To prevent health tourism from leading to a health care system with a higher quality segment catering to wealthy nationals and foreigners and a lower quality segment for the rest of the population, the national government can adopt a number of measures to ensure that part of the revenues generated by exports through Mode 2 are funneled toward the whole domestic health system.

Mode 3—Commercial Presence In order to limit the potential negative impacts of liberalization on equity and access, regulatory measures can be adopted to ensure that foreign investors provide services to the poor; these might include, among other things: universal service requirements, quotas of uninsured patients who must be treated in foreign-owned establishments, and requirements to establish clinics in rural as well as urban areas. Similarly, foreign providers of health insurance can be required to offer a basic package of benefits, be prohibited from excluding people with preexisting conditions or high-risks consumers, and the cost of their premium can be regulated by national governments. These regulations aimed at ensuring equitable access to health services and insurance can be applied to both domestic and foreign providers. Under the GATS, these regulations could apply exclusively to foreign providers, if no national treatment commitments had been undertaken. However, it is difficult to imagine a situation where the regulator would see it as necessary to do so. Finally, to offset the drain of qualified staff from the public system to private establishments, governments can require foreign providers to train additional numbers of staff.

Mode 4—Presence of natural persons One of the most worrying aspects of trade through temporary movement of natural persons is that it may lead to permanent migration and risk exacerbating the shortages of health professionals in developing countries. There are clear limitations to what governments can do to prevent individuals seeking to migrate or work abroad temporarily from doing so. Possible strategies are the adoption of service requirements, where graduates of national medical schools are required to work for the public system for a number of years, or to impose a training levy on individuals, or payment of a bond upon leaving the country, repayable upon return.

At a more systemic level, national governments can work toward providing enhanced employment opportunities at home in order to better retain health professionals. This can be linked to the liberalization of trade in health services through Modes 2 and 3, as these can improve the income of local health workers. Another mitigating measure that can be adopted by countries facing critical shortages is to negotiate agreements with main countries of destination to prevent active recruitment in their territory.

Enhancing Measures

We saw in the causal chain analysis that trade in health services can have several positive impacts in terms of availability of capital for infrastructure, new knowledge, and technology. Enhancing measures are actions that governments can take

Box 6.5: Foreign Private Investment in Health in Low-Income Countries

The prospects of foreign investment in the least-developed countries' health sector confront analysts with a contradictory situation. These are the countries in most need of additional capital and resources, but who may be the least likely to receive it. Indeed, LDCs are faced with acute needs for investment in health (Commission on Macroeconomics and Health, 2001). However, the likelihood that foreign investors will establish a commercial presence in these countries appears to be small. Foreign investors are attracted by social and political stability, ready markets, high rates of return, inexpensive and skilled labor, cheap local inputs, and adequate infrastructure (Schmidt and Culpeper, 2003). Therefore, in general, foreign investment disproportionately goes to higher-income developing countries, because they tend to have bigger domestic markets, an educated labor force, and better infrastructures.

Nevertheless, there are cases of LDCs where Foreign Direct Investment flows, measured relative to GNP, are relatively high; these include Angola, Lesotho, Mozambique, and Cambodia. Given that factors influencing the flows of FDI in poor countries do not operate in a straightforward manner, we are seeing cases of trade in health services in LDCs, such as foreign-owned hospitals opening in Vietnam (Robbins, 2002). In these cases, national governments in these countries need to examine whether they have the regulatory capacity to ensure that trade in health services translates into benefits for the national health system as a whole, not only for a very small share of the population. In terms of the export capacity of health services of LDCs, it appears to be nonexistent, given the constraints on infrastructure and human resources. With a low supply of health professionals (less than 20 physicians per 100,000 people), it is difficult to see how offering services to foreign patients would be possible without further reducing access to services for the local patients.

In a case study in Senegal conducted for this project, Ndiaye (2003) did not observe international trade in health services taking place, except for some foreign investment in the health insurance sector. He also found that the various actors involved with health have diverse views about the potential for, and of, trade liberalization in health services. Actors from the private sectors encourage the complete liberalization of the sector: they see private provision as offering better-quality and better-trained and motivated health workers. Key actors within government and civil society organizations are more sceptical regarding the potential gains of liberalization of health services. They believe that the level of poverty in the country is a major obstacle to the promotion of trade in health services. The scepticism found within the trade ministry also derives from those actors' experience from previous liberalization, which has produced destabilizing and disorganizing effects on the economic system and little gain for poor households. For them, liberalization has highlighted the need for the state to regulate markets, in order to facilitate access to essential services for the low-income populations.

Box 6.5: Foreign Private Investment in Health in Low-Income Countries (Continued)

Officials in the Senegalese health ministry insist on the necessity to increase investment in the health system. Given the modest level of state resources, they believe in the importance of resorting to the private sector. They recognize the limits of the presence of the state in the health sector in Senegal. It cannot ensure the financing of the sector and needs to encourage private initiatives in the provision of health services and in health financing, whether they are individual or community-based initiatives. But, for these officials, given the peculiar nature of the health sector, one must consider liberalization in that sector differently than in other sectors. The state has to guarantee the constitutional right to health by encouraging private initiatives while still being present. Different strategies and measures, such as the greater autonomy of hospitals, the development of contracts, and the promotion of health mutuality, can be used. Will liberalization help to effectively fight poverty? For civil society the answer is no, as they see that the most likely impact will be the exclusion of the poorest of the population from health services. Despite the divergences in the views of the Senegalese actors approached for the country study, one common message comes through: the importance of delineating the limits of liberalization and ensuring access to services for the poor, whatever type of trade reform is adopted.

to ensure that these additional resources are harnessed to benefit the whole national health system.

Mode 1—Cross-border supply National governments can adopt international cooperative agreement to facilitate telemedicine and information-sharing on health services being offered over the Internet.

Mode 2—Consumption abroad Policymakers can consider various measures to ensure that the additional incomes from foreign patients are harnessed to benefit the health system of the country in general. For instance, the national government can restrict provision of health services to foreigners to private clinics, tax their profits, and earmark this revenue for the public health system. Where services to foreign patients are provided by public hospitals, administrative mechanisms can be put in place to ensure that the additional revenue generated from treating foreign patients subsidizes the provision of services to nationals (as is often the case in education).

Mode 3—Commercial Presence In order to take advantage of new services offered by foreign providers that were not available before and make these available to all income groups, national governments can target individual patients and provide subsidies or vouchers for treatments in foreign-owned establishments, treatments that are not available in the public system. Moreover, the additional resources brought in by foreign investors can be harnessed to subsidize the public health system by taxing the profits of foreign providers.

Mode 4—Presence of natural persons In addition to the improvement of skills, one of the key benefits of exporting health services through Mode 4 for developing countries is the potential of remittances. The question is how to harness the private flows of remittances for the development of the health system.

Monitoring and Post-Evaluation

Once the impact assessment is conducted and the policy reforms adopted, Kirkpatrick and Lee (2002) recommend that policymakers add monitoring and post-evaluation to their policy process. They propose considering such post-evaluation as an important mitigation and enhancing measure, as it facilitates the identification and remediation of the negative impacts of reforms and the measures that need to be taken to harness the potential benefits.

Regarding the liberalization of health services, we would propose a set of simple indicators to be tracked by policymakers after the adoption of the new policy. The set of indicators proposed in the scoping section could be used and refined for national assessment (see Table 6.1). Ideally, the results of the monitoring of these indicators would be made publicly available, to facilitate public dialogue on the impact of reforms. Indeed, the process of undertaking a national evaluation of GATS and health should enable civil society organizations to hold their government accountable in the negotiations at the WTO and in the implementation of the agreements. An important part of this process is to ensure that information on GATS and trade in health services is available, as it can also facilitate independent monitoring and evaluation work from civil society organizations.

Notes

1. Policymakers can also decide that their objective is to maximize health status, if it means worsening economic welfare. However, given the large positive impact of improvement in health status on economic development (see CMH, 2001), it is difficult to devise a scenario where a health status-enhancing measure would worsen economic welfare.

2. The literature review on which this section relies was guided by the documents found through the following databases and search terms. In Social Sciences Index 2/83–10/03, with the search key "privat* and health," 133 hits were found, and with "user fees," 30 hits were found. In PubMed (Medline), the search terms "privatization and developing" generated 118 items, while "user fees and developing" led to 151 hits. Some other documents were found by crossing the references of the articles analyzed. Other documents were found on the Web-based database Eldis, in the health service delivery/private sectors section, and on the World Bank's resource, Rapid Response, in the health care section. Some material also comes from the country studies commissioned in the context of this project.

3. The report explains that health systems fail poor people because they are trapped in a web of failed relationships of accountability. Either in their relationship to policymakers or to providers, poor people have less clout when it comes to receiving services. "Poor citizens have little clout with politicians. In some countries, the citizenry has only a weak hold on politicians. Even if there is a well-functioning electoral system, poor people may not be able to influence politicians about public services…. As a result, public services often become the currency of political patronage and clientelism. Politicians offer 'phantom' jobs to teachers and doctors. They build free public schools and clinics in areas where their supporters live…. The lesson seems to be that the citizen-policymaker link is working either when citizens can hold policymakers accountable for public services that benefit the poor or when the policymaker cares about the health and education of poor people. These politics are 'pro-poor'" (World Bank, 2003, pp. 6-7).

4. We should note, however, in this South African example that contractors were able to capture all the efficiency gains in profits, with no savings for the government funding the hospital's services.

5. This section partly relies on Ted Schreker's review of the literature prepared for the paper "The Economic Dimensions of Trade in Health Services" by Chantal Blouin, Ron Labonte, and Ted Schreker, presented at the WHO Workskop on Trade in Health Services, July 2003, Ottawa.

6. The following section relies on a list of measures prepared by Julia Nielson (2003).

References

Adams, O., and C. Kinnon. 1998. A public health perspective. In S. Zarrilli and C. Kinnon, eds., *International trade in health services: A development perspective*. Geneva: UNCTAD and WHO.

Arhin-Tenkorang, D. 2001. Mobilizing resources for health: The case for user fees revisited. Working Paper no. 81. Center for International Development, Cambridge MA.

Audibert, M., and J. Mathonnat. 2000. Cost recovery in Mauritania: Initial lessons. *Health Policy and Planning* 15: 66–75.

Baeza, C., and M. Cabezas. 1999. Es necesario el ajuste de riesgo el los mercados de seguros de salud en América Latina? [Is risk adjustment necessary in health insurance markets in Latin America?]. Santiago, Chile: Centro Latinoamericano de Investigacion para sistemas de salud.

Barrientos, Armando, and Peter Lloyd-Sherlock. 2000. Reforming health insurance in Argentina and Chile. *Health Policy and Planning* 15(4): 417–423.

Bennett, Sara, and Lucy Gilson. 2001. Health financing: designing and implementing pro-poor policies. DFID Health Systems Resource Centre, London.

Benson, John. 2001. The impact of privatization on access in Tanzania. *Social Science and Medicine* 52(12), June.

Bertranou, Fabio. 1999. Are market-oriented health insurance reforms possible in Latin America? The cases of Argentina, Chile and Colombia. *Health Policy* 47.

Bisset, Ron et al. 2003. Sustainability impact assessment of proposed WTO negotiations: Environmental services (with particular reference to water and waste management). May.

Blouin, Chantal, Ron Labonte, and Ted Schreker. 2003. The economic dimensions of trade in health services. Presented at the WHO Workshop on Trade in Health Services, Ottawa, July.

Bratt, John et al. 2002. The impact of price changes on demand for family planning and reproductive health services in Ecuador. *Health Policy and Planning* 17(3).

Broomberg, J., P. Masobe, and A. Mills. 1997 Contracting out district hospital services in South Africa. In S. Bennett, B. McPake, and A. Mills, eds., *Private health providers in developing countries: Serving the public interest?* London: Zed Books.

Brown, D., A. Deardorff, and R. Stern. 2002. Computational analysis of multilateral trade liberalization. The University of Michigan School of public policy discussion paper no. 489.

Buddhasri W, S. Saithanu, and V. Tangcharoensathien. 2003. Private hospital industry in Thailand after the economic crisis, 1996–2001. Research report funded by the Health System Research Institute, Nanthaburi: International Health Policy Programme.

Bushan, Indu, Sheryl Keller, and Brad Schwartz. 2002. Achieving the twin objectives of efficiency and equity: Contracting health services in Cambodia. ERD Policy Brief no. 6, Asian Development Bank, Manila.

Chanda, R. 2001. Trade in health services. CMH Working Paper WG 4: 5. Geneva: World Health Organization, Commission on Macroeconomics and Health.

Chawla, M., and R.P. Ellis. 2000. The impact of financing and quality changes on health care demand in Niger. *Health Policy and Planning* 15, 76–84.

CMH (Commission on Macroeconomics and Health). 2001. Macroeconomics and health: investing in health for economic development. World Health Organization, Geneva. http://www3.who.int/whosis/cmh/cmh_report/report.cfm?path=cmh,cmh_report&language=english (accessed May 27, 2003).

Commander, Simon, Mari Kangasniemi, and Alan Winters. 2002. The brain drain: curse or boon? A survey of the literature. Institute for the Study of Labour, Discussion Paper no. 809.

Creese, A. 1991. User charges for health care: a review of recent experience. *Health Policy and Planning* 6: 309–319.

———. 1995. Lessons from cost-recovery in health. Forum on Health Sector Reform, discussion paper no. 2, WHO, Geneva.

———. 1997. Lessons from cost-recovery in health. In C. Colclough, ed. *Marketizing education and health in developing countries: Miracle or mirage?* Oxford, Clarendon Press.

Dee, P., and K. Hanslow. 2001. Multilateral liberalisation of services trade. In R. M. Stern, ed., *Services in the international economy.* Michigan: University of Michigan Press.

Diop, F. et al. 1995. The impact of alternative cost recovery schemes on access and equity in Niger. *Health Policy Planning* Sep 10(3):223–40.

Drager, Nick, and Cesar Vieira, eds. 2002. *Trade in health services: Global, regional and country perspectives.* Washington, D.C.: PAHO.

Economist, The. 2004. Medical tourism in India: Get well away. October 7.

Fabricant, Stephen J., Clifford W. Kamara, and Anne Mills. 1999. Why the poor pay more: household curative expenditures in rural Sierra Leone. *International Journal of Health Planning and Management* 14: 179–199.

Filmer, Deon. 2003. The incidence of public expenditures on health and education. Background note for *World development report 2004: Making services work for poor people.* The World Bank, May.

Gertler, P.J., and J.S. Hammer. 1997. Strategies for pricing publicly provided health services. World Bank conference on innovations in health care financing, March 10–11, Washington D.C.

Gertler, Paul, and Jacques van der Gaag. 1988. Measuring the willingness to pay for social services in developing countries. Living standards measurement study, working paper no. 45, World Bank, Washington, D.C.

Gilson, L. 1997. The lessons of user fee experience in Africa. *Health Policy and Planning* 12: 273–285.

Gilson, L., and A. Mills. 1995. Health sector reforms in sub-Saharan Africa. *Health Policy* 32: 215–243.

Gilson, L., D. Kalyalya, F. Kuchler, S. Lake, H. Oranga, and M. Ouendo. 2000. The equity impacts of community financing activities in three African countries. *International Journal of Health Planning and Management* 15: 291–317.

———. 2001. Strategies for promoting equity: Experience with community financing in three African countries. *Health Policy* 58: 37–67.

Haddad, S., and Fournier, P. 1995. Quality, cost and utilization of health services in developing countries: A longitudinal study in Zaire. *Social Science and Medicine* 40.

Hardeman, Wim et al. 2004. Access to health care for all? User fees plus a health equity fund in Sotnikum, Cambodia. *Health Policy and Planning* 19(1).

Hoekman, B., and C.A. Primo Braga. 1997. Protection and trade in services: A survey. World Bank policy research working paper. http://www.worldbank.org/research/trade/pdf/wp1747.pdf (accessed June 26, 2003).

HSWG (Health Services Working Group). 2003a. Developing Singapore as the compelling hub for healthcare services in Asia. Ministry of Trade and Industry, Singapore.

HSWG. 2003b. Developing Singapore as the compelling hub for healthcare services in Asia: Potential implications on domestic policy objectives. Ministry of Trade and Industry, Singapore.

Jack, William. 2001. Health insurance reform in four Latin American countries: Theory and practice. World Bank policy research working paper no. 2492.

Janjaroen W, and S. Supakankunti. 2002. International trade in health services in the millennium: The case of Thailand. In: Draker, N., and C. Vieria, eds. *Trade in Health Services, Global, Regional, and Country Perspectives.* Geneva: WHO.

Kipp, W., J. Kamugisha, P. Jacobs, G. Burnham, and T. Rubaale 2001. User fees, health staff incentives and service utilization in Kabarole District, Uganda. *Bulletin of The World Health Organisation* 79.

Kirkpatrick, Colin, and Norman Lee. 2002. Further development of the methodology for a sustainability impact assessment of proposed WTO negotiations. Final report to the European Commission, April.

Konan, Denise Eby, and Keith Maskus. 2004. Quantifying the impact of services liberalization in a developing country. World Bank policy research working paper no. 3193, January.

Leon, David A., Gill Walt, and Lucy Gilson. 2001. International perspectives on health inequalities and policy. *British Medical Journal* 322, 10 March: 591–594.

Leon, Francisco. 2003. The case of the Chilean health system 1983–2003. Paper presented at the WHO workshop on trade in health services, Ottawa, July.

Loevinsohn, Benjamin. 2000. Contracting for the delivery of primary health care in cambodia: Design and initial experience of a large pilot test. World Bank Institute Flagship Program Online Journal, www.worldbank.org/wbi/healthflagship/journal/index.htm.

Lowell, Lindsay. 2001. Some developmental effects of the international migration of highly skilled persons. International migration paper no. 46, International Labour Office, Geneva.

Lozano-Ascencio, F. 1993. *Bringing it back home: Remittances to mexico from migrants workers in the united states.* San Diego: Center for US–Mexican Studies.

Marek, Tonia. 2003. Private health: Policy and regulatory options for private participation. World Bank, Private Sector and Infrastructure Network, note no. 264, June.

Marek, Tonia et al. 1999. Successful contracting of prevention services: fighting malnutrition in Senegal and Madagascar. *Health Policy and Planning* 14(4).

Mattoo, A. et al. 2001. Measuring services trade liberalization and its impact on economic growth: An illustration. World Bank policy research paper, August.

McPake, B., K. Hanson, and A. Mills. 1993. Community financing of health care in Africa: an evaluation of the Bamako Initiative. *Social Science and Medicine* 36: 1383–1395.

Mehrotra, S., and S.W. Jarret. 2002. Improving basic health service delivery in low-income countries: Voice to the poor. *Social Science and Medicine* 54(11).

Meuwissen, Lesbeth Emm. 2002. Problems of cost recovery implementation in district health care: A case study from Niger. *Health Policy and Planning* 17(3).

Meyers, D. W. 1998. Migrants' Remittance in latin america: Reviewing the literature. Working paper of the Inter-American Dialogue and The Tomas Rivera Policy Institute, May.

Mills, A. 1998. To contract or not to contract? Issues for low and middle income countries. *Health Policy and Planning* 13: 32–40.

Mills, Anne, and Jonathan Broomberg. 1998. Experiences of contracting: An overview of the literature. Technical paper, Macroeconomics, Health and Development Series, WHO.

Moses, Stephen, et al. 1992. Impact of user fees on attendance at a referral centre for sexually transmitted diseases in Kenya. *The Lancet* (08/22/92) 340 (881).

Mwabu G, J. Mwanzia, and W. Liambila. 1995. User charges in government health facilities in Kenya: Effect on attendance and revenue. *Health Policy and Planning* 10.

Nanda, Priya. 2002. Gender dimensions of user fees: Implications for women's utilization of health care. *Reproductive Health Matters* 10(20).

Ndiaye, Alfred Inis. 2003. Le Commerce en Matière de Services de Santé: Le Cas du Sénégal. Paper presented at the WHO Workshop on Trade in Health Services, Ottawa, July.

Nielson, Julia. 2003. A rough guide to thinking about commitments on health services under the GATS. Paper presented at the WHO workshop on trade in health services, July.

Nolan, Brian, and Vincent Turbat. 1995. Cost Recovery in Public Health Services in Sub-Saharan Africa. Washington D.C.: The World Bank.

OECD (Organisation for Economic Co-operation and Development). 2000. *Assessing barriers to trade in services: The scheduling of economic needs tests in the GATS: An overview.* TD/TC/WP(2000)11/FINAL, Paris: OECD.

OECD/ GATS. 2002. *The case for open services markets.* Paris: OECD.

Pachanee, Cha-aim, and Wibulpolprasert Suwit. 2003. Trade in health services and GATS: The case of Thailand. Paper presented at the WHO Workshop on Trade in Health Services, Ottawa, July.

PAHO (Pan American Health Organization). 2002. *Profile of the health services system of argentina,* 2nd. ed. Washington, DC: PAHO, Division of Health Systems and Services Development.

Palmer, Natasha, Anne Mills, Haroon Wadee, and Helen Scheneider. 2003. A new face for private providers in developing countries: What implications for public health? *Bulletin of the World Health Organization* 81(4).

Puri, Shivani, and Tineke Ritzema. 2000. Migrants' workers remittances, micro-finance and the informal economy: Prospects and issues. ILO Social Finance Unit working paper no. 21.

Ridde, Valéry. 2003. Fees-for-services, cost recovery and equity in a district of Burkina Faso operating the Bamako Initiative. *Bulletin of The World Health Organisation* 81(7).

Robbins, Yvette. 2002. Dilapidated health care. *Vietnam Business Journal.*

Salvador, Soledad, and Cintia Quiliconi. 2003. Argentina trade in health services and GATS: The Argentinean case study. Paper presented at the WHO workshop on trade in health services, Ottawa, July.

Sanhueza, R., and J. Ruiz-Tagle. 2002. Choosing health insurance in a dual health care system: The Chilean case. *Journal of Applied Economics* 5: 157–184.

Schmidt, Rodney, and Roy Culpeper. 2003. Private Foreign Investment in the Poorest Countries. Ottawa, The North-South Institute.

Shi, Guang. 2003. Trade in health services and GATS in China: Preliminary observation and analysis. Paper presented at the WHO workshop on trade in health services, Ottawa, July.

Singh, Alwyn Didar. 2002. Trade and health related services and GATS: eHealth potential and challenge for healthcare. WHO globalization, trade, and health working paper series.

———. 2003. Framework analysis for national country reports on cross-border trade in health services: Findings from Indian eHealth study. Presentation made at WHO Workshop, July, Ottawa.

Soeters, Robert, and Fred Griffiths. 2003. Improving government health services through contract management: A case from Cambodia. *Health Policy and Planning* 18(1).

Suseno Sutarjo, Untung. 2003. Indonesia moves toward liberalization in trade in health care. Paper presented at the WHO workshop on trade in health services, Ottawa, July.

Thi Hong Ha, Nguyen, Peter Berman, and Ulla Larsen. 2002. Household utilization and expenditure on private and public health services in Vietnam. *Health Policy and Planning,* 17 (1).

UNCTAD (United Nations Conference on Trade and Development). 1995. *World investment report: Transnational corporations and competitiveness.* Geneva and New York.

Yoder, R. 1989. Are people willing and able to pay for health services? *Social Science and Medicine* 29(1).

World Bank. 1993. *World development report 1993: Investing in health.* New York: Oxford University Press.

———. 2003. *World development report 2003: Making services work for poor people.* New York: Oxford University Press.

World Bank/IDB (Interamerican Development Bank). 1997. Argentina: facing the challenge of health insurance reform. Washington, D.C.

WHO (World Health Organization). 2000. The world health report 2000: Health systems—Improving performance.

Wouters, A. 1995. Improving quality through cost recovery in Niger. *Health Policy and Planning* 10(3).

TABLE 6.4   Core and Second-Tier Target and Process Sustainability Indicators

Indicator	Core	Second tier
Economic	Real income	Savings, consumption expenditure
	Fixed capital formation	Economic and other components of fixed capital formation
	Employment	Self-employment, informal sector employment
Social	Poverty	Income and other social dimensions of poverty
	Health and education	Life expectancy, mortality rates, nutritional levels, literacy rates, enrollment rates
	Equity	Income distribution, gender, other disadvantaged age-related groups, indigenous peoples, ethnic minorities
Environmental	Biodiversity	Designated ecosystems, endangered species
	Environmental quality	Air, water, and land quality indicators
	Natural resources stocks	Energy resources, other renewable and nonrenewable resources
Process	Consistency with principles of sustainable development	Polluter pays, user pays, precautionary principles
	Institutional capacities to implement sustainable development strategies	Sustainable development integrated into policymaking, high-level ownership, and commitment to sustainable development objectives

Source: Kirkpatrick and Lee, 2002 page 24.

TABLE 6.5 Public Insurance Portability in OECD Countries

Country	Public Insurance Covers Emergency Care Abroad	Public Insurance Covers Elective Care Abroad
Australia	No[a]	No
Canada	Yes[b]	No[c]
United States	(Medicare) Sometimes for care received in Mexico or Canada	No
Japan	No	No
Germany	Yes[d]	No
Austria	Yes[d]	No
Belgium	Yes[d]	No
Denmark	No	No
Spain	Yes[d]	No
France	N/A	No
Finland	N/A	No
Greece	No	No
Luxembourg	Yes	
Netherlands	N/A	No
United Kingdom	No[e]	No
Sweden	No	No

Note: European citizens are covered for emergency and elective care within the European Economic Area (EEA). However, for elective care, they have to receive prior authorization from their local/national authority; the criteria for authorization vary, but can be very strict.

a. Except in eight countries with whom Australia signed bilateral agreements.

b. Reimbursement with ceilings equivalent to local fees.

c. With exceptions: cancer patients have been sent to neighboring American states to receive treatment.

d. With a preauthorization letter from the insurance provider.

e. Except for countries who signed bilateral agreements and European Economic Area countries.

7

TRADE IN HEALTH SERVICES UNDER THE FOUR MODES OF SUPPLY: REVIEW OF CURRENT TRENDS AND POLICY ISSUES

Chantal Blouin, Jens Gobrecht, Jane Lethbridge, Didar Singh, Richard Smith, David Warner

This chapter provides a summary of four background papers on trade in health services under GATS prepared for the WHO; each paper concentrated on one of the four specific modes of supply (cross-border supply, movement of consumers, commercial presence, and presence of natural persons).[1] The chapter provides information on the nature of trade in health services for each of the four modes of supply, as well as the key policy issues related to each specific mode (the health policy issues related to international trade vary greatly from one mode of supply to another).

Mode 1—Cross-Border Supply

Mode 1 refers to supply where the service crosses a border but the producer and consumer do not. With the rise of information and telecommunications technologies, the feasibility of providing health services through Mode 1 (cross-border supply) is greatly increased. The term often used to describe these activities is "e-health." It encompasses three areas: (1) telemedicine; (2) education and training of health workers and professionals; (3) e-commerce and e-business practices used for health management and health systems, data storage and usage, and using IT in health management (HIT or Health IT) for better delivery and increased efficiency.

The first area covers both existing health care services and new e-health start-ups that offer a range of services from drugs online to telelinked diagnosis and World Wide Web-enabled services such as medical transcription and health insurance. The second involves using the power of IT and e-commerce for improving public health services. These could range from information and data to training and advocacy. The third covers the management aspect of health systems, where the use of IT and e-business is essential to bringing efficiencies in health care and health provision. These could range from using IT and e-commerce for better procurement management, including health supply chains, to better supply of hospital services and patient monitoring, and public relations via the Internet.

E-health in Industrial Countries

E-education in health is one of the most significant uses cited for multimedia technology in health care.[2] The most common or general application in e-education would be the delivery of a lecture by a health expert at any location, that is then made available over the Internet to any number of "students" sharing a common workstation or scattered over a campus, a city, or the world. There are growing numbers of Web sites that offer virtual education in health and health-related areas. Companies such as Unext, Fathom, and notHarvard.com are forging alliances with universities (Stanford University, the London School of Economics, etc.) to offer Web-based courses.

Health information is perhaps the area where the greatest availability and content have grown. Individuals today can access a wealth of health and medical information that was previously available only to health care professionals. The past few years have witnessed an explosive growth of the "informatization" of support to health care, especially in the industrially developed countries. There are a growing number of medical information services on the Internet to help both doctors and individuals to answer health questions, supplementing and potentially displacing printed resources. Databases and sites offering general or specific medical or health facts are the main types of e-heath applications in information.

Medline, Ovid, PubMed, etc. are the major Web databases that search medical literature and offer online versions of papers, books, monographs, and data. There are other examples of databases, such as those sponsored by the United Nations that are used by countries for health care purposes. For instance, the *Qualicare* database enables a large number of countries to exchange specific information on quality indicators and consequences of care for diseases such as diabetes and stroke and for oral health and prenatal and postnatal care. There is also a medical supply database, which provides quarterly data to the donor community on vaccines, essential drugs, and basic medical equipment (WHO, 1997).

In the past, physicians have relied heavily on medical journals, textbooks, and other printed sources for medical references. The Internet and e-health are improving the efficiency of providing medical information for physicians, as more doctors have begun to use the Internet. A well-known e-health Web site is Stanford's E-Skolar. The site provides clinical information online to physicians for $240 a year—the usual cost of just one or two subscriptions to print medical journals.

Moreover, there are an increasing number of Web sites being used in the developed countries to inform people about their personal health risks, to educate them about healthy lifestyles and preventive measures, and to update them on the latest advances in medical research and treatment. For instance, in the fall of 1999, there were only a handful of e-health companies in Europe that offered health products or information over the Web. Six months later, Europe had at least 40 e-health Web sites, according to Warburg Dillion Read, an investment bank. In the study of current e-health Web sites,[3] it appeared that sites offering health information account for the majority of the e-health sites. Most of them offer free access. These sites vary mostly in the type or focus of information posted (for example, some focus on alternative medicine, while others on weight control, etc.). Some also offer consumers the option of chat rooms or interactive question-answer formats. Although most of these sites are only in English, there are a few sites such as Planet Medica[4] that are now beginning to have cross-border aspirations and therefore offer information in other European languages.

E-health in Developing Countries

The use of e-health in developing countries as a whole does not compare in volume or level of usage with that in the industrially developed countries. There are several reasons for this, an important one being the lack of the telecommunications infrastructure required to support e-commerce in general and e-health in particular. In a sense this merely reflects the ground position globally of the health sector today, where the medical and pharmaceutical sectors are largely dominated by the industrialized economies. As it could in so many other sectors of the economy, globalization could result in further widening the gap. In e-health, a comparative advantage may not lie with developing countries unless they work to find niche areas of competency. One such clear field of opportunity is the export of such health-related services as medical transcription, health insurance processing, data mining and storage, etc.

There are currently some successful applications of e-health in developing countries that deserve attention. Some prominent examples are the Onchocerciasis Control Programme (OCP), which works to control river blindness in West Africa; HealthNet, an electronic network that covers 28 African, Asian, and American countries;[5] Soulcity, a multimedia health promotion program in South Africa; and Supercourse, a Web site that acts as the medium in which a global academic faculty can share their views in the area of epidemiology, global health, and the Internet.

In India and the Philippines, medical transcription is a significant industry, and medical insurance and claims processing on behalf of U.S. and European countries is a fast-growing sector. In India alone, it is estimated that more than 25,000 people are employed in industries in these sectors (Singh, 2003).

Unfortunately, such success stories are few and far between. E-health is just beginning to impact developing countries. Even in the area of health information, there is still a great unmet demand. The developing countries suffer many of the world's most virulent and infectious diseases, yet often have the least access to information for combating them. Many universities and medical libraries in the poorest areas of the developing world are severely affected by economic problems; they have had to significantly reduce their subscriptions to medical journals and publications from foreign medical societies. As a case in point, a typical U.S. medical library subscribes to about 5,000 journals, but the Nairobi University Medical School Library received just 20 journals in 1999, down from some 300 a decade ago. In Brazzaville, Congo, the medical university library has just 40 medical books and a dozen journals—all from before 1993. Such cases have a ready-made answer—the power of the Internet and e-health information Web sites—but they can only obtain it once they have access which, unfortunately, still remains impossible for most institutions. In Africa, for example, the cost of Internet access is on average five times that of the cost in OECD countries (ITU, 1999).

There are several reasons for this. The most important is the status of e-commerce itself in the developing countries. The factors that go into determining this status are many, ranging from the telecom infrastructure to the general business environment. After all, if consumers wish to avail themselves of e-health offerings of, for example, a supply of drugs ordered online, there have to be a payment procedure, delivery infrastructure, legal framework, and quality assurance arrangement. Several developing countries are addressing these issues, both from the policy angle and through promoting investment and usage of information and communications technologies (ICTs). Lack of resources, however, continues to be major constraint.

Standards and Certification   Establishing standards to ensure quality in e-health applications is an immediate and critical task. Even today, Web-based health care information in general is not very consistent. The history of *telemedicine* has shown that this is not simple and can be rather problematic due to:

- differing concepts of "health informatics and telematics" and components such as "nursing informatics";
- differing ideas on meaning, which affect terminology, coding schemes, and codes;
- differing "syntax," e.g., in the format of messages to be exchanged; and
- differing communication protocols.

Applications in e-health requiring integration of systems with different standards can be costly since the process of integration often requires at least one of the systems to undo some components of the existing infrastructure and add new components. Although costly, establishment of internationally agreed standards of health service delivery over the Internet and of telecommunication methods and media could enhance the application of e-health and the compatibility of health care systems. The answer to this may lie in the example of the adaptation of Electronic Data Interchange or EDI-based trade and industry transactions to Internet-based communication (through common, compatible, and much cheaper solutions). Many of the standard-setting issues and solutions will come from developed countries, as developing countries have neither the resources nor the expertise to devise them. International agencies must be involved, however, so that solutions bearing the interests of developing countries may be found.

The question of certification raises legal and regulatory issues, at both global and national levels. Not only is health probably the most regulated and controlled sector, it is also one in which the state's responsibility is the highest. Which drug controller of which country will certify an online pharmacy, for example? Who will guarantee the prescribing of a certain treatment plan? Who will help distinguish between qualified doctors and "quacks" offering services on the Internet? These are all real issues, and the basic issue of control vs. free market-driven provision of services on the Internet will also be raised when seeking solutions to these matters.

E-education   Other important challenges in implementing e-health are overcoming people's resistance to the use of new technologies and training people to critically evaluate the information and services offered. The human component and psychological response are important factors for e-health. Resistance to change is often a problem when new technologies are introduced. For example, in the area of supplying clinical information to doctors, the success of the online medical information services will hinge on how often doctors use them. So, it is important to train users and promulgate e-health knowledge to the general public. Thus far, e-health Web sites have been using fairly creative ways to motivate physicians and the public to use their sites. For instance, to keep doctors clicking in, Medscape e-mails weekly newsletters telling specialists about the latest developments in their fields (*The New York Times,* 2000). Others offer "health-tip-of-the-day" or free advice on dieting, for example.

Cross-border e-education in health provides a good example of a horizontal challenge in e-health in a sector-specific environment. Distance learning through telecommunication tools can bring critical knowledge to the participants, particularly to information-poor hospitals and medical schools in developing countries. But the challenges to achieving this are great. A potential obstacle for cross-border application in e-education is that most students and trainees prefer to do their studies in their own countries to avoid the problems of licensure and certification. Language is another obstacle. One of the reasons that there is a lot *less* Web-based training in Europe compared to the United States is the fact that there are many different languages in Europe. Also, the course material has to be redesigned for on-line use and academics trained in lecturing online. This, however, raises the question of the "intellectual property" of the lecture material and can result in tension between academics and university authorities, who are likely to be possessive of their employees. Harvard University has restricted academics in giving on-line courses for outside companies since May 2000 (*International Herald Tribune,* 2000).

Ethical and Privacy Issues

Other obstacles to the growth of e-health are the need to standardize the ethical norms behind e-health, and to protect the privacy of patients and consumers online. Compared to other service sectors, the ethical limits to e-health are more acute because the lives of individuals and the well-being of the population in general are at stake. Unlike telemedicine, which is essentially point-to-point, e-health on the Internet is over an open system. It is therefore exposed to security and privacy breaches. Thus, ethical dimensions and privacy issues associated in e-health need to be carefully evaluated. Are e-health sites just interested in making a fast buck by foisting drugs and treatments on patients? Will patients trust Web doctors? Are personal health records and information safe on the Internet?

The uncertainties around the ethical issues and privacy protection in e-health are deeply rooted. There has always been a lack of trust on the public side toward the public or private institutions that keep their medical records. Collection and processing of consumer or patient information online may pose additional risks to the patient. During the purchase of prescription medications online, a consumer's medical history submitted to the Web site may be examined by a third party and possibly used for other purposes of which the consumer is not aware. Some health Web sites such as WebMD and GetFit.com already store a vast amount of consumer information through applications for free membership to the sites. These sites claim that they don't use the information in any other way, but the information may be accessed by employees, nonmedical staff, or even strangers (i.e., hackers) and also could be summoned by the courts, once it is known that it is available. The issues of who has access to this information will need to be considered and resolved in advance for wider propagation of e-health. Properly employed, heavy encryption and password-driven access can do the job; but the more fundamental problem of the lack of public trust will require greater efforts to overcome (Goldsmith, 2000).

Regulatory Issues

The nature of the Internet makes it difficult to enforce effective monitoring and controls over content and transactions. Currently, there are no discrimination or selection criteria for information posted on the World Wide Web (www). An innocent consumer then may not be able to judge the accuracy of the information and its relevance to his or her use. Another uncertainty of monitoring transactions on the Internet stems from the fact that it may be difficult to determine the physical locations of the client, the middleman, and the provider of the information or service. Considering these difficulties in regulating the Internet, the governance issues in e-health become more significant as health information, services, and goods offered over the Internet affect an individual's health and well-being. It is therefore necessary to address the challenges presented by the governance issues to promote "healthy" development of e-health and establish a framework for its functioning.

Legal and Insurance Issues   It is generally felt that legal uncertainties are the biggest barrier to the growth of online medicine. Changes in the legal framework are necessary to recognize the contractual legality of transactions on the Internet, and also to make these acceptable as evidence in a court of law. The major legal issues concern how to protect consumers against illegally dispensed drugs and malpractice in e-health. The concerns are mainly reactions to the emerging examples of dangerous medicine either prescribed or sold online to patients.[6] Negative stories like these could potentially discourage people from using e-health, if the cases do not result in disciplinary or legal action. At the same time, the problem of prosecuting online malpractice can itself become a very tricky issue, since the regulations imposed by governments could impede the development and growth of e-health.

International organizations, and some governments, have already begun to take action addressing the growing legal concern on e-health. For instance, the International Federation of Pharmaceutical Manufacturers Associations (IFPMA) states that "self-regulation is the method of controlling the type and quality of information provided by pharmaceutical companies over the Internet, on pharmaceutical products."[7] The "distance-selling directive" of the European Union (EU) is a piece of legislation that permits member states to ban mail-order pharmacy, and, by extension, Internet-based sales. The EU also bans advertising prescription drugs to consumers, although since 2000 the European Commission has allowed drug companies to post patient-information packs on their Web sites (*The Economist,* 2000).

Health insurance is another very important issue, especially in countries where health services are largely based on insurance schemes—such as in the United States and Japan. Probably the single most important reason why telemedicine, despite having been introduced some 30 years ago, did not develop to its full potential in these two countries is the lack of reimbursement by the health insurance schemes. This is now being addressed for e-health and recent changes have already been introduced in the U.S. national health scheme.

Mode 2—Movement of Consumers

Since Mode 2 is defined as consumers who go abroad for services, it is helpful to look at categories of such consumers, as well as some who are abroad for other purposes and also consume health services. These categories include:

1. Consumers who travel abroad for medical care (whose motives include seeking higher quality, lower cost, or faster treatment, or to return to their native society, or to receive services unavailable or illegal in their nation of residence);
2. Tourists who incidentally need medical care abroad;
3. Retirees abroad (who often have coverage in another country and who may have retired abroad for the cost or amenities, and who may be either native to the country to which they retire or the country from which they have coverage);
4. Temporary or migrant workers;
5. Cross-border commuters who may have multinational coverage options; and
6. Residents of multinational areas with integrated health systems.[8]

Even if one only counts the expenditures in category 1, consumers who cross the border for the purpose of consuming medical care, Mode 2 accounts for the greatest portion of expenditures in trade in health services. This is unlike most other services because the only formal decision a nation has to make under Mode 2 is whether or not to let their citizens go abroad for medical care. Thus, most nations have in fact made some Mode 2 commitments, either with respect to hospital services, other human services, or medical and dental services (Often these commitments are modified by the caveat that public medical insurance programs will not reimburse medical costs incurred abroad.) Nonetheless, it is crucial to understand the extent and nature of Mode 2 trade in health services since capturing or redirecting this trade is the basis for proposals to invest in infrastructure, and even to privatize facilities or programs in many developing countries, either by attracting additional persons from abroad or encouraging residents of the country to remain at home for health services. This chapter focuses on the first category. Further discussions of the other categories can be found in Warner (2003).

It is difficult to estimate the total amount spent by consumers who travel abroad explicitly to consume health care. Nevertheless, this is the one component of Mode 2 expenditures for which some data exist. Balance of payment statistics have the potential to capture this. About a dozen countries estimate health-related travel in their balance of payment statistics. The Interagency Task Force on Service Statistics, which includes the IMF, the OECD, Eurostat, the United Nations, UNCTAD, and the WTO, have developed the Manual on Statistics of International Trade in Services. With regard to personal travel the manual says:

"Personal Travel covers goods and services acquired by travelers going abroad for purposes other than business, such as holidays, participation in recreational and cultural activities, visits with friends and relations, pilgrimage, and education and health related purposes. The present Manual recommends a breakdown of personal travel into three sub-components—health related expenditure (total expenditure by those traveling for medical reasons), education related expenditure (i.e., total expenditure by students), and all other personal travel expenditure. This breakdown is the same as the supplementary information recommended in BPM5. In addition, separate data collected on, or estimated for, expenditure specifically on health and educational services are useful for analytical purposes and if these are available they should be provided separately"(Interagency Task Force on Service Statistics, 2002. p. 39).

It should be noted that all expenses except passenger fares for international travel of those who are traveling in order to consume health services are included in this health-related Mode 2 estimate. At a joint WTO-WHO workshop, Guy Karsenty presented 1999 estimates for health-related expenditures under this personal travel category. He estimated that, for the countries that reported under this category, health-related travel expenditures amounted to roughly 1.3 percent of total travel expenditures. If that were used as a proxy, it would amount to approximately $6.5 billion annually. Guy Karsenty stated that this number is likely to be an underestimate (see Table 7.1).

TABLE 7.1 **Selected Data on Exports in Health-Related Travel Expenditures, 1999**

	Travel expenditures (in billion US$)	Amount health-related (in million US$)	Share (percent)
United States	89.0	1300	1.5
Italy	28.0	367	1.3
Canada	10.2	62	0.6
Belgium-Luxembourg	7.3	93	1.2
Mexico	7.2	98	1.4
Poland	3.2	7	0.2
Croatia	2.5	36	1.4
Tunisia	1.8	9	0.5
Brazil	1.6	6	0.4
Slovenia	0.9	5	0.5
Lithuania	0.6	4	0.8
Romania	0.2	6	2.4
Senegal	0.2	2	1.2
Total of these countries	153.0	1995	1.3

Source: Data compiled by Guy Karsenty, WTO-WHO consultation on trade in health services, Geneva, January 2002.

Factors Motivating Patients to Seek Care Abroad: Quality

When a consumer travels abroad explicitly to consume medical care, there is usually a push-pull factor. The consumer is going abroad because he or she prefers care abroad to the care available at home. This disparity can be in terms of quality, availability, cost, and/or cultural familiarity. It might be useful to examine some particular examples of this phenomenon. One immediately thinks of world-class facilities like the M.D. Anderson Cancer Center and Methodist Hospital in Houston, or the facilities in London, or the Mayo Clinic when one thinks of people going abroad for medical care. And, indeed, these facilities do attract a number of elite and well-off patients from around the world and probably account for as much as a billion dollars or more annually in medical care. Kuwait and Saudi Arabia are in the process of developing world-class hospitals and medical schools that may attract some of the patients currently going to the United States or London for specialized care. But decisions by developing countries to attract or retain patients don't necessarily have to replicate world-class facilities.

Availability

One approach is to develop a particular service or set of services that people currently have to go abroad to receive. Malta provides an excellent case study of a country that invested in medical technology in order to reap gains from import substitution (N.B. when patients go out of the country one is importing medical care). Prior to 1995, all Maltese patients requiring cardiac surgery had to leave the islands, and MRI machines were not available until 1998. Malta has a unique relationship with the United Kingdom with regard to medical care. U.K. visitors to Malta (roughly 600,000 per year) receive free medical care for acute conditions and U.K. permanent residents receive care at discounted rates. In return, Maltese patients are treated free of charge in specialized hospitals of the National Health Service. Because of the expanded need for specialized care, since 1990 the number of patients has exceeded the agreed levels and Malta has had to reimburse the United Kingdom.

By 1995, Malta had to severely restrict the number of persons being referred to the United Kingdom for specialty care. At that time, Maltese specialists were attracted back to Malta and developed a cardiac surgery program, including a limited number of heart transplants, starting in 1996. Subsequently, a private hospital acquired an MRI machine, followed by the government hospital. As a result of developing these sustainable services, Malta was able to adopt criteria for specialized care comparable to that in a number of EU countries and to shorten waiting times substantially. Although the total cost was higher, the savings from not referring a number of patients to the United Kingdom was substantial and travel costs and lack of continuity were also avoided (Cachia, 2002).

Another example is where facilities may exist but patients nonetheless leave the country in great numbers because they prefer alternatives. In Bangladesh, for example, where the public expenditure for medical care amounted to only $3.60 per capita annually, there is concern that citizens spend as much as US$100–175 million annually abroad for medical care (Hasan et al., 2002, p. 19). Although patients go to Thailand, Singapore, the United Kingdom, the United States, and India, the majority probably go to India. A study that surveyed patients from Bangladesh who used private hospitals in Dacca as opposed to those who go to Kolkata (Calcutta) for care found that those who went to Kolkata were comparable in income to those who went to Dacca. They further found that the reasons for going to Kolkata were that the language was the same and that patients believed that the private sector in Kolkata was more advanced and had professional nursing staff and physicians who were more responsive to their needs than those in the private sector in Dacca. The authors of the study point out that the private sector in Bangladesh had expanded to the point that it comprised 21 percent of the beds in the country, but they believed that these hospitals, while often having technology not available in the public sector, could not afford to assure specialty physician care. The authors concluded that the government in Bangladesh should take initiatives to make physicians more accountable to patients, that the quality of nursing should be upgraded, and that shortages of technicians should be addressed. Finally, they believe that the government should encourage foreign direct investment in the hospital sector in order to be able to compete for Bangladesh patients currently going abroad (Hasan et al., 2002)

Some countries hope to attract paying patients from their region and from further away by developing or expanding specialized facilities. Examples include Thailand (Janjaroen and Supakankunti, 2002); India, where advanced cardiac programs have been developed in several hospitals (Waldman, 2003);[9] Chile, which has increased the numbers of patients from Bolivia, Argentina, and Peru using their facilities (Leon, 2002); and Australia, which has long served as a regional center for medical care and medical education (Benavides, 2002). In one example, Groote Schuur hospital in Capetown, South Africa, has developed an arrangement to treat British patients who need heart operations. "The scheme, which is a move to cut the hefty hospital waiting lists in Britain, could see between 500 and 1,000 British patients sent to Groote Schuur annually for cardiac bypasses alone. The operations would be performed in Groote Schuur's private wards with a 50-50 split of profit between the hospital and the private sector" (Cleary and Thomas, 2002).

Payment Issues

Patients who choose to go abroad for medical care for quality reasons often have to pay out of their own pockets, since the government or private insurance plans will generally not pay unless it is an emergency. Even within the European Union, although there have been several recent court cases that require certain national benefit plans to pay providers as they would providers inside the nation,[10] crossing borders for the purpose of receiving health care will generally not be covered by national health insurance schemes. There are insurance companies, however, that provide coverage in other countries as a benefit. Amil in Brazil and Amedex, based in Miami, which provides services to more than a million, mostly affluent, residents of Latin and Central America, include care in the United States in a number of their policies.[11]

Similarly, some private health insurance policies provide coverage for services both in Mexico and, if the deluxe line is purchased, access to care at participating hospitals in the United States as well. Grupo Nacional Provincial, the largest health insurer in Mexico, has historically offered Linea Azul, which has covered care by physicians and hospitals in Arizona, California, Florida, Louisiana, and

Texas, as well as a number of Mexican states (Aldrete and Williams, 1999, pp.173–196). How much is spent through these policies and out-of-pocket by Mexican citizens residing in Mexico for care in the United States on an annual basis is hard to estimate, but one would think that it would amount to well over $100 million annually.

Geographical Proximity

In some cases the ability of a developing nation to attract a number of paying customers from abroad will be determined by proximity and the characteristics of the neighboring country's health system. The price differential for many services is probably the most important factor in the large migration to Mexico of U.S. residents who are not covered by third-party payment. Schneider cites an analysis by the Sinclair Company in 1993 that "stated that when compared with charges at the 50th percentile in San Diego, the charges of an Exclusive Provider Organization in Tijuana were lower by 38 percent for medical procedures, 31 percent for surgery, 16 percent for pathology and 40 percent for radiology"(Schneider 1997). Primary care visits are generally only one-third to one-half as costly. A number of surveys of U.S. residents crossing to Mexico for medical and dental care and for pharmaceuticals have cited the price differential as extremely important or the most important reason for crossing the border (Arrendondo Vega, 1999). Studies of border communities also have seemed to show that a high percentage of all residents on the border who do not have coverage for dental care or pharmaceuticals are likely to seek services in Mexico. On the other hand, Mexican-Americans are also far more likely to seek medical care on the Mexican side of the border (McConnell et al., 1990). This is probably a function of lower levels of medical insurance coverage among Mexican-Americans as well as the higher level of comfort with culture and language on the Mexican side.

There is no doubt that the fact that Medicare does not cover outpatient pharmaceutical and dental care means that a number of older Americans (eligibility begins at 65) choose to cross the border for these services. In fact, one of the attractions of the lower Rio Grande Valley and southern Arizona for "snow birds" (retirees from the north who spend two to five months in the winter near the border) may be the availability of low-cost pharmaceuticals and dental care.

Mode 3—Commercial Presence

In the GATS, the third way international transactions in services can take place is commercial presence. This is defined as "any type of business or professional establishment, including through i) the constitution, acquisition or maintenance of a juridical person, or ii) the creation or maintenance of a branch or representative office, within the territory of a Member for the purpose of supplying a service" (Article XXVIII). Trade in health services through commercial presence can take different forms. Foreign investment in health facilities such as hospitals and clinics and in the establishment or acquisition of firms offering health insurance are two examples that dominate the literature, but there could be other areas, such as medical education, where foreign investment is relevant.

There are considerable gaps in the knowledge base concerning foreign direct investment (FDI) and health services trade. Most of the issues highlighted are "data free," based on theory, assumption, experience in other sectors, or conjecture. Unfortunately, empirically very little has actually been done on FDI and health. Therefore, it is currently impossible to fully assess the potential impact of FDI on health because of:

- uncertainty—there is no definitive interpretation of what existing agreements mean, together with opaque negotiations;
- lack of experience in cross-border trade in health services;
- lack of data generally; and
- lack of analysis of impact (partly a consequence of the above).

This uncertainty, together with limited experience/evidence and analysis, means that informed decisions cannot be made. This is critical because there is no time limitation on GATS commitments: in principle, commitments made now, on the basis of inadequate information, will still constrain policy indefinitely, whereas circumstances may change profoundly over time. Countries can place any limitations on their commitments they see as appropriate—but they have to specify what they are at the outset. The knowledge to make an informed decision about what limitations may be appropriate or necessary does not exist. A series of logical steps, questions, and items for clarification and research designed to provide an initial discussion of the issues to be addressed are presented below.

The Nature of the Current Public/Private Environment in Health

The basic information for assessing the impact of foreign commercial presence and FDI concerns the basic health care system (the "market") in the country. This includes a description of the level of government versus private funding of health care (with private funding further split by profit and not-for-profit organizations), the current demand and supply situation, the education and professional supply, the rural/urban split, the focus on secondary and primary care, etc. This is required before arriving at any conclusions about what may happen as a result of FDI. In particular, it is important for two reasons.

First, FDI is, by definition, only directly relevant to the *private market*. It is therefore important to establish the (potential) size of this market to assess the scope for FDI and its likely impact, e.g., FDI may *cause* a two-tier system, but one may already exist and the relevance is then on the degree to which it is exacerbated, or regulations are required to militate against it. Second, it could well be that "problems" observed within the health care system/market once FDI is encouraged are not actually related to FDI per se but, for example, to there simply being a highly privatized market. That is, there are two components to Mode 3: the "*commercial*" and the "*foreign*." That is, FDI may strengthen *or* weaken the health care system, but this depends largely on the structure of the *domestic* sector to begin with.

Thus, the first question is not whether or not *presence* in the health care market is *foreign*, but whether or not it is *commercial*. Most of the observed impact is probably not due to whether the country has a foreign presence, but how big the commercial sector is and thus whether we are talking of an increase in the proportion of the commercial presence or actually starting one from scratch.[12] We therefore begin with the idea of whether or not the health *system* is commercial (or the degree to which the commercial sector participates) and the effect that having or increasing the commercial *presence*—such as a two-tier system, or reduced emphasis on public health—will have **before** considering the impact that *foreign* presence will have in the commercial sector.

It is important to establish the regional context with respect to health and FDI. It could be that the decisions of neighboring countries impact upon the national decision, and/or impact upon the cost:benefit ratio of FDI in the domestic circumstance. It may also be that there are valuable lessons to be drawn from neighboring countries on the experience of FDI that may inform the view of FDI in the following sections. Overall, the extent to which FDI is a "regional" phenomenon is unclear, but there may well be scope for mutual benefits when there are shared cultures, language, social factors, and diseases of importance. Further, the status of the health sector in neighboring countries may also provide opportunities for more regional trade in health services via FDI. For example, this is occurring to a degree in the provision of hospital services across countries in Southeast Asia.

The Current Regulatory Environment

The current regulatory environment, and "strength" of a country will determine the effectiveness of safeguard measures and the stability of the GATS commitments. For example, in the case of disputes, would the existing legal establishment be able to deal with them? There is an important issue here of the balance of "power" between the national regulatory system and potential investors; in particular, multinational corporations, which in many cases are economically far larger than the countries they are seeking to invest in (Schaars and Woodward, 2002). The sustainability and cost-benefit balance of FDI will be determined to a large degree by the level, pace, and sequencing of regulatory reform.

In addition to the general regulatory environment, regulations that are directly pertinent to health are also important. These include, for example, regulation concerning the standards of health care and health care establishments; professional accreditation and mutual recognition; cross-subsidization policies; pro-poor regulations in health; restrictions on corporate hospitals; conditions placed upon profits, reinvestment, and resource transfer to the government; the role of professional bodies and the powers they exercise; medico-legal liability issues, and so forth. As indicated earlier, FDI will have a significant impact upon the domestic system as it opens up what may be a largely government sector to one that is contestable by commercial activity. If there is a desire to protect certain aspects of health care provision, and indeed finance, then the current regulatory system is a key variable, as is the level of development in that system that might be necessary if a commercial presence is to be encouraged/allowed.

Information Specific to FDI

Countries need to establish a range of information specifically related to FDI. The first important issue here is to establish what actually *constitutes* FDI. That is, it could be based on the proportion of ownership, in which case what the proportion is (e.g., 10 percent is often the minimum, but could be majority ownership at 51 percent or full ownership at 100 percent). Alternatively, it could be based on the management system being foreign or local, investment on an affiliate or nonaffiliate basis, or some combination. It is critical to establish this, as the "definition" of FDI will not only influence what is measured as FDI, but may also determine the performance of FDI initiatives. For example, equal partnerships appear to do badly in other sectors, as do initiatives with the government as a partner, whereas majority-owned local *or* foreign enterprises appear to perform equally well.

It is similarly important to distinguish between FDI that is "for profit" and that is "not for profit." For example, where nonresident nationals of a country may wish to improve the situation in their homeland, rather than necessarily seek large profits, there may be significant differences in the levels and types of FDI, and of course the cost-benefit ratio. This is a particularly relevant case in health services, as there is a significant amount of nonresident, diaspora-based FDI in health (as the Indian health case shows, where a lot of the equity investment in health is by nonresident Indians and mostly not-for-profit). It might therefore be useful for countries to have a breakdown of FDI in health between nonresident nationals and "foreigners," as this could provide important policy directions for tapping diaspora networks for getting FDI in health.

The second important issue here is to establish whether the core interest of a country is in inward or outward FDI, or indeed a combination/balance of both.[13] This will determine the scope of the analysis with respect to the other issues below, particularly the expected cost:benefit ratio. Related to this is also whether there is an FDI "national strategy," and whether there is an agency leading on this aspect of trade. In addition, it is important to establish, more specifically, whether there is a separate strategy for inducing inward FDI or promoting outward FDI in the health sector (and what relationship, if any, it has to the ministry of health).

The third important issue is to establish whether the country is primarily interested in hospital, and/or other institutional investment, or insurance as, again, this will determine the manner in which most of the remaining issues are approached.[14] Finally, it is important to establish the current extent/magnitude of FDI (unfortunately, there is a lack of this basic information globally at present), and its distribution, geographically and between subsectors.

How FDI is Expected to/Does Affect Health (Status and Distribution) and Health Services

Once the nature of the health system, regulatory environment and FDI, are established, the country is in a position to estimate both the potential and actual "impact" of commercial presence and FDI. Importantly, this should address both efficiency and equity measures, as well as health and other areas. The four key areas for assessment of the impact of FDI are described briefly here.

First, taking the information from the nature of the health system and regulatory system outlined above, **a country will need to establish its "attractiveness" to potential sources of FDI,** and thus identify what would need to change if it is to be made (more) attractive (e.g., tax concessions), and what would need to change to ensure that the "social objectives" with respect to health are protected. This will provide the baseline data to establish not only the impact of FDI per se, but also the impact that changes to the regulatory and/or health system as a result of FDI will have. This second aspect is important, as it is not simply a case of assessing the impact of FDI in isolation, but also the direct and indirect effects of changes in policy that result from FDI.

Second, and most intensive in terms of data collection, **is to establish the potential health and economic impact (costs and benefits) of FDI** (and over what time period—discounting will be an issue, as will risk analysis). This requires data collection concerning various financial, resource, production, outcome, and equity indicators. For example, it will be necessary to establish the impact of FDI on:

1. Health This will be difficult to establish, at least in the short run, but the key variable is the impact of FDI on "health." This may be measured, for example, through routinely collected statistics on mortality or morbidity, or could be obtained in more detail through survey or other work to estimate, for example, Disability Adjusted Life Years (DALYs).

2. Equity of Access to Health Care Services Given that most government intervention in health care is due to concerns over equity of access to services, this is a key question: to what extent will equity of access to health care services be affected by FDI? In order to map this, a series of indicators showing the types of changes that are taking place in the health care sector as a result of FDI would be required (these might include, for example, "cream-skimming," a two-tier system, or exploiting "niches").

3. Health Service Provision FDI will be encouraged principally because of its perceived effect on health services. Here then one needs to assess changes that occur in: (1) the quantity of health service provision, whether capacity increases, and more broadly what services are provided and to whom (for example, although overall capacity may increase, it may be that this increase is wholly concerned with high technology services provided only to the wealthy of a country, and the total capacity increase could mask a deterioration in one area, such as services to the poor); and (2) the quality of health service provision. Although capacity (quantity) may be increased, this may be at the expense of reduced quality of service, either of the new services delivered or in existing services (e.g., if FDI attracts the better professionals away from public services, the quality of these public services may fall).

4. Health Service Financing Health care finance is typically through some form of social or commercial health insurance, together with various levels of out-of-pocket payment. At the most basic level, there is a need to establish the change that might result in the public/private mix of health care financing (e.g., what FDI supplements or replaces domestic government or private finance), which might occur especially through increased FDI in the insurance market. Within the private sector, however, there may also be changes in the level of "competition," such as between hospital services, which may be assessed, for example, by measures of market concentration. There may also be changes in the way in which private services are financed. Within the health care market, there may also be changes in levels of efficiency of service provision, with impacts on financing, as well as relative prices. Finally, there may be an impact on financing of research and development.

5. Wider Socioeconomic Effects Trade in health services, and FDI, will have wider economic effects; these will also require assessing as they will be of particular importance to ministries of trade in their negotiations concerning GATS commitments, and liberalization of trade more generally. Although by no means exhaustive, some key areas where measurement of impact will be required will include foreign exchange, currency, and income (especially of inward FDI); local employment (e.g., is the internal "brain drain" hastened or lessened, are the jobs created unskilled or skilled?); changes in domestic skills and technology (e.g., are they upgraded or depleted? What is the impact on "human capital"?); and infrastructure in general (e.g., in terms of telecommunications, roads, and power generation). Much of this will need to be captured in some form of "FDI-specific" multiplier effect, as the effect of inward FDI should be to increase the size of the domestic economy more indirectly.

In all of the five areas highlighted, the perception of the information (i.e., whether or not FDI is seen favorably) will depend upon the perspective taken, and it might therefore be useful to envisage some form of "summary of FDI impact" categorized according to perspective.

A third key area for assessment is, from this information, **how best to adjust policy and regulations to improve or maintain health.** This is taken as the core objective for the purposes of this volume, but one could see this in the form of either maximizing the health impact of FDI subject to constraints in the others areas, or pursuing objectives in other areas with their effect on health as a "constraint." This might include, for example, maximizing balance of payments subject to ensuring that the population's health status is at least made no worse. In this respect there is arguably a need for some *decision-making algorithm* to balance these different impacts—especially the health and financial.

Finally, a fourth key is the need, from the information collected here, to **establish the impact of FDI attributable to, versus irrespective of, GATS** and therefore the actual impact of GATS per se rather than trade in health services more generally.

Mode 4—Temporary Movement of Natural Persons

GATS defines Mode 4 as "the supply of a service… by a service supplier of one Member, through the presence of natural persons of a Member in the territory of other Members" (Article 1 2(d)). There is a broad definition of "movement of natural persons" in the GATS, which covers all occupations, skills levels, and qualification levels. It can cover foreigners who are employed by a foreign company established abroad and that is supplying services under contract without a permanent presence. It also includes independent or self-employed service providers and foreign nationals employed in domestic companies (Butkeviciene, 2002).

The GATS defines the movement of natural persons as people seeking "nonpermanent" entry or "temporary" stay for the supply of services abroad. There is no specified timeframe for "temporary." Each country may interpret this according to its own specific national legislation, which may be reflected in the GATS-specific commitments (Butkeviciene, 2002). These may extend from a few months to several years, "which may be extended and might be different for different categories of persons" (Butkeviciene, 2002). However, permanent migration is explicitly excluded (Nielson 2002a).

The importance of services suppliers is emphasized. According to Nielson (2002a), Mode 4 is defined as covering:

- self-employed or independent service suppliers (paid by host country);
- employees of a foreign company who are sent to fulfill a contract with a host country client;
- employees of a foreign company established in the host country; and
- business visitors (short-term stays, no remuneration received in host country).

Nielson (2003) also suggests that, although Mode 4 is unclear, a working definition could be "Mode 4 service suppliers gain entry for a specific purpose (to fulfill a service contract as self-employed or an employee of a foreign service supplier), are normally confined to one sector and are temporary (i.e., … are neither migrating on a temporary basis nor seeking entry to the labour market)" (Nielson, 2003, p. 3).

Winters et al. (2002) argue that there is "an important ambiguity at the very heart of GATS." It is unclear whether "movement of natural persons" covers the "employment of foreigners in an economy or merely their ability to provide services via some form of contractual relationship" (Winters et al., 2002, p. 29). It is unclear whether a domestic company employing a foreign worker to deliver a service is covered by the GATS because a transaction takes place between a foreign worker and a company as well as between the company and the service provided. In the health sector, foreign health professionals would be covered if they worked as independent providers or were provided by a recruitment agency, but would not be covered if they were direct employees of a health care institution.

Cautionary Perspectives in Relation to Mode 4

Although countries are still drawing up commitments to Mode 4, there are some concerns about the position of workers who move as a result of GATS Mode 4 agreements. As these workers are not directly employed in the local labor market and are "temporary," their legal position will often be unclear and they may have few rights, especially if they have been recruited by external agencies. Pay levels and terms and conditions of employment may be more limited than they are for permanent workers. The uncertain legal position for temporary workers leaves workers open to exploitation. They may also be subject to racism. There are no core labor standards incorporated into the GATS.

There are also indirect results of temporary migration that lead to "de-skilling" of health workers. Health workers may find that they are unable to use their skills appropriately in the job that they have been recruited for, or that there is no on-the-job training or skills development. Recruitment agencies play a crucial role in helping workers from developing countries find work in developed countries but often charge high fees. Recruitment agency fees are often lower for less skilled jobs than for health professional posts. Health workers sometimes seek less skilled jobs because the agency costs of finding a job are lower.

Although developing countries have lobbied for Mode 4, the implications for the health sector of increasing temporary migration of skilled health workers is expected to result in shortages of skilled health professionals in some countries. In the Caribbean, nurse migration has resulted in nursing shortages in the region, decreased the capacity of health services to deliver health care, increased the costs of recruitment and retention, and lowered the morale of users and health workers.

Sustainable migration policies that address labor rights are considered to depend on the active management of migration and the recognition of mutual benefits between migrant and employer and between sending and receiving countries (Martin, 2003).

Potential for Future Mode 4 Negotiations

At the moment, country commitments to Mode 4 are relatively small and relate to highly skilled migration, which is particularly relevant for the health sector. In the future, negotiations may start to include less skilled migration. The list of service sectors developed for GATS and accompanying rules are connected to how a service is delivered rather than the job being performed or who is delivering it. Winters et al. (2002) suggest that a parallel list for Mode 4 be drawn up that "identifies service occupations relevant to temporary service delivery overseas and to use this to define scheduled commitments." This would help to make countries aware of how Mode 4 can be used and to monitor its effects.

Mutual Recognition Agreements are used to achieve some bilateral agreements on the recognition of qualifications and experience. In the health sector, recognition of qualifications and experience is particularly difficult because the sector is highly regulated in many countries through complex licensing requirements. If the movement of temporary workers is to be facilitated, extensive work needs to be done to develop internationally recognized qualifications, which could cover the specific needs of the health sector. An international system of skills and competency assessment is also needed to cover generic skills, e.g., management skills. In some fields, the adoption of occupational certification is often preferred over professional qualifications because it allows semiskilled and skilled workers to be used in nonprofessional areas (Brown, 2002). This has implications for the changing skill mixes that are increasingly needed to deliver health care.

Implications of Migration of Skilled Health Professionals

Although both developing and developed countries experience highly skilled migration, the effect of the loss of skills is different on the two groups of countries. For developed countries, e.g., the European Union, North America, there is more a process of "circulation", in which professionals will return to their country of origin. Many highly skilled migrants from the United Kingdom, Germany, and Sweden go to the United States and often return to their home countries. The proportion of skilled migrants who leave has an important bearing on the impact on the sending country. When skilled migrants only represent a small percentage of trained staff, the effect on the health sector will be much less than in a country where a significant proportion of highly skilled staff migrate.

For many developing countries, e.g., countries of Sub-Saharan Africa, skilled professionals may never return, so causing a loss of scarce skills and a loss of investment in training. Another form of skill loss is when highly skilled people migrate but they are unable to use their skills in the country to which they have moved (Ouaked, 2002, p. 155). There is an increasing problem of qualified nurses not being employed in posts requiring their skills, but rather being employed as nursing aides at lower rates of pay. Another result of large numbers of highly skilled health workers leaving developing countries for developed countries is that the skills they use and develop are shaped to the needs of developed countries, i.e., older populations, high rates of noncommunicable diseases. If they have the opportunities to develop new skills, these are often related to high technology equipment. This may make them better prepared to work in large urban centers and the private sector if they return to their sending country. They are unlikely to develop skills appropriate for working as primary health care workers at the local level in rural areas or to address health care problems in developing countries.

Migration of health staff from sending countries often lowers the morale of the remaining staff and worsens the health professional shortage. In South Africa, nurse migration has led to frustration and a decline in morale among remaining health staff, a loss of skills impacting on the quality of health services and increasing shortages of staff. In a survey commissioned by DENOSA, the South African nursing union, 60 percent of institutions reported recruitment problems. DENOSA has recommended increasing pay and conditions as a way of limiting the migration of nurses (Buchan et al., 2003). In 1998, the medical doctor vacancy rate in the public sector in Malawi was 36 percent. In Lesotho, public health nurse vacancy rates were estimated to be 48 percent. The loss of one doctor can result in a specialist unit closing.

Finally, the cost implications for developing countries of investing in education and training of health workers are large. It has been estimated that the loss of 82,000 South African doctors between 1989 and 1997 implied an overall loss of training investments of US$5 billion. The loss of investment is also proportionally greater in countries where there is a smaller number of trained health personnel.

There are, however, some positive effects of migration. For some developing countries, highly skilled professionals may return or set up networks with the expatriate community (Ouaked 2002, p. 155). The South African Network of Skills Abroad (SANSA) was launched in 1998 to link skilled South African migrants from a range of sectors and professions (Kaplan, Meyer, and Brown, 1999). It is hoped this will bring positive gains following the migration of skilled workers from South Africa.

Impact on "Receiving" Health Care Systems

The health workforce is aging in North America and Europe. A large percentage of the workforce will retire in many countries in the coming decade, which will lead to a shortage of experienced health staff. Unless this future deficit is addressed by increased training, career breaks, a more flexible home-work balance, and improved working conditions and pay, the demand for temporary health workers will increase.

In the United States, professional nursing bodies and trade unions are questioning whether there is a nursing shortage. They attribute the shortage of nurses to poor working conditions in health care institutions, in which U.S.-trained nurses are increasingly unwilling to work. Foreign trained nurses are being recruited to work in these settings.

In both the United Kingdom and the United States, the recruitment of foreign-trained health staff lessens the motivation to solve the problem of nursing shortages through increasing domestic training and recruitment and long-term human resource planning. In the United Kingdom, the National Health System (NHS) is increasingly dependent on recruiting nurses from abroad. The cost of recruitment per nurse is between £2,000 and £4,000. With more than 20,000 nurses recruited recently, this represents a significant investment of resources (Buchan et al., 2003, p. 36). New highly skilled health migrants can provide an influx of new approaches and skills to receiving countries as well as solving labor shortages. This may provide challenges for the existing health workers.

Trends in Migration of Health Personnel: Examples for Exporting and Importing Countries

Doctors and nurses are the two largest groups of highly skilled health personnel that migrate on short- and long-term bases. The main countries that send skilled health workers on a temporary or permanent basis are the Caribbean states, the Philippines, South Africa, Bangladesh, and India. Eastern Europe, Canada, and, to a lesser extent, the United Kingdom, Sweden, Australia, and New Zealand also send skilled health workers to other developed countries. The main receiving countries are the United Kingdom, the United States, Australia, Canada, and Norway. These countries are characterized by having a growing older population and a shortage of health professionals.

Philippines   The Philippines have experienced high levels of both temporary and permanent migration since the 1970s. The government set up the Philippine Overseas Employment Administration (POEA) to promote migrant labor. It has also developed partnerships with private placement agencies. The aim was to earn foreign exchange through migrant labor and reduce unemployment. There has been in increase in the number of highly skilled migrants, both temporary and permanent (Tujan, 2002). There have also been changes in the types of highly skilled migrants during the last 20 years. The number of nurses and paramedical professionals migrating increased in the 1980s. A large number of migrants are women; and the proportion of female migrants, including nursing and other health workers, has increased through this period (Tujan, 2002).

Another indicator of the numbers of nurses leaving the Philippines is the decrease in the numbers of nurses registered during the period 1995–2000. In 1995, 27,272 nurses were registered but by 2000, only 5,874 were registered (Professional Regulation Commission, Commission on Higher Education (PRC, CHE). Although there was a decline in the number of nurses graduating annually during this period from 49,802 in 1995 to 38,000 in 2000, there were still more than 30,000 nurses in 2000 who graduated but did not register (PRC,CHE).

Tables 7.2 and 7.3 show some of the extent of migration of health personnel, but they do not show the number of nurses and health workers who migrate as

TABLE 7.2   The Number of Temporary Health Workers Leaving the Philippines

Type of health worker	Numbers
Health and life sciences professionals	43,000 (33,000 women)
Hospital aides and caregivers	3,000
Life science and health associates professionals	
Caregivers, personal service workers	104,000

Source: Tujan, 2002.

domestic workers. A fee for the placement of a health worker is US$3000, but for a domestic worker the fee is less and so some health workers choose this route to find work abroad (Tujan, 2002). This results in health workers not using their skills and, in the long term, becoming "de-skilled." Labor recruitment agencies charge recruitment fees to provide labor for health care institutions in developed countries. They also link to job placement agencies, which charge health workers in the Philippines fees for placements in developed countries (Tujan, 2002). This is part of a global process of "contractualization" of labor. Placement fees are often high, causing health workers to mortgage properties or take out large loans. The costs of these loans are then taken out of wages earned. The expansion of recruitment agencies may increase with the implementation of Mode 4.

United States The United States is the focus of migration by health professionals from both developed and developing countries. One of the main routes for temporary health professionals is through the H-1B visa scheme. H-1B visas can be issued in 8 to 12 weeks, are valid for three years, and may be renewed for a further

TABLE 7.3   Main Destinations of Nursing Professionals

Main destinations	2002 March	2001	2000
Ireland	271	1,529	126
Kuwait	33	182	133
Saudi Arabia	1,213	5,045	3,888
Singapore	158	413	292
UAE	176	243	295
United Kingdom	944	5,383	2,515
United States	63	304	89
Total	2,908	13,536	7,583

Source: Tujan, 2002 from POEA data.

three years. From October 1999 to February 2000, 2,635 H-1B petitions were approved for health professionals in the following groups:

Physicians and surgeons	1,155
Occupations in medicine and health	851
Therapists	629
Total	*2,635*

Nursing is a profession that the Department of Labor has decided is experiencing a shortage of workers. Registration to practice is a separate process from applying for a visa. A nurse may apply for a Schedule A Labor Certification, if s/he has passed the Commission on Graduates of Foreign Nursing Schools Examination or if they have an unrestricted license to practice in the state in which they want to work. It is difficult to estimate how many foreign-trained nurses are practicing in the United States. One indication is that 26,506 nurses applied for Registered Nurses Licensure in the period 1997–2000 (see Table 7.4). However, a survey for the Department of Health and Health Services in 2000 estimated that there were about 100,000 foreign-trained nurses living in the United States, with about 86 percent practicing as registered nurses. Of these nurses, 72 percent are working in hospitals, which is a higher proportion than for U.S.-trained nurses.

A nurse may apply for three forms of work permit: an employment based Third Preference Immigrant Visa (green card); H-1B visa; H-1C visa. A nurse is eligible to apply for the H-1B visa if s/he is to work in a supervisory or highly specialized position and can show that the health care institution requires a graduate degree to practice. Five hundred H-1C visas ended in 2003 were issued annually, specifically for nurses, for jobs in underserved areas. They do not require the Commission on Graduates of Foreign Nursing Schools Examination. Visas are issued for three years and cannot be renewed. The scheme Table 7.5 shows the geographic origins of nurses admitted through this scheme.

TABLE 7.4   Nurses Applying for Registered Nurses Licensure, 1997–2000

Country	Percentage
Philippines	32.0%
Canada	22.0%
South Africa and Nigeria	7.4%
Kenya	7.1%
India	5.8%
United Kingdom	4.4%
Total	100% (26,506)

TABLE 7.5   Nurses Admitted through the H-1C Scheme

	Number	Percentage
Asia	190	35.5%
North America	153	28.5%
Europe	124	23.2%
Caribbean	46	8.6%
Africa	12	2.2%
Oceania	11	2.0%
Total	534	100

Source: 1999 Statistical Yearbook of the Immigration and Naturalization Service (in Nielson and Cattaneo, 2002).

GATS and THS Trends and Issues: A Summary Across Modes

Mode	Nature of trade in health services	Key issues discussed
1	Telemedicine and e-health services over the Internet	Ethical and privacy issues
	Health services over the Internet including education and training of health workers	Regulatory issues
	E-commerce and e-business practices used for health management and health systems, data storage and usage, using IT in health management	Legal and liability issues
2	Consumers who travel abroad for medical care	Cross-national disparity of health services quality, availability, cost, and/or cultural familiarity
	Tourists who incidentally need medical care abroad	
	Retirees abroad	Health insurance reimbursements for services
	Temporary or migrant workers	
	Cross-border commuters who may have multinational coverage options	
	Residents of multinational areas with integrated health systems	

(Continued)

(Continued)

Mode	Nature of trade in health services	Key issues discussed
3	Foreign investment in health facilities such as hospitals and clinics Establishment or acquisition of firms offering health insurance	Health impacts Equity of access to health care services Health provision (quantity and quality) Impact on health financing Wider socioeconomic impacts
4	Self-employed or independent service suppliers (paid by host country) Employees of a foreign company who are sent to fulfill a contract with a host country client Employees of a foreign company established in the	Loss of investment in training Health professional shortage in many developing countries Morale of remaining staff Return migration and gains in skills

Notes

1. Jane Lethbridge, "Trade in Health Services, GATS Mode 4: Movement of Natural Persons," WHO Globalization, Trade and Health Working Paper Series, November 2003.

Alwyn Didar Singh et al., "Trade and Health Related Services and GATS: E-health Potential and Challenge for Healthcare," WHO Globalization, Trade and Health Working Paper Series, July 2002.

Richard Smith, "Trade in Health Services: Commercial Presence—Foreign Direct Investment," WHO Globalization, Trade and Health Working Paper Series Background Paper, December 2002.

David Warner, 2003.

2. http://www.nttc.edu/telmed/indust.html

3. Singh, 2003. Sasha Hu, one of the authors of this report, conducted an evaluation of current e-health Web sites by studying 24 sites that were most often visited or mentioned in references.

4. Planet Medica, started in 1999, has launched consumer portals in Britain, France, and Germany, establishing future markets in Spain, the Netherlands, Belgium, and Italy. The Internet company plans to supply physicians in France, Britain, and Germany with technical information and with software for lease. The company's Web sites will also provide clients with information on costs and policies of health insurance.

5. For HealthNet's Web homepage, go to http://www.healthnet.org/hnet/hnet.html

6. *Financial Times* has reported that several online doctors or pharmacies prescribed Viagra to "consumers" (characters made up by *Financial Times*) who gave medical histories that clearly indicated potential health risks with taking Viagra. Similar cases have been reported in both the United Kingdom and the United States.

7. http://www.ifpma.org/Appendix.htm

8. Some analysts have also included temporary trainees and students in health and medical programs, including medical residents or nursing or medical students who go abroad. It appears more appropriate, however, to categorize health and medical students as being Mode 2, trade in educational services, and, to the extent that they provide services, as medical residents do, this should be considered Mode 4 in health services.

9. Dr. Reddi of Appollo Hospitals and Dr. Trehan of Escort Heart Institute come to mind. *See* Amy Waldman, 2003, p. 3.

10. The Kohl and Decker decisions and the Smits-Peerbooms ruling mentioned that undue delay in accessing needed care could be a criterion for requiring coverage of cross-border care.

11. Amedex Web site, http://www.amedex.com.

12. Notwithstanding that foreign commercial presence may affect the competitive structure of the domestic commercial sector, and that foreign providers may behave differently from local commercial providers (e.g., in services provided, market served, pricing, marketing, staffing, etc).

13. In this paper the assumption is that inward FDI is of most relevance to developing countries.

14. Note that health insurance comes into the financial sector for GATS commitments.

References

Aldrete, Horacio, and Ann Williams. 1999. Insurance companies and processes in the mexican insurance market. In David Warner, *Getting what you paid for: Extending medicare to eligible beneficiaries in Mexico.* U.S. Mexican Policy Studies Report No. 10, LBJ School of Public Affairs, Austin, Texas.

Arrendondo Vega, Jorge Augusto. 1999. The use of Mexican private medical services by American nationals in the border city of Tijuana. Doctoral thesis, University of London, May. Asian Pacific Research Network (APRNET), www.aprnet.org/journals/6/4/.htm.

Benavides, D.D. 2002. Trade policies and export of health services: A development perspective. In Drager N., and C. Vieira, eds., *Trade in health services: Global, regional and country perspectives.* Washington D.C.: PAHO.

Brown, E.A. 2002. The Jamaican experience with the movement of natural persons in the provision of services. Paper presented to the WTO symposium on the movement of natural persons, Geneva, 11–12 April.

Buchan, J., T. Parkin, and J. Sochalski. 2003. International nurse mobility: Trends and policy implications. WHO, April.

Butkeviciene, J. 2002. Temporary movement of natural persons (mode 4) under GATS. Presentation to the WTO symposium on the movement of natural persons, Geneva, 11–12 April.

Cachia, John M. 2002. Cost effective specialized hospital care in an island community—A case study of the Maltese islands. Paper given at a conference at Bad Hofgastein, Austria, September 28.

Cleary, Susan, and Stephen Thomas. 2002. Mapping Health Services Trade in South Africa. University of Capetown, TIPS 2002 Annual Forum, http://www.tips.org.za/research/papers/showpaper.asp?ID=569.

Economist, The. 2000. E-health screening. March 25.

Goldsmith, J. 2000. How will the internet change our health system? *Health Affairs* 19 January/February: 148–156.

Hasan, Abu Hena Reza, Sushil Ranjan Howlader, and Khaleda Islam. 2002. Cross-border use of health care by Bangladeshi patients in India: A study of determinants. University of Dhaka, Bangladesh, February.

Interagency Task Force on Services Statistics. 2002. *Manual on statistics of international trade in services, 2002* (Available from the OECD as Series M No. 86 of statistical papers from the statistical division of the Department of Economic and Social Affairs).

International Federation of Pharmaceutical Manufacturers Associations. 1998. The internet and pharmaceutical products: The state of the art and the way forward. IFPMA symposium, 6 Oct., Geneva. In: *International Herald Tribune,* Health web sites to unveil safeguards, May 2, 2000.

International Herald Tribune. 2000. Students log on for virtual education—Internet learning programs emerging as e-commerce's new frontier. June 23.

ITU (International Telecommunications Union). 1999. Challenges to the network: internet for development. Geneva

Janjararoen, W.S., and S. Supakankunti. 2002. International trade in health services in the millennium: The case of Thailand. In Drager, N., and C. Vieira, eds. *Trade in health services: Global, regional and country perspectives.* Washington D.C.: PAHO,

Kaplan, D., J-B. Meyer, and M. Brown. 1999. Brain drain: New data, new options. www.sansa.ac.za/documents/.

Karsenty, G. 2002. International trade in services statistics and trade in health services. Paper presented at Assessment of GATS and Trade in Health Services: An International Consultation on Monitoring and Research Priorities, WHO, 9–11 Jan.

Leon, Francisco. 2002. The case of the Chilean health system, 1983–2000. In Drager, N., and C. Vieira, eds., *Trade in health services: Global, regional and country perspectives.* PAHO, Washington D.C.

Martin, P. L. 2003. *Sustainable migration policies in a globalising world.* International Institute for Labour Studies, Geneva, ILO.

McConnell, et al. 1990. Cooperating in health care across the US–Mexico border: The Palomas Columbus experience. *Border Health* July–September.

Nielson, J. 2002a. Current regimes for temporary movement of services providers: Labour mobility in regional trade agreements. Paper presented at the Joint WTO–World Bank Symposium on Movement of Natural Persons (Mode 4) under the GATS, 11–12 April.

———. 2002b Movement of people and the WTO. OECD Working Paper on Migration, June.

———. 2003. A needle in a haystack: Migration statistics and GATS mode 4. Paper at Joint ECE–Eurostat Work Session on Migration Statistics organized in cooperation with the UN Statistics Division, Geneva, 28–30 April.

Nielson, J., and O. Cattaneo. 2002. Current regimes for temporary movement of service providers case study: The United States of America. Paper presented at the Joint WTO-World Bank Symposium on Movement of Natural Persons (Mode 4) under the GATS, 11–12 April.

New York Times, The. 2000. Physicians now face a wealth of clinical information Online. May 30.

Ouaked, S. 2002. Transatlantic roundtable on high-skilled migration and sending countries issues. *International Migration* 40(4):153–164.

Schaars, C., and D. Woodward. 2002. Measuring globalization of health services. WHO internal discussion paper, WHO/ EIP/HDE, Geneva.

Schneider, Pablo. 1997. Cross-border health services between the U.S. and Mexico: The San Diego-Tijuana region. Master's project, San Diego State University College of Business Administration.

Singh, A. D. 1999. Electronic commerce: issues for the south. South Centre, Geneva.

———. 2000. Background papers for ITC ExecForum.

———. 2003. Framework analysis for national country reports on cross-border trade in health services: Findings from Indian e-health study. Presentation made at WHO Workshop, Ottawa, July.

TeleMedicine Today. 1997. TeleMedicine in Pohnpei http://telemedtoday.com/articlearchive/articles/TeleMedicinepohnpei.htm

———. 1998a. TeleMedicine in Russia http://telemedtoday.com/articlearchive/articles/TeleMedicinerussia.htm

———. 1998b. TeleMedicine in Japan http://telemedtoday.com/articlearchive/articles/TeleMedicinejapan.htm

Tujan, A. 2002. Health professionals migration and its impact on the Phillipines. *APRN Newsletter* 6 (March 2002). http://www.aprnet.org/journals/6/4.htm.

Waldman, Amy. Indian heart surgeon took talents home, *New York Times*, May 10, 2003, p. 3.

Warner, David. 1997. NAFTA and trade in medical services between the U.S. and Mexico. U.S. Mexican Policy Report no. 7, LBJ School of Public Affairs, Austin, Texas.

———. 1999. Health care across the border: The experience of U.S. citizens in Mexico. U.S. Mexican Policy Studies Program, Policy Report No. 4, LBJ School of Public Affairs, Austin, Texas.

————. 1999. Getting what you paid for: Extending medicare to eligible beneficiaries in Mexico. U.S–Mexican Policy Report No. 10, LBJ School of Public Affairs, Austin, Texas.

————. 2003. Trade and health services. GATS Mode 2: Consumption of services abroad. WHO Globalization, Trade and Health Working Paper Series, July.

Warner, David C., and Lauren R. Jahnke. 2001. Toward better access to health insurance coverage for U.S. Retirees in Mexico. *Salud Publica de Mexico* 43 (1): 59–66, Enero-Febrero.

Winters, L.A., T. Walmsley, Z.K. Wang, and R. Grynberg. 2002. Negotiating the liberalisation of the temporary movement of natural persons. University of Sussex Discussion Papers in Economics Discussion Paper No. 87.

WHO (World Health Organization). 1997. Health informatics and TeleMedicine, EB99/INF.DOC/9. Geneva.

8

TRADE IN HEALTH SERVICES AND THE GATS: WHAT NEXT?

Richard Smith, Chantal Blouin, Nick Drager

Introduction

A considerable body of expert opinion and knowledge has been brought together in this book to consider how trade in health services, and GATS more specifically, may best be assessed by countries, and to provide an indication of key aspects in the epidemiology, economics, legal, and political arenas that require careful consideration when countries embark on negotiations for trade in health services, whether under GATS or otherwise. The handbook has defined GATS and which services fall under each mode; described current data that are available; provided an indication of how to collect such data; and suggested how such data may be analyzed and interpreted on a country basis. We hope that all of this will assist policymakers and other interested parties evaluating the liberalization of trade in health services.

Next Steps for Research and Policy

Each of the chapters within this volume highlights specific areas for further work in research and/or policy terms. We do not repeat these here, but rather draw together the common themes that we see as forming the basis for discussion of future research and policy agendas in the area of trade liberalization and health. We then conclude with a core central recommendation.

Research

GATS provides for certain risks and certain opportunities with respect to trade in health services, and the effect of this trade on population health, access to health, and economic factors. The core research requirement is a quantification of these effects. For instance:

- What is the impact of trade liberalization in health services on overall population health status?
- What is the impact of trade liberalization in health services on the distribution of health status in the population?
- What is the impact of trade liberalization in areas other than health services on population health status and its distribution?
- What is the impact of trade liberalization in health services on economic factors, such as GDP, BoP, or unemployment?
- What is the impact of trade liberalization under GATS compared with other agreements?
- What is the "added value" of GATS?

Data are currently scarce, and the annex to this volume provides an indicative framework for countries to use in assessing the impact of such trade. However, a starting point may be to more qualitatively outline the expected risks and opportunities presented by trade in health services, and GATS more specifically, following a format such as that presented in Table 8.1.

TABLE 8.1 Modes of Supply and Illustrative Opportunities and Risks

Supply modes	Opportunity	Risk
Mode 1: Cross-border supply of services	Increased care to remote and underserved areas	Diversion of resources from other health services
Mode 2: Consumption of services abroad	Generate foreign exchange earnings for health services of importing country	Crowding out of local population and diversion of resources to service foreign nationals
Mode 3: Commercial presence/FDI	Create opportunities for new employment and access to new technologies	Development of two-tier health systems, with an internal brain drain
Mode 4: Presence of natural persons	Economic gains from remittances of health care personnel working overseas	Permanent outflow of health workers, with loss of investment in education and training

One of the great challenges in terms of research on trade in health services is the availability of data. Presently, most data available on trade in health services are aggregated numbers of the extent of trade in services in general. To foster further analysis in the health sector, it is necessary to have disaggregated data and statistics on trade relating to the health sector, e.g., it will be necessary to use the GATS modes as well as relevant specifications of sectors and subsectors and types of services. The classification of health services will be a major problem for the task of measuring trade in health services. Since the "4 Modes" typology is part of the GATS agreement and is therefore being used internationally to classify trade in services, it is convenient to use the GATS modes to quantify trade in *health* services. However, it must be noted that the strict application of GATS to classify trade flows in health services can also constitute disadvantages. Indeed, the breakdown of modes of supply in the GATS diverges from the definition of what constitutes an international transaction in the national accounts (Maurer and Chauvet, 2002). Therefore, one has to use other sources to collect the information. At the international level, the balance of payment statistics as well as the Foreign Affiliates Trade in Services Statistics (FATS) can be useful sources of information (see Table 8.2). At the national level, governments should consider improving the collection of statistics on trade in health services in order to better understand the key trends at play. Gobrecht et al. (2004) have proposed a list of potential indicators that national agencies can track in this area (see Table 8.3).

Policy

Governments face key choices concerning the breadth and depth of trade liberalization related to health services. This degree of choice makes it imperative that health policymakers understand the structure, substance, and language of GATS especially, collaborate with other government agencies on GATS negotiations and commitments, and act to ensure that GATS does not adversely affect autonomy in national health policy. From the work undertaken for this book, there are several key points (outlined in box 8.1) that policymakers should therefore become familiar with.

Based on work to date, there are four key messages concerning health policy:

1. National stewardship of the health system in the context of GATS requires a sophisticated understanding of how trade in health services already affects a country's health system and policy.
2. The GATS process can affect many sectors related to health, and this fact places a premium on health ministries understanding the importance of a comprehensive outlook on trade in health services.

TABLE 8.2 Possible Statistical Information on Trade in Health Services from EBOPS and FATS

Modes of trade	Extended balance of payments services classification (EBOPS)	Foreign affiliates trade in services statistics (FATS)
Mode 1: Cross-border supply of services	Health Services under personal, cultural, and recreational services, covering services provided by health professionals, including via telecommunication networks. Most of it represents Mode 1 services. However, this category also indistinguishably covers some Mode 3 services.	
Mode 2: Consumption of services abroad	Health-related expenditure in travel. It covers foreign patients seeking care outside their territory of residence.	
Mode 3: Commercial presence/FDI		Provides information on the market share of foreign companies and their activity in the service sector (e.g., sales).
Mode 4: Presence of natural persons	Health services in personal, cultural, and recreational services. It includes information on services rendered by health professionals going temporarily abroad. However, this category mostly refers to Mode 1 services. Again, a main problem would be the definition of "resident" (e.g., BOP: 12 months; GATS Mode 4: up to 5 years).	Contains information on foreign employees within the foreign company according to the occupation.

A more complete picture of the presence of natural persons would have to be found outside BOP and FATS (e.g., to include migration statistics, employment statistics, as well as statistics on workers' remittances and compensation of employees).

Source: Gobrecht et al., 2004.

TABLE 8.3 Desirable Data Collection by Country

Cross-border trade		Consumption abroad		Commercial presence		Movement of natural persons	
Imports	**Exports**	**Imports**	**Exports**	**Imports**	**Exports**	**Imports**	**Exports**
• Value of traded health services (e.g., eHealth, eEducation, transcripts of medical records, health insurance • Country where service is provided • Type of service (some health related services might be hidden within larger aggregates)	• Value of traded health services (e.g., eHealth, eEducation, transcripts of medical records, health insurance • Country where the service is consumed	• Expenditure for traded health services in currency value (this data might need to be provided by the country providing the treatment) • Number of patients • Country of origin • Type of treatment	• Expenditure for traded health services in currency value • Number of patients Receiving country • Type of treatment	**FDI** • Inflows (currency) • Inward stocks (currency) • Country of origin • Type of investment **FATS** • Value of turnover • Turnover in host country as % of national total turnover of the respective industry • Value added • Country of origin of FA • Number of employees of FA • Employment of FA as % of total national employment in respective industry	**FDI** • Outflows (currency) • Outward stocks (currency) • Receiving country • Type of investment **FATS** • Value of turnover • Turnover in host country as % of national total turnover of the respective industry • Value added • Country receiving FA • Number of employees of FA • Employment of FA as % of total national employment in respective industry	• Number of health personnel (inflows) • Category of health professionals • Inward stocks • Inward stocks as % of national total • Country of origin • Duration of stay • Value of remittances from foreign employees into their home country.	• Number of health personnel (outflows) • Category of health professionals • Outward stocks • Outward stocks as % of national total • Receiving country • Duration of stay • Value of remittances sent home by of domestic health workers employed abroad.

Box 8.1: Key Points for Health Policymakers

- GATS establishes the multilateral legal framework for international trade in services among WTO members.
- The scope of GATS is very broad, which means that it applies to a wide range of health and related services.
- GATS covers policies, practices, and laws that affect trade in services among WTO members.
- GATS contains general obligations and disciplines that apply to all measures affecting services within the scope of the agreement.
- GATS allows WTO members to make specific commitments on market access and national treatment and to tailor those commitments to national policy ends.
- GATS sets the objective of progressive liberalization of trade in services, meaning that WTO mmbers will negotiate over new specific commitments in service sectors subject to the agreement.
- The process of progressive liberalization under GATS requires the active involvement of health policymakers.
- Before making any specific commitment under GATS, governments should ensure that they have thoroughly assessed the implications of opening health systems to foreign services and the potential costs and benefits of making legally binding commitments.
- Countries may wish to experiment through autonomous liberalization of certain aspects of health services, and only make commitments after a careful assessment of the effects of these.

3. GATS provides countries with choices and does not force them to make liberalization commitments that are not in their best interests. If a country is unsure about the effects of making specific commitments, it is fully entitled to decline making legally binding commitments to liberalize.

4. Health principles and criteria, as outlined in Box 8.2, should drive policy decisions on trade in health services in GATS negotiations.

GATS constitutes one of the most important trade agreements from the perspective of health. Unlike the relationship between health and other WTO agreements, the GATS and health interface will be most significantly shaped by the ongoing and subsequent efforts to progressively liberalize trade in services. In light of this reality, countries must develop informed and sophisticated approaches to managing the GATS process, its results, and future liberalization efforts. WHO is developing capabilities to assist countries in this endeavor but, without the commitment by national governments, the protection and promotion of health in the

Box 8.2: Health Policy Principles to Guide Liberalization of Health Services

- Liberalized trade in health services should lead to an optimal balance between preventive and curative health services.
- Involvement of both private industry and civil society is important to ensure that liberalization of health services trade promotes participatory health policy toward achieving national goals.
- Improving access and affordability of health services should be a goal of liberalization of trade in health services.
- Developing countries, and least-developed countries even more, deserve special consideration in the process of liberalizing trade in health services.
- The status of health as a human right should inform and guide proposals to liberalize trade in health services.

GATS process may be compromised. To promote the engagement of health ministries in the issues concerning trade in health services, a checklist, presented in Box 8.3, is suggested to help health policymakers move forward with dealing with trade in health services. Examples from Thailand and Canada are provided in Box 8.4.

Box 8.3: Checklist for Policymakers on Trade in Health Services

- Identify a focal point for trade in health services within the country's ministry of health.
- Establish contacts and systematic interactions (e.g., a GATS working group) with trade and other key ministries and with representatives from industry and civil society.
- Collect and evaluate relevant information on the effects of existing trade in health services within the country (using the framework in the annex of this volume).
- Obtain reliable legal advice not only on GATS but also on other international trade and investment agreements (e.g., bilateral investment agreements) that may affect trade in health services.
- Develop a sustainable mechanism for monitoring the impact of trade in health services generally, and GATS specifically.
- Utilize the information and technical assistance provided by WHO on matters concerning trade in health services.
- Subject all requests for, and offers of, liberalization of trade in health services to a thorough assessment of their health policy implications

> ## Box 8.4: Trade and Health: The Institutional Process in Thailand and Canada
>
> The process of making policy on trade and health entails institutional innovations for many national governments. Indeed, since services are now included in trade negotiations, officials from trade and health ministries had to find ways to collaborate to develop national trade strategies, a departure from the previous situation where trade ministries often monopolized trade policymaking. For instance, in Thailand, the Ministry of Commerce was the only institution involved in the GATS negotiation at the WTO for Thailand until 1995–96 (Wibulpolprasert and others, 2004). However, in 1997, the structure for international trade negotiation in Thailand was reformed and began to involve many more stakeholders, including all concerned ministries, private sectors, academics, and civil society organizations. The Ministry of Commerce is still the main agency, responsible for the secretariat of the National Committee on International Trade Policy, but the new infrastructure provides an umbrella for the human capacity developments as well as the networking of all stakeholders. Thus, in 1998, the Ministry of Public Health established a Ministerial Committee on Health Impact from International Trade, with three subcommittees related to TRIPs, SPS/TBT (sanitary and phytosanitary measures/technical barriers to trade), and GATS; each was assigned a secretariat. These are all ad hoc structures with inadequate expertise on a noncontinual basis, but these subcommittees have provided useful outcomes. The most important one is the realization among officials of the significance of international trade in health in Thailand and the networking of stakeholders. The regular meetings resulted in a better understanding of GATS among stakeholders, as well as a clearer national position for the national negotiation focal point, i.e., the Department of Trade Negotiation, Ministry of Commerce.
>
> Public health experts and academicians in Thailand as well as civil society organizations also started to get involved and build up technical capacities on international trade and health, through research, workshops, and meetings. For instance, in 1997, the Thailand Research Fund, a public independent fund, supported two separate studies on GATS and Health Services. In 1998, in response to the new Foreign Business Bill and the attempt at creating discipline for professional licensing by GATS, the Thai Medical Council sponsored a study on the possible implications of international trade on the national health system. This resulted in the amendment of the Foreign Business Bill.
>
> In Canada, one also observed increasing collaboration between the trade ministry and the health ministry in order to deal with the GATS negotiations. Hence, Health Canada has dedicated full-time staff in several parts of the department to address the linkages between health system policy and trade policy, as well as health protection activities that may be affected by trade (e.g., labeling of health products). International Trade Canada (ITCAN) regularly consults with domestic federal departments such as Health Canada regarding sector-specific issues across all of the negotiations Canada undertakes. Health Canada and

(Continued)

ITCAN officials are in regular contact when issues of key concern come up in trade fora such as the WTO, and may involve officials from other federal government departments (e.g., the access to medicines issue under the TRIPS Agreement, which involved many departments and/or agencies). Topic-specific workshops and consultation sessions are hosted by this group of health/trade policy experts with colleagues and stakeholders who have the specialized expertise needed to evaluate the general policy implications of any given trade or health policy option. Research projects are undertaken by this group of officials, either directly or via some other means (e.g., a research project led by an academic or academics skilled in a relevant field, such as trade law). Finally, federal, provincial, and territorial officials participate in the Federal-Provincial-Territorial Committee on Trade, which meets quarterly to exchange information and develop Canadian positions on a range of trade policy issues, including negotiation.

We should note that, in addition to that interdepartmental collaboration, the Canadian government has been taking measures to increase the transparency of its trade policymaking process as well as its engagement with civil society organizations. The government consults with nongovernmental organizations representing a broad cross-section of interests, including business, labor, environmental, human rights, international development, academic, consumer, youth, and gender groups. So how has the Government of Canada ensured that Canadians play a role in setting trade policy? It has expanded transparency and engagement by:

- facilitating closer attention by parliamentary committees;
- seeking broader political and social goals through trade policy, not just economic ones; undertaking extensive consultations with Canadians, and especially key stakeholders, through a myriad of formal and ad hoc consultative mechanisms;
- working in close partnership with provincial and territorial governments across the waterfront of trade policy, but especially in regard to the areas of trade policy, such as health care, that fall within provincial jurisdiction pursuant to Canada's Constitution.

On Canada's health system, the message received from this engagement is clear: Canadians seek assurances that their health system will remain intact for them and for their children into the future. Therefore, Canada took a somewhat unique position when the current round of GATS negotiations commenced in April of 2001 by proactively announcing that it would not take commitments in the health sector.

Core Recommendation

The core recommendation from this book is that members who would like to open their health sector to foreign providers should consider "sampling" liberalization outside of GATS before making GATS commitments. Members can liberalize trade in health-related services unilaterally, if they wish, without accepting binding commitments in their national GATS schedules of specific commitments. Such unilateral liberalization would allow WTO members to experiment with such policies in a way that permits them to reverse course on market access or national treatment if the experiment produces unsatisfactory results. The reversal of a unilateral liberalization of trade in health-related services would not be subject to GATS rules on providing compensation to WTO members affected by the change in market access or national treatment. For WTO members also bound by bilateral or regional treaties affecting trade in services, unilateral liberalization policies may have greater legal significance than under GATS.

In simple terms, using a common market adage, we recommend that countries should "try before you buy"!

References

Gobrecht, Jens, Richard D. Smith, and Nick Drager. 2004. "Measuring Trade in Health Services.", WHO Working paper.

Maurer, A., and P. Chauvet. 2002. "The magnitude of flows of global trade in services." In B. Hoekman, A. Mattoo, and P. English, eds., *Development, trade and the WTO*. The World Bank:235–246.

Wibulpolprasert, S. C. Pachanee, S. Pitayarangsarit, and P. Hempisut. 2004. "International service trade and its implications for human resources for health: a case study of Thailand." *Human Resources for Health* 2:10.

TRADE IN HEALTH SERVICES AND GATS: A FRAMEWORK FOR POLICYMAKERS

Rupa Chanda, Richard D Smith

Introduction

This appendix presents a framework[1] that has been designed to capture a wide range of issues that have a direct or indirect bearing on trade in health services generally, and more specifically in the context of the GATS.[2] The framework aims to guide policymakers toward: (1) a holistic and comprehensive understanding of the state of trade in health services across all four modes of the GATS; (2) relevant mode-specific aspects of trade in health services, by drawing linkages between the general economic and health environment and the modal characteristics of trade in health services; and (3) institutional, legislative, infrastructural, and other shortcomings in assessing trade in health services and preparedness for the GATS negotiations.

The framework is designed to achieve these aims through assisting countries in gathering information to help policymakers understand the nature and implications of international trade in the health sector, and thus assist them in formulating trade policy as well as in international negotiations concerning the health sector. In doing so, the framework will also assist in the identification of information and data gaps, and thus help prioritize, streamline, and coordinate data collection in this area, as well as helping to avoid duplication of information and effort in assessing the opportunities and risks involved in engaging in wider trade liberalization in health services. It is hoped that the framework will also help in the systematic collection of comprehensive qualitative and quantitative information on trade in health services for a wide range of countries across different regions.

The rationale followed in the development of this framework is that trade in health services, in general as well as in the context of the GATS, is a complex subject. It requires an understanding of numerous interconnected facets that concern the health system, the domestic economy, health and trade policy, and international relations, among others. Although each country faces a unique context in terms of its current development status, the opportunities and challenges it faces with regard to trade in health services, and its larger objectives with regard to trade, economic development, and health, some fundamental factors underpin each of these specific contexts. These fundamental factors include the state of the domestic health care system, the trade and sectoral policy framework, the infrastructural and regulatory framework within which health services are traded, and the availability of information in this regard.

For example, the nature and impact of trade liberalization in health services is likely to depend on prevailing domestic economic conditions and health systems. Similarly, the impact (expected or realized) of each specific mode of trade is likely to be influenced by a variety of factors, such as the prevailing trade and health sector policies that pertain to each mode, the human and physical infrastructure of the health system that facilitates or constrains trade in each mode, and the regulations that ensure gains and mitigate costs associated with trade in each mode. Finally, assessment of this impact and an understanding of the implications of trade liberalization in health services will depend on the availability of data on the health sector and trade as well as evidence from other countries and sectors in this area.

The role of this framework is to draw out the "common" elements that can be useful to all countries and that can be built upon and adapted to suit country-specific circumstances. Thus, the framework provides a generic structure for analysing trade in health services, but a structure that is flexible and easily adaptable to different local contexts, concerns, and priorities. This flexibility is key to the successful adoption and use of the framework.

Framework Structure

The framework that is proposed addresses the principal issues that are a prerequisite to analyzing trade in health services. It also serves as a guideline for identifying gaps that need to be addressed if countries are to undertake autonomous or GATS-specific liberalization in health services, benefit from such liberalization, and address potential adverse consequences of such liberalization. By offering a common format and a standard questionnaire, the framework is designed to facilitate the establishment of a common database and data collection techniques; it is also designed to allow greater sharing of experiences and data across countries, and enable cross-country learning and comparative assessment of the effects of autonomous or GATS-related liberalization.

Figure A.1 Proposed Framework for Policymakers.

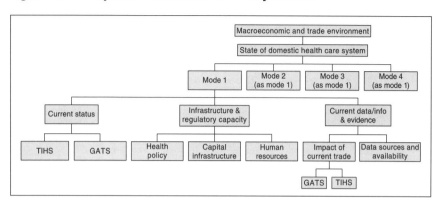

The framework is structured to provide a logical flow from general issues that are relevant across modes to mode-specific issues. Each of the mode-specific issues is structured in a similar fashion, in order to generate familiarity with the framework and comparable results obtained. The overall framework structure is illustrated in the figure A.1.

Starting at the top, the first element within the framework establishes the relevant background details on the general macroeconomic and trade environment in the country concerned. In order to understand the nature and the implications of trade in health services, it is necessary to first collect basic background information on the macroeconomic and trade environment within which this trade occurs. It is this environment that shapes the impact of health services trade and influences the adoption of policies to regulate/promote such trade. This includes information on the macroeconomic status and stability of the country; its trade and balance of payments position; the degree of openness of its trade and investment regime, both overall and specifically in the case of services; and overall policy objectives. Thus, a mix of quantitative and qualitative information is required under this category.

At the next level, the second element narrows down from the general environment to the state of the domestic health system more specifically. Since the implications of trade in health services under any of the modes is shaped by prevailing conditions in the health sector and in related areas, it is important to collect information on the state of the domestic health care system. This includes such aspects as the amount of investment in the health care sector; demand and supply conditions; the public-private balance in health care; the policy environment; infrastructure conditions; the regulatory framework; human resource capabilities; and labor market conditions in the sector. The important aspect here is to identify the factors that constrain and facilitate trade in health services and how trade in health services may impact on these factors, positively or adversely. Using this information, one is then "streamed" toward one or more specific modes, depending on what is most relevant to each country, given available information.

The third level comprises the mode-specific elements. There are three aspects that are covered under each mode. The first concerns the current status of trade and investment in the health sector and the direction of policies in this regard, as well as the current status of GATS commitments and proposed liberalization in the context of the GATS, for the mode in question. The framework builds upon this core set of mode-specific background information and raises a large number of optional, supplementary questions that are aimed at collecting more detailed information on trade and investment in the health sector, including the extent and nature of trade and investment in health services, associated policies, areas and modes of comparative advantage within the health sector, perceived/realized benefits and challenges from opening up the health sector, and the existing and proposed nature of GATS commitments in the health sector as well as in related sectors.

The second aspect of the mode-specific element of the framework concerns the institutional capacity with regard to trade in health services, both within and without the context of the GATS. The framework raises core questions about the state of the country's regulatory, legislative, economic, analytic, and administrative capacity for assessing trade in health services and for undertaking domestic policy measures and initiatives at the bilateral/regional/international levels to promote and regulate this trade. These core questions are supplemented by optional questions on the effectiveness, use, nature, strengths, and weaknesses of this institutional capacity. The aim is to help countries identify gaps in their institutional capabilities and structures and strengthen them accordingly so as to deal more effectively with liberalization of health services.

The third aspect of the mode-specific part of the framework concerns data sources and availability of information in the health sector. The core questions on this aspect concern the state of data and information on the health sector in general and specifically with respect to trade and investment in health services. This is followed by supplementary questions on key sources and quality of data and other information on the health sector in general, and more specifically on trade and investment in health services, and the institutional framework at the national and international levels for data collection and dissemination in this regard. The aim is to help highlight gaps and ways to improve the state of information in this sector and thus enable more effective assessment of trade liberalization in health services.

The framework is thus structured in a layered and hierarchic format, starting with the broader economic and sectoral context within which trade in health services takes place, followed by the mode-specific aspects of this trade, with a set of core and supplementary questions at each stage. It is expected that all countries will answer the core or basic questions and use these to determine which supplementary questions are appropriate for them to answer, given their specific interests and concerns, as the supplementary questions are designed to delve deeper into the issues raised by the core questions.

The figure below illustrates the questionnaire structure that is used both in the general and mode-specific parts of the framework.

This tiered structure is aimed at:

(a) highlighting linkages between the broader economic and sectoral context within which trade in health services occurs and the mode-specific aspects of this trade;

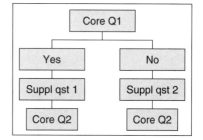

(b) helping policymakers prioritize across modes and steer them toward the most relevant modes; and

(c) helping countries focus on specific policies, strategies, and issues within each mode and address their particular needs and concerns.

Using the Framework

Although it is recognized that countries will differ in how they administer the framework, certain organizational and procedural aspects are suggested as common across countries.

Organizational Steps

The first organizational step in using the framework should be the establishment of a Framework Task Group. This group would consist of a range of experts who would guide the development, administration, and analysis of the framework. This group might include a representative from the appropriate WHO regional body, an expert from WHO headquarters who is familiar with the use of the framework in other areas, a representative from the health ministry, a representative from the trade ministry, a representative of the health providers (both public and private), and representatives from other stakeholder groups, depending on the modal focus of the framework.

This group would initiate, monitor, review, and finalize the framework and report, and would also be responsible for carrying the issues, such as making recommendations for the GATS negotiations, forward to the next stage. This group might also initiate a program of capacity building, such as by raising awareness about the GATS among the health community, and about health services among the trade community, and bring these two key groups together to ensure more effective use of institutional capabilities.

The next organizational step would be to delegate the management of the framework process to an individual or group, perhaps someone in-house or an external consultant. This individual/group, assisted by the Task Group would be charged with implementing the framework questionnaire and presenting the results to the Task Group.

Procedural Steps

Procedurally, the first step would be for the Task Group to assess those elements within the framework that would be most relevant, given the specific country context concerned. As noted earlier, the framework is designed and presented in a generic form. Hence, it does not distinguish, for example, between elements that may be more or less relevant to countries according to their stage of economic development, nor does it focus specifically upon either the export or import of services or on any one particular mode more than any other. As the various elements highlighted in the framework would have varying significance for different countries, the Task Group would need to identify the key elements of interest to the country, prioritize across them, and steer the questionnaire toward the most relevant issues and modes. It is hoped that the framework, by taking a tiered approach consisting of core and supplementary components, will permit such country-specific adaptation.

The second procedural step in using the framework would be to identify the sources of data for the questionnaire. This will mostly include a mix of readily accessible national data, which the group managing the project may complete by itself or employ a national data collection organization to do, as well as data obtained through interviews. In each case, the idea would be to seek the best possible source of information available. Of course, sources of information will differ across countries, ranging from quantitative data collected on a regular basis, to qualitative information obtained from different stakeholders, to simply anecdotal evidence, perceptions, and views. For the purposes of this framework, all of these forms of data or information would be "valid," as the aim is to enable the best possible assessment of the status and impact of trade in health services and liberalization commitments under GATS.

To assist the process, indicative responses to each question, such as whether the answer should be qualitative or quantitative and whether it is a closed or open-ended question, have been provided in the questionnaire. In addition, possible sources of data or information, such as whether information should be sought from national and international statistics, existing publications, stakeholders, and so forth, are also indicated for each question. Given the nature of most of the questions, it is expected that much of the information sought in the questionnaire will be best obtained through interviews with concerned stakeholders and experts. Thus, it is further recommended that relevant parts of the framework, which cannot be readily filled through available information sources, be administered through detailed semistructured interviews and discussions with relevant stakeholders, and that this task be assigned to a trained interviewer. It is important to note that the framework cannot be self-administered through postal or other impersonal methods, as it is potentially demanding. Approaches other than personal interviews are likely to yield very poor response rates or poor quality information. Moreover, since many parts of the questionnaire have deliberately been kept open-ended and flexible, to permit adaptation to specific country contexts, such as by permitting rephrasing or removal of questions, an interview-based approach would be able to elicit more-appropriate and better-quality information. About 20 such semistructured and detailed in-person interviews should suffice to complete the framework.

It is also important to note that, despite the built-in flexibility of the questionnaire, there may be questions that are difficult to answer, as data may not be available from existing sources or may prove difficult to obtain even from interviews and discussions. However, inability to do so may also serve a purpose, by helping countries identify information gaps and institutional limitations, and therefore guiding further developments in such areas. Overall, the entire process can be expected to take around two to three months to complete, from establishment of the Task Group to drafting of the final report.

Analyzing the Results for Policy Analysis of GATS

As the questionnaire gathers together information from a variety of sources, and in a variety of formats (quantitative and qualitative), it is not possible or desirable to produce a "mathematical" algorithm for determining a country's approach to trade liberalization in health services (within or without the context of GATS). Rather, the framework pulls together, in a systematic manner, the most relevant items of information that policymakers will need to assist them in this respect and to work through the complex economic, sectoral, social, and international issues that surround trade liberalization and health services.

The information that is gathered based on this framework and questionnaire is therefore expected to serve three broad purposes. The first purpose is awareness creation and sensitization. It is expected that the process of completing this framework will help bring countries up-to-date on the current status and characteristics of trade and investment in health services and their country's prospects for liberalization in this regard; this process should also sensitize them to the associated benefits and challenges, whether realized or perceived. Such awareness creation would help countries understand their interests and concerns and their strengths and weaknesses in this area.

The second purpose is policy identification and formulation, at the national, bilateral, regional, and multilateral levels. It is expected that the results will help countries to identify areas and issues on which to focus and prioritize in terms of policy measures and initiatives at various levels, with a view to facilitating trade in health services and ensuring the associated gains, and mitigating the associated adverse effects. In addition to guiding the decisions as to whether or not they should liberalize, or make GATS commitments, the results from the application of the framework may also be used to identify restrictions to be included in the schedule of commitments. One example would be helping policymakers identify regulatory measures they want to protect in the health system, even if they make liberalization commitments.

The third purpose is to identify gaps in data and information, and existing data collection systems and procedures. It is expected that identification of such limitations will provide the basis for establishing appropriate procedural, organizational, and institutional structures and systems to improve the state of data and information relevant to understanding and assessing trade in health services.

Framework Questionnaire

This section presents the general as well as mode-specific questionnaire, consisting of core and supplementary questions. It is important to note at the outset that:

1. The definitions of the modes are as laid down in the GATS, and thus are as described in chapter 7 of this handbook.
2. Many of the issues are highly interrelated and thus may appear duplicated across the modes. Although there are variations in the presentation of these issues depending on the theme or mode in question, the associated questions are largely similar, mainly because of the similarity in the underlying core issues. Such repetition, however, is likely to help in consistent data gathering across the modes and enable quicker familiarity with the questionnaire.
3. The relative emphasis is on *inward*, as opposed to *outward*, trade and investment (i.e., on imports as opposed to exports of health services), as the former is likely to be more important for a larger number of developing countries.

However, it is also recognized that for several developing countries, export of health services, particularly via certain modes, is important. Given the adaptable nature of the framework, this relative emphasis can easily be addressed, as required, with minimal changes to the questionnaire.

As outlined earlier, there are three parts to the framework; the general macroeconomic and trade context, the health sector-specific context, and the mode-specific aspects of trade in health services. These three parts are denoted in the questionnaire as Element G (for general), Element H (for health), and Element M (for mode-specific), respectively. Element M is further subdivided into Elements M1, M2, M3, and M4 for the four GATS modes. For elements G and H, the core questions are numbered consecutively, starting with G.1 and H.1, respectively. Under each of the mode-specific elements, there are three further subparts, namely, the current status of trade and investment, the institutional and regulatory capacity, and the state of data and information. The core questions in each of these subparts for the four modal elements are consecutively numbered as M1.1 to M1.3, M2.1 to M2.3, M3.1 to M3.3, and M4.1 to M4.3, respectively. These are followed by supplementary questions that flesh out the basic information sought by the core question and provide a richer set of information. However, the supplementary questions may be omitted if found to be inappropriate, or too cumbersome or difficult to answer, and the responder is free to move on directly from one core question to the next. It is, however, expected that countries will address at least some of the supplementary questions so as to have some level of detail and richness in the information gathered to be useful for further analysis. Moreover, it is also expected that countries will tailor all questions, core and supplementary, to suit their specific contexts and work through the questionnaire in the manner most appropriate to their needs and interests.

Notes

1. The discussion in this annex draws upon mode-specific frameworks and background papers that were prepared under the WHO Trade in Health Services project, and summarized in chapter 7. This annex pulls together the key aspects of these individual papers and frameworks to provide a general schematic that can be followed by different countries and fine-tuned to their individual interests and concerns.

2. It is important to note that although the framework presented here makes use of the GATS' modal structure to frame the relevant issues, this framework can also be used outside the GATS context for a general assessment of trade in health services.

ELEMENT G: General Macroeconomic and Trade Environment

CORE QUESTION G.1	1. TYPE OF ANSWER	POSSIBLE DATA SOURCE
At what level of economic development is your country?	OECD classification: —High income —Middle income —Low income	National accounts OECD classification Multilateral sources—UN, World Bank, IMF
SUPPLEMENTARY QUESTIONS G.1	**2.**	
1. What is your country's GDP?	Level in US$ (nominal exchange rate, purchasing power parity)	National accounts International sources
2. What is your country's GDP per capita?	US$ per person (nominal exchange rate, purchasing power parity)	National accounts International sources
3. What has been your country's recent overall performance?	Real GDP growth rate for the last 3 years Inflation rate for the last 3 years	National accounts International sources
4. Is the economy generally stable?	There have been periods of economic instability (meaning balance of payments crises, debt default, external shock): —In the last year —In the last 3 years —In the last 5 years —Earlier	National accounts Policy documents Minister of Trade International sources Media
CORE QUESTION G.2	**3. TYPE OF ANSWER**	**POSSIBLE DATA SOURCE**
How would you characterize your country's trade regime?	—Open —Moderately open —Closed	Interview with Trade Minister Policy documents Existing trade data from national, WTO, and other international sources
SUPPLEMENTARY QUESTIONS G.2	**4.**	
What is the pattern of trade?	Geographic and sectoral distribution of trade	National, WTO, and other international ources

ELEMENT G: General Macroeconomic and Trade Environment (Continued)

What has been the general trend in your country's trade policy over the past few years?	Ratio of trade to GDP, average tariff rate Use of quantitative restrictions have been: —Increasing —Stable —Decreasing	National accounts Policy documents WTO and other international sources
What is your country's general trade policy orientation toward the service sector?	—Trade promoting —Trade inhibiting —Indifferent to trade	Interview Minister of Trade National policy documents WTO sources
Does your country belong to any regional or other trading arrangements?	If yes, specify which ones	Minister of Trade Policy documents
Do these agreements cover service sector trade and investment?	If yes, what is the extent of trade and investment in services (inward and outward) under these agreements?	Minister of Trade Policy documents
What are the perceived/expected benefits and challenges to the economy from liberalizing services trade?	Open-ended response: —Generally —In the regional/bilateral context —In the multilateral context	Minister of Trade Minister of Health Other stakeholders
CORE QUESTION G.3	**5. TYPE OF ANSWER**	**POSSIBLE DATA SOURCE**
What has been the recent (past 3 years) trade performance of your country's service sector?	Value of services exports as percent of GDP, as percent of total exports Value of services imports as percent of GDP, as percent of total imports Services trade as a percent of total trade Rate of growth of services exports Rate of growth of services imports	National accounts BoP statistics International sources

(Continued)

ELEMENT G: General Macroeconomic and Trade Environment (Continued)

SUPPLEMENTARY QUESTIONS G.3	6.	
What is the trend in service sector trade over the past few years?	Ratio of services trade to GDP, total trade has been: —Increasing —Stable —Decreasing	National accounts BoP statistics International sources
What are the main characteristics of service sector trade in your country?	Major source and destination markets, regional and subsectoral composition	National accounts International sources
CORE QUESTION G.4	**7. TYPE OF ANSWER**	**POSSIBLE DATA SOURCE**
What is your country's overall approach to multi-lateral trade liberalization of services under the GATS?	Forward looking (phased or precommit-ment approach to liberalization) Status quo (commit to existing policies) Conservative (more restrictive commitments than prevailing policies)	Ministry of Trade officials and GATS negotiators WTO Commitment schedules
SUPPLEMENTARY QUESTIONS G.4	8.	
What are your main interests and concerns under the GATS, in terms of specific sectors and modes?	Interests: Export opportunities, market access, foreign exchange earnings, FDI, technology transfer, employment creation, increased competitiveness, and efficiency Specific sectors and modes where comparative advantage	Ministry of Trade officials and GATS negotiators, commitment schedules, and GATS 2000 request and offer documents

ELEMENT G: General Macroeconomic and Trade Environment (Continued)

	Concerns: Higher prices, forced opening up of sensitive sectors, consumer interests, equity, hurt domestic suppliers Specific sectors and modes where such concerns most applicable, where weaknesses	
What is the current state of your country's commitments under the GATS?	Number of sectors scheduled, percentage of commitments unrestricted, partial, unbound, common types of restrictions scheduled, commitments relative to status quo	Ministry of Trade officials, GATS negotiators, WTO documents on Uruguay Round commitments, GATS 2000 offers
What is the current state of requests received by your country under the GATS 2000 negotiations?	Number of requests received Main countries making requests Most important sectors featuring in requests Kinds of requests (full, partial, and mode-wise)	Ministry of Trade officials, GATS negotiators, WTO documents, requests
What offers have been made by your country thus far under the GATS 2000 negotiations?	None If offers made, specify in which sectors, modes, types of offers, common limitations maintained	Ministry of Trade officials, GATS negotiators, WTO documents
What are the expected/ realized gains and challenges from liberalizing service sector trade and investment under the GATS, over and above other trade agreements?	Gains: Increased export volume and earnings, increased market access, employment, competitiveness, efficiency Challenges: Import competition,	Ministry of Trade officials, GATS negotiators, health experts and practitioners, professional associations

(Continued)

ELEMENT G: General Macroeconomic and Trade Environment (Continued)

	higher prices, affecting public/private monopoly providers, employment displacement	
What are the main areas of comparative advantage within the service sector in terms of GATS modes of supply and sectors/types of services?	Modes 1, 2, 3, 4 Sectors	Ministry of Trade officials, professional associations, health experts and practitioners
CORE QUESTION G.5	**9. TYPE OF ANSWER**	**POSSIBLE DATA SOURCE**
How would you characterize your country's overall investment regime?	—Open —Moderately open —Closed	Concerned ministry or agency, policy documents, industry representatives/ associations
SUPPLEMENTARY QUESTIONS G.5	**10.**	
What has been the general trend in your country's foreign investment policy over the past few years?	—Increasingly liberal —Stable —Increasingly restrictive Number of sectors completely open, on negative list, on case based approval, etc.	Concerned ministry or agency, policy documents, industry representatives/ associations
What is the extent of foreign investment (portfolio and direct) in your country and by your country? What is the pattern of this foreign investment in terms of sectors and source/destination markets?	Volume of FDI (latest, cumulative for past 5 years) Rate of growth of FDI over past 5 years, latest year Sectoral allocation of FDI Regional distribution of FDI	Concerned ministry or agency, policy documents, industry representatives/ associations
What is your country's general foreign investment policy orientation toward the service sector?	—Promotion —Regulation/inhibition —Indifferent	Concerned agency/ministry

**ELEMENT G: General Macroeconomic and Trade Environment
(Continued)**

What is the extent of FDI in your country's service sector? What is the trend in this regard over the past few years?	Volume of FDI (cumulative for past 5 years and latest)	Concerned agency/ministry
What are the main characteristics of service sector FDI in and by your country, in terms of service activities, key source/destination markets?	Sectoral shares Country/regional shares	Concerned agency/ministry
What is your country's overall view toward liberalizing foreign investment in general, and specifically with regard to the service sector?	—Rapid liberalization desirable —Gradual liberalization desirable —Conservative and cautious approach	Ministry or concerned agency for investment, industry associations and representatives, consumer interest groups
What are the perceived/expected benefits and challenges to the economy from liberalizing foreign investment in services?	Benefits: Increased capital flows, employment creation, technology transfer, increased competitiveness, upgrading of standards, export spillovers of FDI Challenges: Hurt monopoly providers, adverse effects on equity, higher prices, distortions in resource allocation	

ELEMENT H: State of the Domestic Health Care Syste

CORE QUESTION H.1	11. TYPE OF ANSWER	POSSIBLE DATA SOURCE
How would you characterize your country's health system?	—Predominantly public —Predominantly private —Equal public/private	Ministry of Health officials, private sector representatives, professional associations, establishments
SUPPLEMENTARY QUESTIONS H.1	12.	
What is the budgetary allocation to the health sector?	Total $ value Percent of GDP	National accounts Treasury/Ministry of Finance
Is there a demand-supply gap in health care services?	Yes No If yes, indicate in what sense? You may use indicators such as number of doctors/nurses/hospitals per thousand patients, qualitative sense of shortages in supply of health care services	Ministry of Health, professional associations, practitioners and experts, establishments
Is supply of services equitable?	Yes No If no, indicate whether income bias, geographic bias, service bias (curative, preventive, tertiary versus primary)	Ministry of Health, professional associations, practitioners and experts, establishments
What is the nature of demand?	—Wealthy or poor —Urban or rural —Type of service —Public or private	Ministry of Health, professional associations, practitioners and experts, establishments
Are supporting facilities and equipment in the health sector accessible and affordable?	Yes No If no, note in what sense	Ministry of Health, professional associations, practitioners and experts, consumer interest groups, establishments

ELEMENT H: State of the Domestic Health Care System
(Continued)

13. CORE QUESTION H.2	14. TYPE OF ANSWER	POSSIBLE DATA SOURCE
What is your country's current trade policy with regard to health services?	—Seen as an important tradable sector —Indifferent—end —Restrictive—end	Ministries of Trade and Health
SUPPLEMENTARY QUESTIONS H.2	**15.**	
What are the recent trends in trade policy toward health services?	—More liberal —Unchanged —Restrictive	Ministries of Trade and Health, budget and trade policy documents, establishments, professional associations, experts
How do health services fit within your country's overall trade policy toward the service sector? Are health services a priority area?	Specific policies and initiatives, budget directives, duties on equipment and supplies, etc.	Ministries of Trade and Health, budget and trade policy documents, establishments, professional associations, experts
What are the recent trends in investment policy toward health services?	—More liberal —Unchanged —Restrictive	Ministry of Health, concerned agency for foreign investment, policy documents, establishments, professional associations, experts
How do health services fit within your country's overall investment policy toward the service sector? Are health services a priority area?	Specific initiatives and policies, directives, announcements	Ministry of Health, concerned agency for foreign investment, policy documents, establishments, professional associations, experts
What are the perceived/realized gains and costs from autonomous liberalization of trade and investment in health services?	Gains: Increased competitiveness and efficiency, employment, higher standards, technology upgrading, etc. Costs: Equity, higher prices, hurt domestic suppliers, distortion in resource allocation	Ministry of Health, concerned agency for foreign investment, policy documents, establishments, professional associations, experts

(Continued)

ELEMENT H: State of the Domestic Health Care System (Continued)

16. CORE QUESTION H.3	17. TYPE OF ANSWER	POSSIBLE DATA SOURCE
What is the magnitude of your country's trade in health services?	Breakdown by exports and imports, by subsectors within health services, by modes (as per GATS), and by regions, if available	Ministry of Health, BoP statistics, Ministry of Trade, professional associations, establishments, experts, international sources/partner country data sources
What is the magnitude of foreign investment in and by your country in health services?	Provide breakdown by inflows and outflows, by subsectors, and by regions, if available	Ministry of Health, BoP statistics, ministry or agency dealing with foreign investment, professional associations, establishments, experts, international sources/ partner country data sources
SUPPLEMENTARY QUESTIONS H.3		
Are there any niche areas/activities that have been targeted in this sector as part of trade and investment policy toward health services?	Types of services (specialized, alternative medicine) Target groups (diaspora, other specific countries/ regions)	Ministries of Health and Trade, ministry or agency dealing with foreign investment, professional associations, establishments, experts
What are your country's main areas of comparative advantage within the health sector?	Types of services (curative, preventive, specialized, rehabilitative, tertiary, primary) Types of resources (human, physical)	Ministries of Health and Trade, ministry or agency dealing with foreign investment, professional associations, establishments, experts
What are your country's main GATS modes of comparative advantage within the health sector?	Modes 1, 2, 3, 4 Specific subsectors and activities within health services as per GATS classification	Ministries of Health and Trade, ministry or agency dealing with foreign investment, professional associations, establishments, experts
What are your country's main sources of *weakness* with regard to trade and investment in health services?	—Endowment —Locational —Policy based —Infrastructure	Ministries of Health and Trade, ministry or agency dealing with foreign investment, professional associations, establishments, experts

ELEMENT H: State of the Domestic Health Care System (Continued)

	—Regulatory environment —Human resource capabilities	
What are your country's main sources of *strength* with regard to trade and investment in health services?	—Endowment —Locational —Policy based —Infrastructure —Regulatory environment —Human resource capabilities	Ministries of Health and Trade, ministry or agency dealing with foreign investment, professional associations, establishments, experts
CORE QUESTION H.4	**18. TYPE OF ANSWER**	**POSSIBLE DATA SOURCE**
Is the current regulatory environment in health sufficient to deal with greater liberalization of trade?	Yes—end No—continue	Ministries of Health and Trade, ministry or agency dealing with foreign investment, professional associations, establishments, experts, consumer interest groups
SUPPLEMENTARY QUESTIONS H.4	**19.**	
What are the relevant government, professional, and industry bodies/institutions in the health sector?	List names with some details of type of body, how old, number of members, activities undertaken	Ministry of Health, professional associations, establishments, experts, consumer interest groups
Which are the main pieces of legislation/acts that are relevant to the regulation of health services?	Name relevant acts, constitutional provisions, professional charters	Ministry of Health, professional associations, establishments, experts, consumer interest groups
What measures are in place to: Ensure equity in the provision of health care services? Ensure widespread availability of services? Regulate costs and ensure affordability? Ensure adequate quality and minimum standards?	Name specific acts/legislative measures (e.g., drug price controls, standards, certification requirements and licensing issues)	Ministry of Health, professional associations, establishments, experts, consumer interest groups

(Continued)

ELEMENT H: State of the Domestic Health Care System (Continued)

CORE QUESTION H.5	20. TYPE OF ANSWER	POSSIBLE DATA SOURCE
How would you characterize the availability and quality of supporting infrastructure such as power and telecommunications facilities in the health sector? What are the major problems in regard to these?	Good OK Bad (Can use international norms for benchmarking or give qualitative answers) E.g., high cost, irregular supply, low reliability	Institutions, professional associations, experts, and practitioners
SUPPLEMENTARY QUESTIONS H.5	**21.**	
How would you characterize the availability and quality of technology, equipment, and supplies in the health sector?	Good OK Bad	Institutions, professional associations, experts, and practitioners
What are the major problems in regard to these?	(Can answer as indicated in the question above)	
How would you characterize the availability and quality of training institutions and related facilities in the health sector?	Good OK Bad	Institutions, professional associations, experts, and practitioners
What are the major problems in regard to these?	(Can answer as indicated in the question above)	
CORE QUESTION H.6	**22. TYPE OF ANSWER**	**POSSIBLE DATA SOURCE**
What do you perceive as the main problems within the health sector?	Lack of facilities/ resources (go to Mode 3, Mode 1) Lack of technology (go to Mode 3, Mode 1) Shortage of manpower (go to Mode 4)	Minister of Health, Minister of Trade, health professionals, professional associations, and establishments

**ELEMENT H: State of the Domestic Health Care System
(Continued)**

SUPPLEMENTARY QUESTIONS H.6	23.	
How do you think trade in health services and its liberalization would help in addressing these problems?	Would not help—end Help attract inward FDI (Mode 3) Help raise quality of manpower (Mode 4) Upgrade standard and quality of infrastructure (Mode 3)	Minister of Health, Minister of Trade, health professionals, professional associations, and establishments
What do you perceive as the main factors that would make it difficult to *realize gains* from trade in health services and its liberalization?	Lack of regulatory framework and capacity, public-private imbalance, underinvestment in health sector, etc.	Minister of Health, Minister of Trade, health professionals, professional associations, establishments, and consumer interest groups
Do you feel these problems are likely to be aggravated by liberalizing under GATS rather than autonomously?	Yes No If yes, give a qualitative sense of why	Minister of Health, Minister of Trade, health professionals, professional associations, establishments, and consumer interest groups

ELEMENT M1.1: Current Status of Trade in Health Services and GATS

CORE QUESTION M1.1.1	24. TYPE OF ANSWER	POSSIBLE DATA SOURCE
Are e-health or telehealth part of a national plan or strategy?	No—end Yes—what are plans for next 3 years?	Ministries of Health, IT, and Telecom, policy documents, institutions, associations
SUPPLEMENTARY QUESTIONS M1.1.1	**25.**	
What agency leads the e-health initiative?	Ministry of Health Ministry of Telecom-munications Ministry of Information Technology Others	Officials in these institutions
Is e-commerce being used for development and is health covered in this initiative?	No—end Yes—detail plans and activity	Ministries of Health, IT, Telecom, policy documents, institutions, associations, experts
Is e-government being used, and is health covered?	No—end Yes—detail plans and activity (e.g., info to population via www)	Ministries of Health, IT, and Telecom, policy documents, institutions, associations, experts
Are any public-private partnerships established or planned for e-health?	No—end Yes—detail plans and activity	Ministries of Health, IT, and Telecom, policy documents, institutions, associations, experts
CORE QUESTION M1.1.2	**26. TYPE OF ANSWER**	**POSSIBLE DATA SOURCE**
What are your country's existing and proposed GATS commitments on Mode 1 in health services?	Subsectors within health services where Mode 1 commitments undertaken; percent of full, partial, unbound entries in Mode 1; kinds of limitations maintained on Mode 1; views on further commitments	Ministries of Trade and Health, GATS negotiators

ELEMENT M1.1: **Current Status of Trade in Health Services and GATS (Continued)**

SUPPLEMENTARY QUESTIONS M1.1.2	27.	
What are your country's existing and proposed GATS commitments in other services, namely, health insurance, telecommunications, computer-related services and business services, which have bearing on Mode 1 and health services?	List other related sectors where commitments undertaken, types of commitments (percent of full, partial, unbound— especially on Modes 1 and 3), limitations maintained, views on further commitments	Ministries of Trade and Health, GATS negotiators
What are the perceived benefits and costs of GATS?	Benefits: Increased market access, increased export volume and earnings, employment generation, technology transfer Costs: Greater import competition, higher prices, adverse equity effects, displacement of service suppliers	Ministries of Trade and Health, GATS negotiators, experts, professional associations
Are health services a priority area for e-health?	Yes No If yes, note any specific e-health initiatives or programs	Ministries of Health, IT, and Telecom, institutions, professional associations, experts
What are the major policy incentives/concessions for Mode 1-related health care?	List special incentives or concessions in areas such as supporting infrastructure, procurement procedures, subsidies, tax treatment, etc.	Ministries of Health, IT, and Telecom, institutions, professional associations, experts
What are the major policy disincentives for Mode 1-related health care?	Note disincentives with regard to supporting infrastructure, procurement procedures, subsidies, tax treatment, etc.	Ministries of Health, IT, and Telecom, institutions, professional associations, experts

ELEMENT M1.2: Infrastructure and Regulatory Capacity

CORE QUESTION M1.2.1	28. TYPE OF ANSWER	POSSIBLE DATA SOURCE
What are the existing mechanisms for regulation of e-health?	Note specific acts and legislation relating to e-health regulation, relevant institutional bodies	Ministries of Health, IT, and professional associations, establishments, experts, concerned regulatory bodies
How effective are they?	Effective Ineffective	
SUPPLEMENTARY QUESTIONS M1.2.1	**29.**	
What is the strength of legal protection for processing and storage of information?	Good Bad (You may note the reason for your answer, such as inadequacy/ absence of appropriate legislation or its enforcement)	Ministries of Health and IT, regulatory bodies, professional associations, experts
What is the strength of legislation to prosecute cyber-crimes (e.g., breaches of security and privacy, authorize digital signatures, etc)?	Good Bad (You may note the reason for your answer, such as inadequacy/ absence of appropriate legislation or its enforcement)	Ministries of Health and IT, regulatory bodies, professional associations, experts
Is there (effective) protection for intellectual property rights?	Yes No If no, you may want to provide some detail	Ministries of IT and Health, IPR-related regulatory bodies, professional associations, experts, establishments
What measures are available to protect the consumer, and do they cover health and/or Internet transactions?	—Legal/liability-related —Payments for Mode 1 transactions —IPR —Confidentiality and privacy of information	Ministries of Health and IT, consumer interest groups, related regulatory bodies, professional associations, experts, establishments
Is there regulation that allows or restricts foreign investors in e-Health (see also Mode 3)?	FDI legislation in health and related sectors	Ministries of Health and IT, concerned agencies for foreign investment, establishments

**ELEMENT M1.2: Infrastructure and Regulatory Capacity
(Continued)**

CORE QUESTION M1.2.2	30. TYPE OF ANSWER	31. POSSIBLE DATA SOURCE
How would you characterize your country's IT infrastructure?	Good OK Bad	Ministries of IT and Telecom, establishments
SUPPLEMENTARY QUESTIONS M1.2.2	**32.**	
How widely is IT used within the health system?	No. of facilities at primary, secondary, and tertiary level with PC and Internet connections Level of use of these facilities	Ministries of IT and Telecom, establishments
How widely is IT used within the country?	Total number of users with ISP address	Ministries of IT and Telecom
Is there effective competition among IT providers (including Internet service providers)?	Public monopoly Open to all providers	Ministries of IT and Telecom
How affordable is network access?	Cost of network connectivity	Ministries of IT and Telecom, establishments
Is there an existing e-finance network to support e-health?	Electronic funds transfer Credit card "culture"	Ministries of IT and Telecom, establishments
How reliable is network access?	Speed of access, whether interruptions or not	Ministries of IT and Telecom, establishments
How reliable is the electricity supply?	Regular/interrupted supply, use of alternative sources and backups	Ministry of Power, establishments
Is capital available for e-health?	Yes No If yes, how much, at what kinds of interest rates, from what sources	Establishments, professional associations, experts, Ministries of Health and IT
What is the present level of e-health among the private health industry?	Number of establishments with e-health facilities, number of users, revenues from e-health	Establishments, users, practitioners, experts, Ministry of Health

(Continued)

ELEMENT M1.2: Infrastructure and Regulatory Capacity (Continued)

CORE QUESTION M1.2.3	33. TYPE OF ANSWER	POSSIBLE DATA SOURCE
What is the availability of professionals for e-health?	Estimated number of such professionals Quality, level of training	Ministries of Health and IT, establishments, professional associations, experts
SUPPLEMENTARY QUESTIONS M1.2.3	**34.**	
Are the skill levels of the health workforce sufficient to cover e-health needs?	Yes—end No—what would be needed to make them so?	Ministry of Health, professional associations, establishments, experts
	(e.g., more investment in training, better equipment, investment in telecom infrastructure, more establishments with such facilities)	
How would you characterize existing levels of IT training in the education system?	Sufficient Insufficient	Ministry of IT, relevant industry associations, establishments
Does the country produce IT professionals?	Yes No If yes, note how many and what type	Ministry of IT, relevant industry associations, establishments
What is the level of e-literacy among the population?	Low Medium High	Ministry of IT, relevant industry associations, establishments
Is the structure of the health system conducive to e-health?	Yes—why No—why (e.g., for reasons of public-private balance, type of health care needs, who is served, etc.)	Ministry of Health, professional associations, experts, establishments

ELEMENT M1.3: Current Data/Information and Evidence

CORE QUESTION 1.3.1	35. TYPE OF ANSWER	POSSIBLE DATA SOURCE
Does any cross-border trade in e-health take place?	Yes—go to M1.3.1a No—go to 1.3.1b	Ministries of Health and Trade, establishments, professional associations, practitioners
SUPPLEMENTARY QUESTIONS 1.3.1a	**36.**	
What is the extent of this trade?	Value in $ terms, exports and imports	Ministries of Health and Trade, establishments, professional associations, practitioners
What health-related IT services are traded?	Telemedicine, teleconsultations, telediagnosis, etc.	Ministries of Health and Trade, establishments, professional associations, practitioners
Where and with whom does this trade take place?	—Hospitals (public, private) — Insurance companies —Main partner countries/institutions/ health systems	Ministries of Health and Trade, establishments, professional associations, practitioners
What is the source of competitive advantage for trade in e-health services?	Infrastructure, manpower, costs, quality	Ministries of Health and Trade, establishments, professional associations, practitioners
Are there examples of success in e-health?	No—end Yes—describe evidence of such cases and their impact	Ministries of Health and Trade, establishments, professional associations, practitioners
SUPPLEMENTARY QUESTIONS M1.3.1b		
What are the existing barriers to e-health?	—Legal —Financial —Infrastructural —Human resource —Technical	Ministries of Health and Trade, establishments, professional associations, practitioners
CORE QUESTION M1.3.2	**37. TYPE OF ANSWER**	**POSSIBLE DATA SOURCE**
Are data on Mode 1 and health services available for your country, nationally and/or internationally?	Yes—see below No—end	Ministries of Health and Trade, international sources like WHO and WTO

(Continued)

ELEMENT M1.3: Current Data/Information and Evidence (Continued)

SUPPLEMENTARY QUESTIONS M1.3.2	38.	
Which are the concerned national (governmental or otherwise) and international *agencies* who collect this information?	Ministries of Health, IT and Telecom, WHO, WTO	Ministries of Health, IT and Telecom, WHO, WTO, establishments
Which national and international *publications* provide this information?	National accounts, ministry or sectoral publications, WHO, documents concerning information and communication technology	Ministries of Health, IT and Telecom, WHO, WTO, experts, establishments
What are the extent and nature of interaction between the concerned agencies at the national and international levels, in terms of data collection, data sharing, and data dissemination?	—Close cooperation and frequent interaction —Loose, ad hoc cooperation and periodic interaction —No coordination at all (In each case, describe in what respects there is cooperation or lack thereof)	Ministries of Health, IT and Telecom, WHO, WTO, experts, establishments
Are the data on Mode 1 and health, at the national and international levels, of good quality?	Yes No Answer with regard to aspects such as reliability, consistency, accuracy, timeliness, and coverage of this data	Ministries of Health, IT and Telecom, WHO, WTO, experts, establishments
What are the existing mechanisms and organizational procedures for gathering information on Mode 1 and health in your country?	Note procedures for data gathering, time frame, division of responsibilities across concerned agencies	Ministries of Health, IT and Telecom, WHO, WTO, experts, establishments
What are the identified gaps/limitations in your country's data on Mode 1 and health?	Answer with regard to quality of coverage, level of detail, accuracy, timeliness, frequency, consistency, etc.	Ministry of Health and Trade, professional associations, experts

ELEMENT M1.3: Current Data/Information and Evidence (Continued)

What are the identified problems with the organizational structures and mechanisms for data collection and dissemination for Mode 1 and health in your country?	Lack of timeliness, poor coverage, poor coordination, lack of trained manpower, lack of consistency, etc.	Ministries of Health, IT and Telecom, WHO, WTO, experts, establishments

MODE 2 QUESTIONS: M2
ELEMENT M2.1: Current Status of Trade in Health Services and GATS

CORE QUESTION M2.1.1	39. TYPE OF ANSWER	POSSIBLE DATA SOURCE
To what extent does the population deliberately seek health services overseas, and vice-versa?	Imports: —Lot —Little Exports: —Lot —Little	Central Bank, establishments, Ministry of Health, national health agencies of selected trade partners, insurance companies, experts, Ministry of External Affairs/Foreign Relations, professional associations, practitioners
SUPPLEMENTARY QUESTIONS M2.1.1	**40.**	
What is the extent of consumption abroad by nationals (import)?	Number who go abroad for health services Where they go Expenditures by them Services they consume Who pays Why they do so	Sample survey of the general population or the population that might go abroad for care[a] Hospitals/clinics abroad that cater to the country's nationals[b] Some of the other sources given in core question M2.1.1

[a]Limitation is that people may not answer truthfully, especially if there are currency controls.

[b]Many hospitals and clinics may be protective of their patients' privacy and may not divulge relevant information.

ELEMENT M2.1: Current Status of Trade in Health Services and GATS (Continued)

What is the extent of consumption abroad or at home by retirees living abroad?	Number who consume care in country of residence Number who return to the country for care	Survey retirees in country coming from abroad Establishments catering to such retirees diaspora networks Some of the other sources given in core question M2.1.1
What is the extent of consumption in country by foreigners (export)?	Number who consume health services in the country Where they come from Expenditures by them Services they consume Who pays Why they do so	Hospitals or clinics in the country that serve foreign nationals, nonresident nationals who come back for treatment, diaspora networks Some of the other sources given in core question M2.1.1[c]
What are the insurance coverage arrangements for those seeking care abroad, or seeking care here?	Describe portability of insurance—private and public Arrangements between national health systems or establishments	Insurance companies that cover a country's citizens as well as companies that cover those who come from abroad to consume care (Note the possibility of proprietary concerns in providing such information.)
Would tourists choose to stay in your country for treatment if they got sick?	Number who would Number who wouldn't Why	Survey tourists (Some existing surveys could be expanded to ascertain attitudes toward and likely use of the country's health services by tourists.)
CORE QUESTION M2.1.2	**41. TYPE OF ANSWER**	**POSSIBLE DATA SOURCE**
What are your country's existing and proposed GATS commitments on Mode 2 in health services?	Subsectors covered by Mode 2 commitments, type of commitments (percent full, partial, unbound entries), types of limitations maintained, restrictive	Ministries of Trade and Health, GATS negotiators

[c]Again, private clinics and hospitals might be proprietary about providing such information and public hospitals may not wish to do so for political reasons.

ELEMENT M2.1: Current Status of Trade in Health Services and GATS (Continued)

	or liberal relative to existing policies covering Mode 2, views on further commitments	
SUPPLEMENTARY QUESTIONS M2.1.2	**42.**	
What are your country's existing GATS commitments in other services, namely, health insurance, telecommunications, and business services, that have bearing on Mode 2 and health services?	Other related subsectors covered by commitments, nature of these commitments (especially in Modes 1 and 3), types of limitations scheduled	Ministries of Trade and Health, relevant line ministries, GATS negotiators
What are the perceived benefits and costs of GATS?	Benefits: Increased export earnings and volumes, higher standards, better technology, more investment, employment Costs: Higher prices, adverse equity impact, resource diversion	Ministries of Trade and Health, GATS negotiators, establishments, practitioners, professional associations
What are the major policy *incentives/concessions* that affect Mode 2-related health care?	E.g., setting up of hospitals, procurement of supplies and equipment, insurance portability, subsidies, and tax treatment	Ministries of Trade and Health, establishments, practitioners, professional associations
What are the major policy *disincentives* that affect Mode 2-related health care?	E.g., foreign exchange restrictions, lack of insurance portability, price restrictions, taxes	Ministries of Trade and Health, establishments, practitioners, professional associations

ELEMENT M2.2: Infrastructure and Regulatory Capacity

CORE QUESTION 2.2.1	43. TYPE OF ANSWER	POSSIBLE DATA SOURCE
Does the policy and regulatory system provide cover to those seeking care abroad, or foreigners seeking care in the country?	Yes—continue No—end	Ministry of Health, insurance companies (public and private)
SUPPLEMENTARY QUESTIONS M2.2.1	**44.**	
What level of coverage are citizens entitled to in consuming services abroad?	Type of care, limits on coverage, deductibles, types of establishments where entitled to coverage	Ministry of Health, insurance companies, partner countries' national health systems, establishments abroad
What level of coverage are foreigners entitled to within the country?	Type of care, limits on coverage, deductibles, types of establishments where entitled to coverage	Ministry of Health, insurance companies, establishments
CORE QUESTION M2.2.2	45. TYPE OF ANSWER	POSSIBLE DATA SOURCE
Does the health system facilitate consumption of services abroad by nationals and/or by foreigners in the country?	Yes—continue (Note existing arrangements with other governments, nature of these arrangements with regard to payments, liability cover, etc.) No—end	Ministry of Health, concerned agencies in partner countries, establishments, insurance companies, practitioners, professional associations
SUPPLEMENTARY QUESTIONS M2.2.2	**46.**	
Does the health system have the capacity to administer claims from nationals abroad and/or vice-versa?	Highly effective Limited effectiveness Ineffective	Ministry of Health, concerned agencies in partner countries, establishments, insurance companies, practitioners, professional associations
How does the cost of care in this country compare with that found in neighboring countries?	High Comparable Low	Ministry of Health, concerned agencies in partner countries, establishments, insurance companies, practitioners, professional associations

**ELEMENT M2.2: Infrastructure and Regulatory Capacity
(Continued)**

Are there particular services for which this country is at a comparative advantage or disadvantage in terms of quality or cost?	E.g., alternative medicine, specialized care, tertiary services, rehabilitative, etc.	Ministry of Health, insurance companies, partner country health systems/relevant agencies, establishments, practitioners, professional associations
Is your health system a barrier to tourism?	Yes No If yes, answer with regard to access, quality, range of services	Ministry of Health, establishments, Ministry of Tourism, practitioners
CORE QUESTION M2.2.3	**47. TYPE OF ANSWER**	**POSSIBLE DATA SOURCE**
How important are your human resource capabilities as a factor driving your country's Mode 2-related trade in health services?	Important factor Not an important factor	Ministry of Health, establishments, professional associations, experts, practitioners
SUPPLEMENTARY QUESTIONS M2.2.3	**48.**	
In what ways have human resource capabilities influenced Mode 2-related trade in health services?	Exports: Quantity and quality of manpower available, Specialized skills available Imports: Lack of the above	Ministry of Health, establishments, professional associations, experts, practitioners
Is the supply of health professionals in the country sufficient to provide services to foreign patients without affecting services for the local population?	Yes (why?) No (why?)	Ministry of Health, establishments, professional associations, experts, practitioners

ELEMENT M2.3: Current Data/Information and Evidence

CORE QUESTION M2.3.1	49. TYPE OF ANSWER	POSSIBLE DATA SOURCE
How would you characterize the use of health care by foreign citizens in your country to date?	Success—go to M2.3.1a Failure—go to M2.3.1b	Ministry of Health, establishments, experts, practitioners, professional associations
SUPPLEMENTARY QUESTIONS M2.3.1a	**50.**	
Have they helped in improving the health system?	Range of services Quality of care Standards Range of health professionals	Ministry of Health, establishments, experts, practitioners, professional associations
Has it been possible to reallocate some of the additional resources generated from foreign patients to health care for the local population, especially poorer populations?	Yes (which ones?) No (why?)	Ministry of Health, establishments, experts, practitioners, professional associations
Have they contributed in any significant way to the economy?	Yes—detail (e.g., BoP, employment) No—end	Ministry of Health, BoP data, Central Bank, establishments, professional associations, experts, practitioners
To what degree has this impact been due to GATS as opposed to autonomous/other liberalization?	Open ended, based on perceptions	Ministries of Health and Trade, professional associations
What has been the key to these successes?	E.g., infrastructure, manpower, regulations, insurance sector policies, standards, etc.	Ministries of Health and Trade, professional associations
SUPPLEMENTARY QUESTIONS M2.3.1b		
Have they been a failure in health terms?	Cost of services Quality of services Access to services Access to health professionals	Ministries of Health and Trade, professional associations, experts, practitioners, establishments

ELEMENT M2.3: Current Data/Information and Evidence (Continued)

	Impact on the public health system and allocation of resources Drain on revenues	
Have they been a failure in economic terms?	Employment, revenues, BoP impact	Ministries of Health and Trade, professional associations, experts, practitioners, establishments
To what degree has this impact been due to GATS as opposed to autonomous/other liberalization?	Open ended, based on perceptions	Ministries of Health and Trade, professional associations
What has been the key to these failures?	Lack of infrastructure, regulatory capacity, manpower, insurance portability, poor standards, lack of mutual recognition	Ministries of Health and Trade, professional associations
CORE QUESTION M2.3.2	**51. TYPE OF ANSWER**	**POSSIBLE DATA SOURCE**
Are data on Mode 2 and health services available for your country, nationally and/or internationally?	Yes—see below No—end	Ministries of Health and Trade, BoP statistics
SUPPLEMENTARY QUESTIONS M2.3.2	**52.**	
Which are the concerned national (governmental or otherwise) and international *agencies* that collect this information?	WHO, WTO, IMF, Ministry of Health, professional bodies, Central Bank	Publications and documents of the listed agencies
Which are the national and international *publications* that provide this information?	National accounts, BoP statistics, IMF statistics, WTO documents	As given in column 2
What other institutions are data available from?	Private establishments Insurance companies Tourism Board Ministry of External Affairs Experts/researchers	As given in column 2

(Continued)

ELEMENT M2.3: Current Data/Information and Evidence (Continued)

What are the extent and nature of interaction between the concerned agencies at the national and international levels, in terms of data collection, data sharing, and data dissemination?	Close coordination and frequent interaction Loose coordination and periodic interaction No coordination and interaction	Ministries of Health and Trade, WHO, WTO, professional associations, national accounts statistical sources, establishments
How good are the data on Mode 2 and health, at the national and international levels?	Good Bad Answer in terms of the coverage, timeliness, consistency, accuracy of the data	Ministries of Trade and Health, WHO, WTO, professional associations
What are the existing mechanisms and organizational procedures for gathering information on Mode 2 and health in your country?	Note procedures for data gathering, time frame, division of responsibilities across concerned agencies	Ministries of Trade and Health, professional associations, establishments
What are the identified gaps and/or limitations in your country's data on Mode 2 and health?	Answer with regard to quality of coverage, level of detail, accuracy, timeliness, frequency, consistency, etc.	Ministries of Health and Trade, professional associations
What are the identified problems with the organizational structures and mechanisms for data collection and dissemination for Mode 2 and health in your country?	Lack of timeliness, poor coverage, poor coordination, lack of trained manpower, lack of consistency, etc.	Ministries of Trade and Health, professional associations, establishments

ELEMENT M3.1: Current Status of Trade in Health Services and GATS

CORE QUESTION M3.1.1	53. TYPE OF ANSWER	POSSIBLE DATA SOURCE
How do you define FDI in the health services sector?	Foreign equity, joint venture, collaborative arrangements, partnerships and tie-ups, etc.	Agency concerned with foreign investment clearances and promotion, Ministry of Health, establishments, professional associations
SUPPLEMENTARY QUESTIONS M3.1.1	**54.**	
What is the extent of inward and outward FDI in the health sector?	Stock of FDI (latest, cumulative over past 3 years) Number of foreign collaborative arrangements/investors Volume of sales, employment, profits in FDI-related establishments	Agency concerned with foreign investment clearances and promotion, Ministry of Health, establishments, professional associations
What has been the growth rate of FDI inflow and outflow over the last five years?	Estimated growth rate	Ministry of Health, agency dealing with foreign investment
Where is this inward/outward FDI based in the health sector?	Hospitals Nursing homes, clinics Type of care	Ministry of Health, agency dealing with foreign investment, establishments
What is the geographic and income distribution of this outward/inward FDI?	Urban or rural Rich or poor	Ministry of Health, agency dealing with foreign investment, establishments
What are the key sources/destinations of this FDI?	Countries, corporations, diaspora abroad, returnees	Ministry of Health, agency dealing with foreign investment, nonresident population and diaspora organizations
What proportion of this FDI is acquisition of existing facilities versus creation of new facilities?	If unable to provide quantitative answer, give a qualitative answer	Surveys, agency dealing with foreign investment, Ministry of Health
What have been the main objectives in allowing inward/outward FDI in health services in your country?	Inward: —Technology transfer —Upgrading standards —Setting up infrastructure	Ministry of Health, agency dealing with foreign investment, professional associations, establishments

(Continued)

ELEMENT M3.1: Current Status of Trade in Health Services and GATS (Continued)

	—Employment generation —Improving quality and range of services Outward: —Profits, exports, and assistance	
Are there any niche areas within health services that are being/have been targeted for FDI?	Specialized tertiary services, primary, preventive, curative, etc.	Ministry of Health, agency concerned with foreign investment, professional associations
What is the breakdown between private (domestic) and private (foreign-owned) establishments in the health sector, in terms of total expenditures, investment, capacity, market demand, supply and location (rural/urban)?	High/low with respect to the shares in total expenditure, investment, capacity, market demand, supply, and rural/urban distribution where possible provide numerical answers	Ministry of Health, agency concerned with foreign investment, professional associations
How does this breakdown compare with the breakdown in these same respects for the public and private health care segments overall?	More skewed toward private, urban segments More skewed toward higher-end, specialized services	Ministry of Health, agency concerned with foreign investment, professional associations
CORE QUESTION M3.1.2	**55. TYPE OF ANSWER**	**POSSIBLE DATA SOURCE**
What are your country's existing and proposed GATS commitments on Mode 3 in health services?	—Liberal/forward looking —Status quo —Restrictive Note number of subsectors covered under Mode 3, type of commitments made in Mode 3 (percent full, partial, unbound entries), types of limitations maintained	Ministries of Trade and Health, GATS negotiators

ELEMENT M3.1: Current Status of Trade in Health Services and GATS (Continued)

SUPPLEMENTARY QUESTIONS M3.1.2	56.	
What are your country's existing GATS commitments in other services, namely, health insurance, telecommunications, construction, and business services, which have bearing on Mode 3 and health services?	—Liberal/forward looking —Status quo —Restrictive Same as in core question M3.1.2 where bearing on Mode 3 and health services	Ministries of Trade and Health, relevant line ministries, GATS negotiators
What are the perceived benefits and costs of GATS?	Benefits: Improved standards, increased availability of capital and resources, employment creation, improved quality, and range of services Costs: Adverse equity impact, higher prices, distortions in resource allocation, worsen public-private imbalances	Ministries of Trade and Health, GATS negotiators, professional associations
Are health services a priority area for FDI?	Note any specific initiatives or programs concerning FDI in health services	Ministry of Health, agency concerned with foreign investment, professional associations, foreign investors, establishments
What are the major policy *incentives/concessions* for Mode 3-related health care establishments and how do these incentives compare with those granted to domestic private health care establishments?	E.g., incentives concerning supporting infrastructure, procurement procedures, subsidies, tax treatment —More liberal —Similar —Less liberal	Ministry of Health, agency concerned with foreign investment, professional associations, foreign investors, establishments
What are the major policy *disincentives* for Mode 3-related health care establishments and how do these compare with those for domestic private health care establishments?	E.g., disincentives concerning supporting infrastructure, procurement procedures, tax treatment —More of a disincentive —Similar —Less of a disincentive	Ministry of Health, agency concerned with foreign investment, professional associations, foreign investors, establishments

ELEMENT M3.2: Infrastructure and Regulatory Capacity

CORE QUESTION M3.2.1	57. TYPE OF ANSWER	POSSIBLE DATA SOURCE
How effective are mechanisms for regulation of FDI?	—Very effective —Somewhat effective —Ineffective	Ministry of Health, agency concerned with foreign investment, establishments, professional associations
SUPPLEMENTARY QUESTIONS M3.2.1	**58.**	
What are the main professional and governmental bodies involved in regulating FDI-related establishments in the health services sector?	List concerned bodies	Ministry of Health, agency concerned with foreign investment, establishments, experts, professional associations
What are the main pieces of legislation/acts that are relevant to the regulation of FDI in health services?	List relevant pieces of legislation	Ministry of Health, agency concerned with foreign investment, establishments, experts, professional associations
Are there measures to: —Ensure equitable access to FDI-related health care establishments? —Regulate the costs/prices of health care in such establishments? —Ensure adequate quality and standards of operations and facilities in such establishments? —Protect consumer interests and prevent malpractice in such establishments? —Ensure transfer of resources from foreign private health care establishments to other parts of the health system? —Control repatriation of profits? —Regulate wages and other earnings in these establishments?	Name specific acts and their objectives Note how effective these acts are (good, bad, OK)	Ministry of Health, agency concerned with foreign investment, establishments, experts, professional associations

ELEMENT M3.2: Infrastructure and Regulatory Capacity (Continued)

Regulate labor flows between the public health care segment and FDI-related health establishments?		
In what ways do these measures differ from those affecting domestic establishments?	More restrictive Comparable Less restrictive	Ministry of Health, agency concerned with foreign investment, establishments, experts, professional associations
What is the monitoring and supervisory framework for ensuring implementation of regulations in FDI-related health care establishments?	Multiple agencies responsible, nodal agency, coordinated approach across agencies, etc.	Ministry of Health, agency concerned with foreign investment, establishments, experts, professional associations
CORE QUESTION M3.2.2	**59. TYPE OF ANSWER**	**POSSIBLE DATA SOURCE**
How would you characterize your country's capital infrastructure?	Good OK Bad	Establishments, professional associations, agency concerned with foreign investment
SUPPLEMENTARY QUESTIONS M3.2.2	**60.**	
What is the availability of power supply and telecommunication facilities for FDI-related health establishments?	Better than for domestic health establishments Comparable to domestic health establishments Worse than for domestic health establishments	Establishments, professional associations, Ministry of Health, agency concerned with foreign investment
What is the access to real estate/land, buildings, and other support facilities for Mode-related health establishments?	Better than for domestic health establishments Comparable to domestic health establishments Worse than for domestic health establishments	Establishments, professional associations, Ministry of Health, agency concerned with foreign investment

(Continued)

ELEMENT M3.2: Infrastructure and Regulatory Capacity (Continued)

What is the availability of specialized equipment, technology, medical supplies, clinical, and R&D facilities for FDI-related health establishments?	Better than for domestic health establishments Comparable to domestic health establishments Worse than for domestic health establishments	Establishments, professional associations, Ministry of Health, agency concerned with foreign investment
What is the availability of training institutions and facilities in FDI-related health establishments?	Better than for domestic health establishments Comparable to domestic health establishments Worse than for domestic health establishments	Establishments, professional associations, Ministry of Health, agency concerned with foreign investment
CORE QUESTION M3.2.3	**61. TYPE OF ANSWER**	**POSSIBLE DATA SOURCE**
What is the nature and extent of employment of local personnel in foreign-owned establishments compared with the rest of the health care sector?	Medical professionals Technical Managerial Support staff (Absolute numbers or share in total staff) Higher/lower/ comparable to employment in rest of health care sector	Establishments, Ministry of Health, agency concerned with foreign investment, professional associations, practitioners
SUPPLEMENTARY QUESTIONS M3.2.3	**62.**	
How does the workforce in foreign-owned establishments compare in skill level and/or productivity with the rest of the sector?	Same Better Worse	Establishments, Ministry of Health, agency concerned with foreign investment, professional associations, practitioners

ELEMENT M3.2: Infrastructure and Regulatory Capacity (Continued)

How do the prospects for professional advancement, further training, international networking, and development of specialized skills in such establishments compare with the rest of the health care sector?	Same Better Worse	Establishments, Ministry of Health, agency concerned with foreign investment, professional associations, practitioners
To what extent are returning migrant health care workers employed in FDI-related health care establishments?	Higher share than in rest of health care sector Comparable to that in rest of health care sector Lower share than in rest of health care sector	Establishments, Ministry of Health, agency concerned with foreign investment, professional associations, practitioners
How mobile is labor between other segments of the health care sector and the foreign private segment?	Highly mobile Not mobile	Establishments, Ministry of Health, agency concerned with foreign investment, professional associations, practitioners
What is the wage structure between foreign versus domestic private health care establishments? How does this compare with the general public-private wage structure in the health services sector?	Higher/lower in foreign private establishments compared to domestic private establishments or Comparable Compares favorably with general public-private wage structure Compares unfavorably with general public-private wage structure	Establishments, Ministry of Health, agency concerned with foreign investment, professional associations, practitioners

ELEMENT M3.3: Status of Current Data/Information

CORE QUESTION M3.3.1	63. TYPE OF ANSWER	POSSIBLE DATA SOURCE
Has FDI in health in your country to date been a success overall?	Yes—go to 3.3.1a No—go to 3.3.1b	Agency concerned with foreign investment, Ministry of Health, professional associations, experts and practitioners
SUPPLEMENTARY QUESTIONS 3.3.1a	**64.**	
Has it helped in improving the health system?	Yes No If yes, answer in terms of the improvements in: —Availability and quality of health services —Standards of operation/management, technology, and the general infrastructure —Skill and efficiency levels and competence of health-related manpower —Opportunities for training, research, professional advancement and networking —Development of niche areas and specialization	Agency concerned with foreign investment, Ministry of Health, professional associations, experts and practitioners
Has it contributed significantly to the economy?	Yes No If yes, answer in terms of its contribution to: —Foreign investment inflows to the country —Availability/saving of financial resources —BoP position of the country	Agency concerned with foreign investment, Ministry of Health, professional associations, experts and practitioners

ELEMENT M3.3: Status of Current Data/Information (Continued)

	—Employment generation —Technology transfer	
To what degree has this impact been due to GATS as opposed to autonomous/other liberalization?	Open ended, perception-based answer	Agency concerned with foreign investment, Ministry of Health, professional associations, experts and practitioners, GATS negotiators, Ministry of Trade
What has been the key to these successes?	Regulatory framework, manpower, quality of services, FDI legislation and incentives, etc.	Agency concerned with foreign investment, Ministry of Health, professional associations, experts and practitioners
SUPPLEMENTARY QUESTIONS M3.3.1b		
Has it adversely affected the health system?	Yes No If yes, answer in terms of the impact on: —Equity-availability and affordability of services for the low-income population, and the public-private, rural/urban balance —Differences in the wage structure between this segment and other parts of the health sector —Labor outflows from other parts of the health sector and health sector employment and earnings —Diversion of financial resources for investment from other parts of the health sector	Agency concerned with foreign investment, Ministry of Health, professional associations, experts and practitioners

(Continued)

ELEMENT M3.3: Status of Current Data/Information (*Continued*)

Has it adversely affected the economy?	Yes No If yes, answer in terms of the adverse impact on: —BoP position (e.g., through imports of costly supplies and equipment or repatriation of earnings) —Employment and earnings	Agency concerned with foreign investment, Ministry of Health, professional associations, experts and practitioners
To what degree has this impact been due to GATS as opposed to autonomous/ other liberalization?	Open ended perception-based answer	Agency concerned with foreign investment, Ministry of Health, professional associations, experts and practitioners, GATS negotiators, Ministry of Trade
What has been the key to these failures?	Lack of regulatory capacity and institutional framework, lack of manpower, inadequacies in the public health system, underinvestment in the health sector	Agency concerned with foreign investment, Ministry of Health, professional associations, experts and practitioners, GATS negotiators, Ministry of Trade
CORE QUESTION M3.3.2	**65. TYPE OF ANSWER**	**POSSIBLE DATA SOURCE**
Are data on FDI/Mode 3 and health services available for your country, nationally and/or internationally?	Yes—see below No—end	Ministry of Health, agency concerned with foreign investment, WHO
SUPPLEMENTARY QUESTIONS 3.3.2	**66.**	
Who are the concerned national (governmental or otherwise) and international *agencies* that collect this information?	Ministry of Health, agency concerned with foreign investment, establishments, Central Bank	As given in column 2

ELEMENT M3.3: Status of Current Data/Information (Continued)

Who are the national and international *publications* that provide this information?	National accounts, FDI statistics, Ministry of Health documents, BoP statistics, WHO, investor/recipient country sources, establishments	As given in column 2
What is the comparability of data available at the national and international levels and with other countries?	High Low Answer in terms of the coverage, level of disaggregation and detail, timeliness, definitions	Ministry of Health, agency concerned with foreign investment, establishments, investor/recipient country sources, WHO
What are the extent and nature of interaction between the concerned agencies at the national and international levels, in terms of data collection, data sharing, and data dissemination?	High degree of coordination and frequent interaction Loose coordination and periodic interaction No coordination at all (Note whether multiple agencies work together, the division of responsibilities, whether there is a nodal agency, etc.)	Ministry of Health, agency concerned with foreign investment, establishments, investor/recipient country sources, WHO
How good are the data on FDI/Mode 3 and health, at the national and international levels?	Good OK Bad Answer in terms of the coverage, timeliness, consistency, accuracy of these data	Ministry of Health, agency concerned with foreign investment, establishments, investor/recipient country sources, WHO
What is the level of disaggregation of the data on FDI/Mode 3 and health, in terms of origin, destination, employment, profits, revenues, and other variables?	High Low (Note the kind of disaggregation that is available)	Ministry of Health, agency concerned with foreign investment, establishments, investor/recipient country sources, WHO
What are the existing mechanisms and organizational procedures for gathering information on FDI/Mode 3 and health in your country?	Strong, loose, no coordination Frequent and close interaction, Periodic interaction,	Ministry of Health, agency concerned with foreign investment, establishments, investor/recipient country sources, WHO

(Continued)

ELEMENT M3.3: Status of Current Data/Information (Continued)

	No interaction (Note as above the hierarchy, nodal, multiple agencies responsible for such data gathering)	
What are the identified gaps/limitations in your country's data on Mode 3 and health?	Answer with regard to quality of coverage, level of detail, accuracy, timeliness, frequency, consistency, etc.	Ministry of Trade, agency concerned with foreign investment, professional associations
What are the identified problems with the organizational structures and mechanisms for data collection and dissemination for FDI/Mode 3 and health in your country?	Lack of timeliness, poor coverage, poor quality of manpower and administrative arrangements, lack of resources, poor institutional setup, lack of coordination across agencies	Ministry of Health, agency concerned with foreign investment, establishments, professional associations, experts

MODE 4: M4
ELEMENT M4.1: Current Status of Trade in Health Services and GATS

CORE QUESTION M4.1.1	67. TYPE OF ANSWER	POSSIBLE DATA SOURCE
To what extent is there movement of health workers into or out of your country?	None-end Little Lot	Ministries of Health, and Labor/Employment, professional associations, practitioners, establishments, manpower export and other agencies, recipient/origin country sources, ILO, WHO
SUPPLEMENTARY QUESTIONS M4.1.1	**68.**	
What is the nature of this movement of workers?	Temporary migrants Self-employed Employees of foreign-owned enterprise Business visitors Specialists Researchers Medical trainees Part of technical and government assistance programs Part of government-government or private institutional collaborative arrangements	Ministries of Health, and Labor/Employment, manpower export and other agencies, professional associations, establishments, Ministry of External Affairs/Foreign Relations, recipient/origin country sources
What is the breakdown by sector?	Number in primary, secondary, and tertiary facilities	Ministries of Health, and Labor/Employment, manpower export and other agencies, professional associations, establishments, recipient/origin country sources
What is the breakdown by occupation/trade?	Number of doctors, nurses, technicians, generalists, specialists, etc.	Ministries of Health, and Labor/Employment, manpower export and other agencies, professional associations, establishments, recipient/origin country sources

(Continued)

ELEMENT M4.1: Current Status of Trade in Health Services and GATS (Continued)

What is the breakdown by import and export?	Number coming into country Number leaving country	Ministries of Health, and Labor/Employment, manpower export and other agencies, professional associations, establishments, recipient/origin country sources
What is the geographic pattern of cross-border labor flows in your country's health sector?	Specify in terms of key source and destination markets and distinguish by temporary versus permanent labor flows.	Ministries of Health, and Labor/Employment, manpower export and other agencies, professional associations, establishments, recipient/origin country sources
What are the extent and nature of return migration in your country's health sector?	Large Small Virtually none Nature: medical graduates after completing training, persons returning after many years of experience in senior positions, etc.	Ministries of Health, and Labor/Employment, manpower export and other agencies, professional associations, establishments, diaspora organizations
Total number of nationals working abroad in health sector	Estimated number or as share of total domestic health workforce	Ministries of Health, and Labor/Employment, manpower export and other agencies, professional associations, establishments, ILO, WHO
Status of employment in receiving country	Trainee, intern, practitioner, researcher and trainer, technical assistance/charitable work, etc.	Ministries of Health, and Labor/Employment, manpower export and other agencies, professional associations, establishments, Ministry of External Affairs/Foreign Relations, recipient country sources, diaspora networks
Length of stay	More than 5 years Between 1and 5 years Less than 1 year	Ministries of Health, and Labor/Employment, manpower export and

ELEMENT M4.1: Current Status of Trade in Health Services and GATS (Continued)

		other agencies, professional associations, establishments, Ministry of External Affairs/Foreign Relations, recipient country sources, diaspora networks
Remuneration received/repatriated	Estimated value in absolute terms or as percent of earnings in sector	Ministries of Health, and Labor/Employment, manpower export and other agencies, professional associations, practitioners, recipient country sources
Total number of foreigners working in country	Estimated number or as share of domestic health care workforce	Ministries of Health, and Labor/Employment, manpower export and other agencies, professional associations, establishments, Ministry of External Affairs/Foreign Relations, ILO, WHO
Source country	List main countries of origin	Ministry of Health, Ministry of External Affairs/Foreign Relations, establishments, professional associations, ILO, WHO
Status of employment in country	Trainee, intern, practitioner, researcher and trainer, technical assistance/charitable work, etc.	Ministries of Health, and Labor/Employment, manpower export and other agencies, professional associations, establishments, Ministry of External Affairs/Foreign Relations, origin country sources
Length of stay	More than 5 years
Between 1 and 5 years
Less than 1 year	Ministries of Health, and Labor/Employment, manpower export and other agencies, professional associations, establishments, Ministry of External Affairs/Foreign Relations, origin country sources

(Continued)

ELEMENT M4.1: Current Status of Trade in Health Services and GATS (Continued)

Remuneration received/repatriated	Estimated value in absolute terms or as percent of earnings in sector	Ministries of Health and Labor/Employment, manpower export and other agencies, professional associations, practitioners, origin country sources
CORE QUESTION M4.1.2	**69. TYPE OF ANSWER**	**POSSIBLE DATA SOURCE**
What are your country's existing and proposed GATS commitments on Mode 4 in health services?	Subsectors covered by Mode 4 commitments, share of full, partial, unbound entries in Mode 4, types of limitations maintained, nature of commitments relative to existing policies, views on further commitments	Ministries of Trade and Health, GATS negotiators
SUPPLEMENTARY QUESTIONS M4.1.2	**70.**	
What are your country's existing GATS commitments in other services, namely, health insurance, telecommunications, construction, and business services, which have bearing on Mode 4 and health services?	Relevant sectors covered by commitments, share of full, partial, unbound entries in such sectors in relevant Modes, types of limitations maintained, nature of commitments relative to existing policies.	Ministries of Trade and Health, GATS negotiators, relevant line ministries
What are the perceived benefits and costs of GATS?	Benefits: Foreign exchange earnings, training, improvements in quality of manpower, increased availability of manpower	Ministries of Health, Trade and Labor/Employment, GATS negotiators, professional associations, experts, practitioners (including migrating professionals)

ELEMENT M4.1: Current Status of Trade in Health Services and GATS (Continued)

	Costs: Loss of human capital investment and brain drain, reduced availability of manpower, adverse effects on equity	
Are health services a priority area for Mode 4?	Yes No If yes, note any specific initiatives and programs concerning Mode 4	Ministries of Health, Trade, and Labor/Employment, professional associations, experts, practitioners
What are the major policy *incentives/concessions* to facilitate inward or outward trade in health services via Mode 4?	E.g., understanding with other governments/national health systems, institutions, signing of mutual recognition agreements, special labor market/immigration/work permit arrangements with other countries	Ministries of Health and Labor/Employment, manpower agencies, professional associations, recipient/origin country sources, immigration authorities
What are the major policy *disincentives* to trade in health services via Mode 4?	E.g., lack of recognition, immigration and labor market restrictions, lack of certification and equivalent training	Ministries of Health and Labor/Employment, manpower agencies, professional associations, recipient/origin country sources, immigration authorities

ELEMENT M4.2: Infrastructure and Regulatory Capacity

CORE QUESTION M4.2.1	71. TYPE OF ANSWER	POSSIBLE DATA SOURCE
How would you characterize the mechanisms for regulating immigrant workers?	Highly effective Somewhat effective Ineffective	Ministries of Health and Labor/Employment, manpower agencies, professional associations, recipient/origin country sources, immigration authorities
SUPPLEMENTARY QUESTIONS M4.2.1	**72.**	
Which bodies are responsible for licensing and recognition in the health sector, by type of health care provider?	Medical council or association, nursing council or association, technician's council or association, etc.	As given in column 2 as well as establishments, practitioners, Ministry of Health
What are the qualification and licensing procedures in your country's health sector, by type of health care provider? What is the purpose of these regulations?	Common certification exam within country, international certification exam, number of years for training, residency requirements, etc. Ensure standards and quality, consumer protection, accountability	Ministry of Health, professional bodies
Does your country have mutual recognition agreements in the health sector? What is the purpose of these agreements?	If so, provide details of the countries with which you have such agreements, the main provision in these agreements, the requirements for according mutual recognition, and the exceptions. Ensure standards and quality, consumer protection, accountability	Ministry of Health, professional bodies, relevant agencies in partner countries
What kinds of labor laws and wage regulations are applicable to health services in your country?	Wage parity conditions, economic needs tests, quantitative restrictions, residency/nationality conditions on foreign health care providers	Professional associations, immigration and labor market authorities, Ministries of Health and Labor/Employment, practitioners, establishments

ELEMENT M4.2: Infrastructure and Regulatory Capacity (Continued)

Are there measures to regulate labor flows between different parts of the health care system in your country?	Yes No If yes, specify these measures (such as minimum service conditions in public health system) and purpose.	Professional associations, immigration and labor market authorities, Ministries of Health and Labor/Employment, practitioners, establishments
CORE QUESTION M4.2.3	**73. TYPE OF ANSWER**	**POSSIBLE DATA SOURCE**
Does the health system have sufficient human capital?	Yes—end No—continued	Ministry of Health, professional associations, establishments
SUPPLEMENTARY QUESTIONS M4.2.3	**74.**	
What is the available supply of health care providers in absolute and per capita terms?	Provide the breakdown for this supply by different occupational categories, for primary, secondary, and tertiary, by rural and urban areas, and by public and private segments within the health sector (You may use usual international indicators like number of doctors, nurses, hospitals per thousand population, etc.)	Ministry of Health, professional associations, establishments
What is the nature of employment within the heath sector (fixed term, contractual, permanent, etc.)?	Distinguish by type of occupational category and by public and private segments	Ministry of Health, professional associations, establishments
What are your policies with regard to training and human resource development and related investments in the health sector?	No special policies Subsidized training in government institutions	Ministry of Health, professional associations, training institutions

(Continued)

ELEMENT M4.2: Infrastructure and Regulatory Capacity (Continued)

What are the current wage levels (broad ranges) in the health sector, by type of health care provider, type of establishment, by public and private segment, by rural and urban areas? Would you characterize labor costs in this sector as being high, moderate, or low in your country?	Note whether average wages and costs in each segment are —High —Moderate —Low	Ministry of Health, professional associations, establishments, practitioners
What are the extent and nature of labor flows within your country's health sector, between the public and private segments, between rural and urban areas?	Lot Little Direction of this movement: —Public to private —Rural to urban	Ministry of Health, professional associations, establishments, practitioners
What are the average skill level and productivity of the workforce in the health sector?	High Moderate Low Distinguish by type of occupational category and by public and private segments	Ministry of Health, professional associations, establishments, practitioners
What are the quality, nature, and extent of training of this manpower?	High Moderate Low Distinguish by type of occupational category and by public and private segments	Ministry of Health, professional associations, establishments, practitioners
What are the prospects for professional advancement, further training, international networking, development of specialized expertise, and upgrading of skills in your country's health care sector?	Good Bad Distinguish between the public and private segments	Ministry of Health, professional associations, establishments, practitioners

Element M4.3: Status of Current Data/Information

CORE QUESTION M4.3.1	75. TYPE OF ANSWER	POSSIBLE DATA SOURCE
Has temporary migration of labor in health in your country to date been a success overall?	Yes—go to M4.3.1a No—go to M4.3.1b	Ministry of Health, Labor/Employment, professional associations, practitioners
SUPPLEMENTARY QUESTIONS M4.3.1a	**76.**	
Has it helped in improving the health system?	Yes No If yes, answer in terms of the impact on: —Availability and quality of health services —Standards of operation/management, technology, and the general infrastructure —Skill and efficiency levels and competence of health-related manpower —Opportunities for training, research, professional advancement and networking —Promotion and development of niche areas and specializations	Ministry of Health, professional associations, establishments, practitioners
Has it contributed significantly to the economy?	Yes No If yes, answer in terms of its contribution to: —Foreign investment inflows to the country —Availability/saving of financial resources — BoP position of the country	Ministry of Health, professional associations, establishments, practitioners

(Continued)

Element M4.3: Status of Current Data/Information
(Continued)

To what degree has this impact been due to GATS as opposed to autonomous/other liberalization?	Open ended perception-based	Ministry of Health, professional associations, establishments, practitioners, GATS negotiators, Ministry of Trade
What has been the key to these successes?	Standards, quality of manpower, presence of mutual recognition agreements, special labor market and immigration arrangements, etc.	Ministry of Health, professional associations, establishments, practitioners, GATS negotiators, Ministry of Trade
SUPPLEMENTARY QUESTIONS M4.3.1b		
Has it adversely affected the health system?	Yes No If yes, answer in terms of the adverse effect on: —Equity-availability and affordability of services for the low-income population, and the public-private, rural/urban balance —Differences in the wage structure between this segment and other parts of the health sector —Labor outflows from other parts of the health sector —Availability and distribution of financial resources for investment in other parts of the health sector	Ministry of Health, professional associations, establishments, practitioners

Element M4.3: Status of Current Data/Information
(Continued)

Has it adversely affected the economy?	Yes No If yes, answer in terms of the adverse impact on: —BoP position (e.g., through imports of costly supplies and equipment or repatriation of earnings) —Employment —Earnings	Ministry of Health, professional associations, establishments, practitioners
To what degree has this impact been due to GATS as opposed to autonomous/other liberalization?	Open ended perception-based	Ministry of Health, professional associations, establishments, GATS negotiators, Ministry of Trade, practitioners
What has been the key to these failures?	Lack of regulatory framework, low wages, underinvestment in health sector, etc.	Ministry of Health, professional associations, establishments, GATS negotiators, Ministry of Trade, practitioners
CORE QUESTION M4.3.2	**77. TYPE OF ANSWER**	**POSSIBLE DATA SOURCE**
Are data on Mode 4 and health services available for your country, nationally and/or internationally?	Yes—see below No—end	Ministries of Health and Labor/Employment, professional associations
SUPPLEMENTARY QUESTIONS M4.3.2	**78.**	
Which are the concerned national (governmental or otherwise) and international *agencies* that collect this information?	Ministries of Health, Labor, professional associations, establishments, WHO, ILO, IOM	As given in column 2
Which are the national and international *publications* that provide this information?	National accounts and sectoral statistics, ILO, IOM, WHO publications	As given in column 2

(Continued)

Element M4.3: Status of Current Data/Information
(Continued)

What is the comparability of data available at the national and international levels and with other countries?	High Low Note in terms of coverage, detail, accuracy, timeliness, consistency of these data	Ministries of Health and Labor, professional associations, establishments, WHO, ILO, IOM
What are the extent and nature of interaction between the concerned agencies at the national and international levels, in terms of data collection, data sharing, and data dissemination?	High degree of coordination and frequent interaction Loose coordination and periodic interaction No coordination at all	Ministries of Health and Labor, professional associations, establishments, WHO, ILO, IOM
What are the existing mechanisms and organizational procedures for gathering information on Mode 4 and health in your country?	Multiple agencies with different responsibilities, duplication of effort across agencies, nodal agency to supervise and streamline information, no lead agency, etc.	Ministries of Health and Labor, professional associations, establishments, WHO, ILO, IOM
What are the identified gaps/limitations in your country's data on Mode 4 and health?	Answer with regard to quality of coverage, level of detail, accuracy, timeliness, frequency, consistency, etc.	Ministries of Health and Labor, professional associations, establishments, WHO, ILO, IOM
What are the identified problems with the organizational structures and mechanisms for data collection and dissemination for Mode 4 and health in your country?	Answer with regard to quality of coverage, level of detail, accuracy, timeliness, frequency, consistency, etc.	Ministries of Health and Labor, professional associations, establishments, WHO, ILO, IOM

INDEX